Judgment at the Smithsonian

The editor is grateful for permission to reprint excerpts from:

Hiroshima Diary by Michihiko Hachiya, translated and edited by Warner Wells, M.D., copyright ©1955.
Reprinted by permission of University of North Carolina Press.

"London Diary" by Martin Peretz, copyright ©1995.
Reprinted by permission of New Republic Inc.

Letter by William M. Detweiler, copyright ©1995.
Reprinted by permission of the American Legion.

Nota Bene: The publication *The Crossroads: The End of World War II, The Atomic Bomb and the Origins of the Cold War*, is unauthorized. No one at the Smithsonian Institution was involved in the preparation of this book.

ISBN 1–56924–841–9

"On the Steps of the Smithsonian," copyright © 1995 by Philip Nobile

The Crossroads: The End of World War II, The Atomic Bomb and the Origins of the Cold War, copyright © 1995 by Marlowe & Company

"The Struggle Over History," copyright © 1995 by Barton J. Bernstein

CIP information forthcoming.

Printed in the United States of America

Judgment at the Smithsonian

Edited and introduced by Philip Nobile

Smithsonian script by
the curators at the National Air
and Space Museum

Afterword by Barton J. Bernstein

Marlowe & Company

New York

DEDICATION

THIS BOOK IS FOR
Leo Szilard who tried to stop the bomb in 1945

AND FOR
The curators at the Smithsonian Institution's
National Air and Space Museum who tried to fill a hole in
American memory in 1995.

ACKNOWLEDGMENTS

Judgment At The Smithsonian is the work of a team of free press enthusiasts who moved small mountains to put the Smithsonian Institution's history of the atom bombings of Hiroshima and Nagasaki into swift circulation.

When mainstream companies turned down the project, I contacted Greg Ruggerio of the Open Magazine Pamphlet Series in Westfield, New Jersey, who recommended Arthur Naiman of Adonian Press in Berkeley, California, who passed the buck on to Randy Fleming of Publishers Group West, in Emeryville, California, and thence to John Weber, publisher of Marlowe & Company, who felt that the citizens who support the Smithsonian with their tax money deserved a look at its script on the bomb.

When I called Edward Sorel for advice about the book's design he suggested Seymour Chwast, director of The Pushpin Group. Chwast's cover illustration is worth many thousand words. Gene Smith, an art director with Pushpin, designed the text, and could not have been more agreeable or more efficient in the final demanding hours.

Pauline Neuwirth of Neuwirth & Associates, Inc. supervised production splendidly. Lawrence Deneault, Marlowe's Managing Editor handled the inside game with aplomb.

Victor Navasky, publisher of *The Nation*, referred me to attorney Leon Friedman for legal advice, which was duly extended. His counsel was encouraging.

The Bombs of August were not on the front burner of journalism when I began writing about them three years ago. And so I thank Jonathan Larsen, former editor-in-chief of *The Village Voice,* who sponsored my initial research. I also salute Margaret Talbot and Judith Shulevitz, former editors of *Lingua Franca,* for commissioning an A-bomb survey of David McCullough's *Truman.* Linda Leavitt, my editor at *The Scarsdale Inquirer,* was likewise ahead of her time.

I have had the pleasure of conversation and correspondence with several historians, each of whom is distinguished by his intellectual kindness: Gar Alperovitz, Kai Bird, Alonzo L. Hamby, William L. O'Neill, Paul Boyer, Richard Minear, John Dower, Robert Donovan, James Hershberg, Walter Isaacson, Edward Linenthal, and Richard Rhodes.

People on both sides of the controversy were cooperative in the extreme. Jack Giese of the Air Force Association sent me a copy of the exhibition script published here and supplied me with several related documents including memos leaked from the Smithsonian. Phil Budahn of the American Legion was also helpful in the flow of paper and information. Jo Becker, Executive Director of the Fellowship of Reconciliation, closely monitored the revisions in the script, and provided me with her analysis of the changes.

As time collapsed, I depended on the generosity and background of Greg Mitchell, co-author (with Robert Jay Lifton) of *Hiroshima in America: Fifty Years of Denial*.

Father John Dear, S.J., Monsignor William Smith of the Archdiocese of New York, and Jack Deedy, my sainted former colleague at *Commonweal*, enlightened me on the Catholic tradition on the atom bomb.

Brian Kenney, A.J. Weberman, Beverly Smith, Greg Knopp, Pat Donovan, Josh Swiller, Ron Bittel, Jeffrey Obler, Eric Nadler, Bruno Kavanagh, Viscount Luke Hinchingbrooke, Louis Theroux, Bruno Maddox, Ron Plotkin, Doug Simmons, Judi Strom, Ron Rosenbaum, Fabio Bertoni, Michael Nobile, George Dadakis, David Pravda, Bruce Goldstone, Stacy Asip, Maureen Nappi, Peter Noel, Ben Mapp, Ross Wetzsteon, Nicola Lee, Evelyn and Isadore Cooper, Chuck Jagoda, Elaine Navien, Golden R. Triever, Phil Rachelson, Bernard Miller, Christine Kelly, John Valadez, Peter Maguire, and Les Payne were important in ways only they know.

Barton J. Bernstein, the first refuge of Hiroshima students and scholars and the last word on the Hiroshima myth, has been a one-man advisory board. Although we have discussed bomb history for some three years, our essays, which bear on similar themes and individuals, were written independently. While immersed in his own composition and teaching, Bernstein commented on my introduction. His afterword is a major contribution to the field.

Glen Hartley of Writers' Representatives Inc., agented in his fashion.

My dear friend Johanna Lawrenson was an early and vital collaboratrice.

Caitlin Nobile, the second of three daughters, performed significant duties in Washington, D.C., including asking President Bill Clinton the apology question. As always, her sisters Megan and Maeve, brought joy to a writing father's heart.

Throughout the making of this book I was supported in the editorial and sweetness of life departments by Carole Shapiro.

Contents

ABOUT THIS BOOK

The Smithsonian Institution, America's national museum, has been complicit in an act of censorship.

In a controversy somewhat reminiscent of the Pentagon Papers, the United States government has attempted to suppress an unflattering war report written by government analysts. The current case involves the Smithsonian's 50th anniversary exhibition of the *Enola Gay*, the B-29 that rendezvoused with destiny over Hiroshima.

The Smithsonian's National Air and Space Museum—the hallowed last hangar of the Wright brothers 1903 *Flyer,* the *Spirit of St. Louis,* and other totems of American aviation—was to display the *Enola Gay* along with a probing explanatory script, and an array of evocative photographs and artifacts from Ground Zero. But funny un-Jeffersonian things happened as the august museum prepared to review, in the words of Israeli Nobel Peace Laureate Shimon Peres, "the Japanese Holocaust."

Averse to perturbing questions about Truman's decision to drop the A-bomb, the Air Force Association and the American Legion lobbied intently against the exhibit and forced many revisions—for example, the erasure of Dwight D. Eisenhower's criticism of the bombings and the removal of all but one photo of the dead at Ground Zero.

The Smithsonian's surrender to the military caste fell apart at the last minute in January 1995, when Martin Harwit, Director of the National Air and Space Museum, overruled the veterans' undocumented claim that the atomic bomb spared up to a million American lives. Harwit's honesty on this all-important point—after the war Truman and Churchill justified the massacre of an estimated 200,000 Japanese with inflated six- and seven-figure casualty estimates for Allied invasion armies—incited a nightmare of recrimination.

William M. Detweiler, the National Commander of the American Legion, called for a cancellation of the exhibit as then designed, and eighty-one members of the House of

Representatives demanded Harwit's firing.

On January 30, in this heated political atmosphere and with threats of defunding floating around Capitol Hill, Smithsonian Secretary I. Michael Heyman—on the advice and consent of the President and Vice President, the Senate majority leader, the Speaker of the House, the Chief Justice of the Supreme Court, and the Institution's Board of Regents—banned the troublesome script and eliminated the powerful images and relics from the exhibit. The *Enola Gay,* the greatest killing machine in the history of combat, would be presented without context, commentary, or physical reminders of the apocalyptic damage left in its wake, just as the military had always wanted.

Heyman's decision to revoke the academic freedom of his curators and to abolish their work fit with a bipartisan nostalgia for the bombings. For instance, President Bill Clinton expressed approval of Truman's atomic order at an April press conference, and Newt Gingrich boasted in *New Republic* of personally spiking the "anti-American" text. Regrettably, no politician's voice was heard in complaint. The press, often resistant to government censorship and skeptical of military information, enlisted with the anti-Smithsonians. In its editorial and news pages, the *Washington Post* earned special un-Pulitzers. After dangling in the Washington winds for three months, Director Harwit resigned his position in early May. In the same month, Alaska Republican Senator Ted Stevens, chair of the Senate Committee on Rules and Administration, hauled before his panel Secretary Heyman and Tom Crouch, the head curator of the *Enola Gay* exhibit, "to explain what went wrong with their management practices, and what steps have been taken to correct the revisionist and 'politically correct' bias that was contained in the original script." Senator Stevens invited five members of the military lobby, including the pilot of the Nagasaki plane, to give their opinions of the museum's work, but not one A-bomb historian was allowed to testify.

Victory over the Smithsonian Papers appeared total. Although Crouch defended the integrity of the initial script, emphasizing the positive reaction of most expert readers, particularly military historians, his careful statement was crafted to appease the museum's critics rather than to vindicate his and his colleagues' labors. "While the exhibit was never intended to attack the justification for the use of the bomb, it did suggest that the decision has been the subject of considerable study and analysis over the past half-century," he related, long drained of defiance and reconciled to rout. "For many, it seemed that the staff members of a treasured national institution were questioning an article of national faith. As though that were not enough, consider how a veteran who believes that he might have lost his life in an invasion of Japan may react to that unit of the exhibition [composed by Crouch himself] which described the suffering in the two cities. Would it not seem to him that the planners of the exhibition valued those lives more than his own? That was clearly not our intent. At the same time it is also clear that we failed to appreciate the deep and powerful links that bind the memory of the bomb to the incredible sense of joy and relief at the end of the war."

Nevertheless, in the interest of American memory, we publish *Judgment at the Smithsonian* containing the complete, original, uncensored script that was intended to tell visitors to the Air and Space Museum the generally untold story behind the Bombs of August.

My introduction takes a hard look at the unseemly battle to oblige the Smithsonian to bend history to patriotism. Since the curators purposely avoided the rights and wrongs of August 6 and 9, 1945, I also examine the moral issues and explore the associated idea of an American apology to Japan.

Barton J. Bernstein's afterword is a meta-analysis of the historical literature. He shows how the Hiroshima narrative was developed over five decades and demonstrates that dissent existed virtually from the beginning. According to Bernstein, who participated in the historians' protest against the Smithsonian's unprofessionalism, the first script distilled the prevailing scholarship, hedged on some disputed matters and, despite some problems, was a respectable piece of written history overall.

ON THE STEPS
OF THE SMITHSONIAN

HIROSHIMA DENIAL
IN
AMERICA'S ATTIC

BY PHILIP NOBILE

ONE

How the Smithsonian Was Forced To Stop Worrying and Love the Bomb

"You have no idea of the forces opposing this exhibit, not in your wildest dreams."
Tom Crouch, Project Manager of the Enola Gay *exhibition*

In the closing paragraphs of *Hiroshima*, John Hersey's report on the first atomic holocaust, a Japanese physician lashed out at President Harry S. Truman and his circle: "'I see,' Dr. Sasaki once said, 'that they are holding a trial for war criminals in Tokyo just now. I think they ought to try the men who decided to use the bomb and they should hang them all.'"

While many Axis war crimes were rightly prosecuted, there was no counter-tribunal. The United States, Great Britain, and the Soviet Union were also responsible for many atrocities during World War II—a conflict that left about 40,000,000 noncombatants dead—but the special horror of the Final Solution and the extreme barbarity of Japan's military methods curbed comparisons. "It would be difficult to find a wartime leader who was not a war criminal—something always pushes armies over the edge," said Telford Taylor, a former American chief prosecutor at the Nuremberg trials, in *The New York Observer*. As for the absurd notion of prosecuting the Allies, Taylor remarked, "Somebody would have to come down from heaven to do that."

The verdict of history, however, has often been harsh. The official government explanation for the events of August 6 and 9, 1945—that the U.S. was forced to kill somewhere between 100,000 and 200,000 Japanese civilians with an apocalyptic weapon in order to shock the enemy into surrender and thus redeem a million American boys from being slaughtered in an invasion—has collapsed like a bad alibi. Since the Sixties, a steady stream of diaries, memoirs, interviews and declassified documents has moved revisionism solidly into the mainstream. Among academic historians, conventional wisdom holds that dropping the bomb was probably a strategic blunder and a moral disaster.

J. Samuel Walker, chief historian of the U.S. Nuclear Regulatory Commission, surveyed the major literature on Hiroshima/Nagasaki and found virtual unanimity on two core matters. "The consensus among scholars is that the bomb was not needed to avoid an invasion of Japan and to end the war within a relatively short time," Walker commented in the journal *Diplomatic History* (Winter, 1990). "It is clear that alternatives to the bomb existed and that Truman and his advisors knew it."

Even Robert H. Ferrell, an anti-revisionist who edited Truman's private papers and letters, has been severely critical. "In retrospect it is clear that there should have been an explicit advance warning to the Japanese, followed by a demonstration of the awesome power of the new weapon," Ferrell wrote damningly of HST's failure of nerve in *Truman: A Centenary Remembrance*. "An Anglo-American-Chinese warning issued from Potsdam was simply a general statement that said nothing about a new weapon. If in the name of humanity, the Americans should have waited, uncertainty drove them on. With the Manhattan Project underway, it was unlikely that one man, even a President, could have stopped it. Research and development had cost $2 billion, an unprecedented sum for a single military or civilian purpose, and scientists and military leaders were eager to use the product. Had Truman refused to go ahead, he might well have been impeached."

McGeorge Bundy, former national security advisor to JFK and LBJ, has unexpectedly edged toward revisionism. As the amanuensis of Henry Stimson, Truman's aged Secretary of War, and the son of Harvey Bundy, Stimson's assistant on the bomb, McGeorge Bundy's move came as a surprise. After all, Bundy *fils* had been knee deep in the government's early disinformation campaign.

The architect of the immediate damage control was James B. Conant, President of Harvard and member of the Interim Committee. As the first of the group to propose a mixed military-civilian target, Conant may have been sensitive to the high negatives that the bombings were getting among the university class. Stung in particular by a Norman Cousins editorial in *The Saturday Review* (September 14, 1946) that called the bombings unnecessary and meant to intimidate the Soviets, Conant groused in a letter to his friend, Bundy *pere*, that "... this type of sentimentalism, for I so regard it, is bound to have a great deal of influence on the next generation. ...[A] small minority, if it represents the type of person who is both sentimental and verbally minded and in contact with our youth, may result in a distortion of history."

In order to protect his own reputation and to keep the bomb safe for continued diplomatic moves against the Soviets, Conant arranged for the recently retired Stimson, then composing his memoirs in concert with McGeorge Bundy, to construct an apologia for the bombings to be published in *Harper's*.

Poor Stimson. He was a fellow of the old school: Phillips Andover, Yale College, Harvard Law, Wall Street, the cabinets of Taft and Hoover. He hated the idea of total war and felt guilty about the air force's indiscriminate bombing. Although relatively passive in war councils about the human costs of military actions, he personally scratched Kyoto, Japan's treasured temple city, from the A-bomb list. Satisfying Conant's wish to defend the twin massacres was not easy. Private qualms wrestled with the rationalizations required by *raisons d'etat*. "I have rarely been connected with a paper about which I have so much doubt at the last moment," the seventy-eight year old statesman confided to Supreme Court Justice Felix Frankfurter in December of 1946. "I think the full enumeration of the steps in the tragedy will excite horror among friends who heretofore thought me a kindly minded Christian gentleman but who will, after reading this, feel I am coldblooded and cruel."

"The Decision to Use the Atomic Bomb" (February, 1947),

heavily rewritten and edited by Conant and both Bundys, was infiltrated with bright, shining untruths and gaping evasions. Asserting that the obliteration of Hiroshima and Nagasaki was "the least abhorrent choice" arrived at only after "a searching consideration of alternatives," Stimson made an authoritative, utilitarian case that the bombs prevented "over a million [U.S.] casualties." *Tout entendre* was *tout pardonner*: "In light of the alternatives which, on a fair estimate, were open to us I believe that no man, in our position and subject to our responsibilities, holding in his hands a weapon of such possibilities for accomplishing this purpose and to save lives, could have failed to use it and afterwards looked his countrymen in the face."

The *Harper's* article slanted history for decades to come. James G. Hershberg noted in *James Conant: Harvard to Hiroshima and the Making of the Nuclear Age*, which detailed the old boy conspiracy behind Stimson's brief, that Stimson's spin was warmly received: "Readers were struck not only by his forceful marshalling of facts…and other previously unknown events and information, but also by Stimson's stern yet humane tone, melancholy over the tragedy of war but not apologetic over the measures necessary to end it."

But some forty years later, Stimson's chief ghostwriter has clarified the record and conceded the revisionists' major complaint. "After the war Colonel Stimson, with the fervor of a great advocate, and with me as his scribe, wrote an article intended to demonstrate that the bomb was not used without a searching consideration of alternatives," Bundy admitted in *Danger and Survival: Choices About the Bomb in the First Fifty Years*. "That some effort was made, and that Stimson was its linchpin, is clear. That it was as long or wide or deep as the subject deserved now seems to me most doubtful."

Nagasaki's hurried appointment in Samarra, an act called "doubly unethical" by double Nobelist Linus Pauling, was likewise censured by Bundy: "It is hard to see that much could have been lost if there had been more time between the two bombs. … Such a delay would have been relatively easy, and I think right."

Philip Morrison, the physicist who assembled the core of "Fat Man," the plutonium device that obliterated Nagasaki, has acknowledged his complicity in a war crime in the *Village Voice*. This writer read him Taylor's trenchant comment on the second bomb from *Nuremberg and Vietnam: An American Tragedy*:

> The rights and wrongs of Hiroshima are debatable, but I have never heard a plausible justification of Nagasaki. It is difficult to contest the judgment that Dresden and Nagasaki were war crimes, tolerable in retrospect only because their malignancy pales in comparison to Dachau, Auschwitz, and Treblinka.

Morrison did not flinch from the implication. "That's a very beautiful statement," he said. "That's more like what I feel. I imagine if we had lost the war, I'd be tried for it."

In other words, Hiroshima/Nagasaki-bashing is not confined to the friends of Noam Chomsky. Americans as establishmentarian as Albert Einstein, Dwight D. Eisenhower, Douglas MacArthur, John Foster Dulles, John McCloy, Herbert Hoover, and Bishop Fulton J. Sheen have expressed distaste for the Bombs of August. Admiral William Leahy, Truman's personal military aide in the White House and later the Chairman of the Joint Chiefs of Staff, participated in the fateful deliberations. But in his 1950 memoir, *I Was There*, Admiral Leahy regretted Truman's order, saying that the last-minute bombings were "of no material assistance in our war against Japan. The Japanese were almost defeated and ready to surrender…. [I]n being the first to use it, we…adopted an ethical standard common to the barbarians of the Dark Ages."

Yet what is believed by the intellectual elite and taught in the university can be subversive in the public square, especially when the subject is wrapped in patriotic myth and surrounded by a bodyguard of lies. Witness the struggle that Japan has experienced in facing its wretched history of atrocities: the genocidal occupation of China, the kidnapping and rape of "comfort women," the torture and murder of Allied POW's (one-in-three died in Japanese camps compared to less than one-in-twenty in German hands). And so when the venerable Smithsonian Institution, the so-called nation's attic and Washington's top tourist attraction, endeavored to commemorate the 50th anniversary of the end of the Pacific War with an exhibit titled *The Crossroads: The End of World War II, The Atomic Bomb and the Origin of the Cold War*, it was bound to raise vexing questions and provoke fierce nationalistic sentiments. The centerpiece of the exhibit, scheduled to open in June 1995 at the Smithsonian's National Air and Space Museum, is the forward section of the *Enola Gay*. The gleaming airplane, restored to the tune of $1,000,000, was to be accompanied by rare photographs and objects, many lent by the peace museums of Hiroshima and Nagasaki, showing the impact of the bombs on the people and buildings at Ground Zero. This reliquary was designated the "emotional center" of the original 5,000-square foot exhibition. But it was the explanatory script that aroused the most commotion and led to the eventual purge of the exhibit.

The historical quarrel pitted the mighty military-political complex including the White House, the Congress, the Pentagon, and the veterans lobby against Martin Harwit, the Director of the National Air and Space Museum, and a team of curators who put the exhibit together. At issue was point of view, that is, the ideas and information contained in the script and conveyed by graphic photos of Japanese victims. Chopped into reading bites designed for wall and display labels, the inaugural text appeared to be a *tour de force* of popularization, that is, an immensely learned and clearly composed digest of the final days of the Pacific War concentrating on the bomb—the decision-making, the deployment, and the effects.

Script One, completed in January 1994, was painstakingly balanced and imparted a tragic sense of the U.S.'s atomic endgame. The weight of history hardly allowed otherwise. Nothing had emerged from the Truman Library or war archives that supported the government's story of the massacres. Truman's and

Stimson's best card—that the bomb spared a million American soldiers from the valley of death—was trumped by Stanford revisionist Barton J. Bernstein who located the true estimates in the files of the Joint War Plans Committee, a high level advisory group to the Joint Chiefs of Staff. In an air-clearing 1986 article titled "A Postwar Myth: 500,000 U.S. Lives Saved" in the *Bulletin of the Atomic Scientists* (June/July), Bernstein disclosed that "in June of 1945, while the Okinawa battle was winding down, U.S. military planners estimated that, at most, 46,000 might die in the various possible invasions of Japan."

The President's men, and certainly the President himself, knew that the shifting 500,000 to 1,000,000 count was impossible. Wrote Bernstein: "In fact, in early June 1945, when a layman suggested such a high number as a half million dead, army planners bluntly replied in a secret report: '[such an] estimated loss ... is entirely too high.' Studying this planners' report General George C. Marshall, army chief of staff, agreed with their assessment and so informed Secretary of War Henry L. Stimson."

The anonymous layman, whom Bernstein named in a footnote, was former President Herbert Hoover whom Truman had invited to the White House on May 28 to discuss food relief in Europe and how to end the war in Japan. Although Hoover was unaware of the bomb, he urged Truman to negotiate peace with the Japanese.

Fighting on to "the bitter end," Hoover said in a follow-up memorandum, would only satisfy "the vengeance of an excited minority of our people." Stating the obvious, he explained, "there can be no American objectives that are worth the expenditure of 500,000 to 1,000,000 American lives." Hoover sent an expanded four-page version of his thoughts to Stimson, his former Secretary of State, saying that a settlement with Japan would mean that "America would save 500,000 to 1,000,000 lives and an enormous loss of resources." It was this prediction that army experts had specifically negated as "entirely too high."

David McCullough, president of the Society of American

Historians and host of PBS's *The American Experience*, seemed to rescue the credibility of the million-man number in his cordial, prize-winning 1992 biography, *Truman*. According to McCullough, the skyhigh estimate was no *ex post facto* invention to camouflage a guilty conscience. There was purported proof that Truman's and Stimson's alarms were real. "Where I differ with the so-called revisionists is their argument that the figures given by Truman, Marshall and Churchill of saving upwards of 100,000 to 250,000 to even a half-million lives came after the fact and were used as a justification," McCullough said. "But I made an effort to try and discover if any such figures were in currency in the high command in Washington or on paper prior to the decision to use the bomb. And in fact, they were. Absolutely no question about that."

The smoking gun that had apparently eluded all prior researchers was a top secret War Department document that McCullough turned up at the National Archives in Washington, D.C. Describing this important find, he wrote in *Truman*:

But a memorandum of June 4, 1945, written by General Thomas Handy of Marshall's staff, in listing the advantages of making peace with Japan, said America would save no less than 500,000 to 1 million lives by avoiding the invasion altogether—which shows that figures of such magnitude were then in use at the higher levels.

Unfortunately for Truman and his defenders in the anti-Smithsonian crowd, McCullough was wrong. What he had "discovered" was old news to revisionists, and he had amateurishly mangled the details as well. Specifically, he had misconstrued Hoover's memo—previously unearthed by Bernstein—as an actual War Department study allegedly authored by General Handy; and compounding the error, he had neglected to cite Handy's reply-memo okayed by Marshall that repudiated the 500,000–1,000,000 figure. When Tony Capaccio of *Defense Week* called McCullough on the error in October of 1994, the biographer admitted that he had mishandled the purportedly exculpating June 4 memo. "My mistake was that in finding the 500,000 to one million casualty estimate in the material at the National Archives, I failed to read carefully on to the place where Gen. Handy calls the figures 'entirely too high,'" he told Capaccio. "General Handy's contrary opinion casts a different light on the numbers and should have been included."

This was not McCullough at his most candid. His error was hardly just failing to "read on" to Handy's refutation—the far larger lapse was misattributing Hoover's unsigned but easily identifiable memo to Handy himself. But acknowledging the Hoover–Handy bungle would highlight both his thin grasp of the literature (Hoover's authorship was already a part of the record) and his dereliction in testing out his allegedly history-shaking goods ("I don't quote anybody because I think they may have said it," he avowed in *U.S. News & World Report*. "If I find something that is controversial or shocking, it must be substantiated by at least three sources.").

Hugely embarrassed by the howler in the center of his defense of Truman, which this writer had privately documented for him in the summer of 1993 and to which the biographer had reluctantly conceded *on tape*, McCullough subsequently attempted to cover it up. In November of 1993, in response to a question from this writer, McCullough misled a lecture audience at Sarah Lawrence about his understanding of the Hoover and Handy memos. "He objects to the fact that I have mislabeled, he says, a memo which said that there would be 500,000 casualties if we proceeded with an invasion," McCullough insisted. "There is in fact no way to tell who wrote that memo, and it may have been General Handy as I have said in my book." Apparently, he was somewhat more forthcoming with *Defense Week* a year later.

Despite stacks of history disputing Truman's atomic order, NASM's curators strained for balance in what they termed "the intellectual heart of the exhibit," that is, the treatment of the decision to drop the bomb. "The draft script offered only a glimpse into the declassified top-secret documents that have compelled historians to rewrite wartime history of the atomic bomb project," observed Martin Sherwin author of *A World Destroyed: Hiroshima and the Origins of the Arms Race*, in *The Nation*. "To those of us familiar with those documents, it appeared as if the curators were giving undue attention to established myths at the expense of historical research. In a word, the draft script was *cautious...*" [emphasis in original].

Reckoning with a nervous Smithsonian hierarchy and perhaps anticipating a hostile reception from air force veterans, the authors frequently pulled punches and injected textbook qualifiers on delicate matters addressed in a series of labels dubbed "historical controversies." On the central question of whether the drops were justifiable, that is ethical, the curators bent over backwards in equivocation (see page 56 in *Crossroads*):

It is also clear that there were alternatives to both an invasion and dropping atomic bombs without warning—for example, guaranteeing the Emperor's position, staging a demonstration of the bomb's power, or waiting for the blockade, firebombing and a Soviet declaration of war to take their toll on Japan. Since these alternatives are clearer in hindsight and it is speculative whether they would have induced the Japanese government to surrender quickly, the debate over "the decision to drop the bomb" will remain forever controversial.

As for Truman's personal guilt, the curators were exceedingly lenient, more so than many Truman experts (see page 23 in *Crossroads*):

...Furthermore, [Truman] was faced with the prospect of an invasion and was told that the bomb would be useful for impressing the Soviet Union. He therefore saw no reason to avoid using the bomb. Alternatives for ending the Pacific war other than invasion or atomic bombing were available, but are more obvious in hindsight than they were at the time.

Allusions to crimes of war or Nuremberg principles or any type of moral approbation were notably absent from the script. "The Smithsonian Institution can take no position in that regard," said a 1993 planning paper penned by Tom Crouch, chair of the NASM's Aeronautics Department and project manager of the exhibit. "All the exhibit can do is to provide visitors with information needed to think more deeply about these questions."

Crouch understood, of course, that merely *posing* disturbing queries about Hiroshima and Nagasaki would reveal the vast carelessness of Truman and his men, and thereby put the heat on the Smithsonian, which depends on federal funding for more than 70 percent of its operating budget. Even while the first draft was in progress, there were internal rumblings.

On July 17, 1993, the outgoing Secretary of the Smithsonian, Robert McCormick Adams, warned Martin Harwit, the director of NASM and Crouch's boss, that focusing on Hiroshima and Nagasaki rather than the end of the Pacific war in general, would be dicey considering the veterans' credo that the bombs were instruments of salvation, *their own*. "It is precisely my feeling that such an ordering greatly—and I think unacceptably—increases the risk to SI [Smithsonian Institution]," Adams memoed Harwit. "[By switching the emphasis] we can reply to critics concerned about the atom bomb as the subject of an exhibit from any direction that this is essentially an exhibit commemorating the end of World War II and naturally also examining its sequela."

Crouch read Adams' note with misgiving. "It is a mistake to think that by tweaking the introduction to the present exhibition we can delude visitors into thinking that it is not really about the atomic bomb...," he wrote to Harwit on July 21. "...You and the Secretary are the ones who will have to accept responsibility for whatever we do. Do you want to do an exhibition intended to make veterans feel good, or do you want to have an exhibition that will lead our visitors to think about the consequences of the atomic bombing of Japan? Frankly, I don't think we can do both."

Deep thoughts did not imbue the victorious anti-Smithsonian campaign. A Nixonian vapor hung over the ten-month siege that was replete with dirty tricks and political highsticking. The Speaker of the House, who is something of an intellectual, bragged to Fred Barnes in *New Republic* that he had helped to kill the Smithsonian Papers. Sounding a lot like RN himself, Newt Gingrich said that the sophisticated, anti-massacre presentation represented "the enormous underlying pressure of the elite intelligentsia to be anti-American, to despise American culture, to rewrite history and to espouse a set of values which are essentially destructive."

Gingrich's lowbrow ridicule stood in contrast to the praise lavished on the original text by Dr. Richard Hallion, chief of the USAF Center for Air Force History. At the first and only gathering of the Exhibition Advisory Board, a ten-man circle of consultants including Bernstein, Sherwin of Dartmouth, and Richard Rhodes, author of *The Making of the Atomic Bomb*, Hallion put his endorsement in handwriting when the curators came under fire.

Sherwin had ignited an unexpected row at the February 7 conclave when he ambushed the enterprise from the left. He asserted that the *Enola Gay* in all its shining glory would overwhelm the script and serve only to celebrate the bombing. Hallion thought that Sherwin was off the wall. From the air force's vantage, he considered the text a swell fit. Feeling sorry for Neufeld, the recipient of Sherwin's barrage, Hallion slipped him a note of confidence: "Mike: Chin up—you've got a great script, and nobody except Marty is out to emasculate it." Underlining his support after the meeting, Hallion gave the curators a three-page memo—coauthored by his assistant Herman Wolk—suggesting a few changes of emphasis in theme and context. "Overall, this is a most impressive piece of work, comprehensive and dramatic, obviously based on a great deal of sound research, primary and secondary," the memo began. In a handwritten postscript, Hallion piled on approval: "Again—an impressive job! A bit of 'tweaking' along the lines discussed here, should do the trick…" (ellipsis in original).

With cover like this from the air force's topgun scholar, the Smithsonian should have been protected on its military flank. But Hallion had been prematurely honest. Faster than you can say Pearl Harbor, he got with the Pentagon program, and morphed into an ardent enemy of the Smithsonian. "They started with an exhibit that was an outright failure and have taken it maybe to a 'C'," Hallion subsequently said to *The American Legion* magazine.

The coprolite hit the propeller in the spring of 1994 when the Air Force Association, a deep pocket aerospace lobby with a membership of 180,000, declared war on the script. The two organizations had been in communication since September of 1993 when Crouch's planning memo was slipped to the AFA by a Deep Throat within the Smithsonian. General Monroe Hatch, Jr., USAF (Ret.), the AFA's executive director, had marched a platoon of objections into a private meeting with the curators the following November. Basically, what upset Hatch and his comrades was the exhibit's perceived "anti-American" shading, that is, too much Monday morning quarterbacking about Truman's actions and too little concern for the casualties of the Japanese sword. In a letter of complaint to Harwit, the general wrote that the "museum treats Japan and the United States as if their participation in the war were morally equivalent. If anything, incredibly, it gives the benefit of opinion to Japan, which was the aggressor."

Hatch was hyperventilating. Blind to American folly and deaf to the cries of innocent victims of war, the general would have deemed any independent inquest into Hiroshima and Nagasaki unbecoming. When the curators completed their script in January without paying much heed to his opinions, the AFA retaliated by leaking copies of the script while simultaneously misrepresenting its contents.

The all-out raid was led by John Correll, editor-in-chief of the AFA's *Air Force Magazine*. In a series of published articles and unpublished script evaluations, Correll borked the Smithsonian's exhibit as "politically correct curating" and a "rigged horror show." The initial salvo in the expensive propaganda offensive exploded in the April 1994 *Air Force*. "Despite some balancing material added in January, the curators still make some curious calls," Correll wrote. "'For most Americans,' the script says, 'it was a war of vengeance. For most Japanese it was a war to defend their unique culture from Western imperialism.' Women, children, and mutilated religious objects are strongly emphasized in the 'ground zero' scenes from Hiroshima and Nagasaki. The museum says this is 'happenstance,' not an ideological twist."

Correll's description of the script contained a seed of deception that grew into a strangling vine over the next few seasons. Not to put too fine a point on Correll's journalistic ethics, his quote from the script was torn out of context and suspiciously cropped. The entire wall label with the exact wording read (see page 3 of *Crossroads*):

A FIGHT TO THE FINISH

In 1931 the Japanese Army occupied Manchuria; six years later it invaded the rest of China. From 1937 to 1945, the Japanese Empire would be constantly at war.

Japanese expansionism was marked by naked aggression and extreme brutality. The slaughter of tens of thousands of Chinese in Nanking in 1937 shocked the world. Atrocities by Japanese troops included brutal mistreatment of civilians, forced laborers and prisoners of war, and biological experiments on human victims.

In December 1941, Japan attacked U.S. bases at Pearl Harbor, Hawaii, and launched other surprise assaults against Allied territories in the Pacific. Thus began a wider conflict marked by extreme bitterness. For most Americans, *this war was fundamentally different than the one waged against Germany and Italy*—it was a war of vengeance. For most Japanese, it was a war to defend their unique culture against Western imperialism. As the war approached its end in 1945, it appeared to both sides that it was a fight to the finish [emphasis indicates words dropped by Correll].

Correll's misquotation, which lacked an ellipsis for the absent and strongly qualifying words, had the sign of foul play.

Clearly, the sentence about Japan's defending itself against Western imperialism was a reference to the summer of 1945 when the xenophobic island nation was surrounded by U.S. ships, pounded by U.S. planes, and about to lose its divine Mikado per the Potsdam Proclamation. Hallion had also noted the compression of the label, but he did not contest its accuracy or impute a pro-Japanese slant. Instead, he recommended elaborating upon Japan's evil conquests before Pearl Harbor. "Four or five sentences take us from 1931 to 1941," he observed in his February 7 memo. "Japanese aggression associated with the drive for a Greater East Asia Coprosperity sphere, and the brutality against subject peoples, resulted in a severe reaction in the United States, among other nations. This brutality, especially in China, a country that Americans were generally sympathetic to, and the reaction to it, seem to be missing here."

Correll's critique dovetailed with bad vibrations about a concurrent exhibit at NASM titled "Legend, Memory, and the Great War in the Air," an unromantic analysis of the broken promise of strategic bombing. Speaking for his troops, Correll called it a "strident attack on airpower in World War I." Apparently preexisting tensions between the Smithsonian's cadre of civilian academics and the nuts and bolts aviation enthusiasts who kept NASM humming would pervert negotiations over *Crossroads*. A 8,000-signature petition by the ad hoc Committee for the Restoration of the *Enola Gay* indicated a widespread distrust among veterans for the rocket scientists in the nation's attic. "One could easily conclude that the visitors to the display will be required to leave their shoes at the door," declared Ned Humphreys, the head of Bombardiers Incorporated, in a memo to Correll.

At the beginning of the battle, Crouch fought back on the

ground of intellectual honesty. The 51-year-old historian who curated the Smithsonian's 1984 exhibit on the internment of Japanese–Americans compared his institution's frank approach to history with the peace museums of Japan that have traditionally covered up Japanese infamies in the Pacific. "I'm really bothered, angered, by the way the Japanese find it so difficult to put wartime issues in real context," he said to *The Wichita Eagle* on April 24. "Their view is to portray themselves as victims. As I listen to the folks who criticized this [the Smithsonian exhibit], I hear something similar to that. There's real discomfort about looking at destruction on the ground....I hear critics saying, 'Don't tell part of the story.'" In a later interview with the *St. Louis Post-Dispatch* on July 12, he said: "The *Enola Gay* exhibit is a tightrope. On both sides of the Pacific, the sensitivities on this subject run very deep."

Director Harwit was torn between his curators and, it must have seemed, the rest of the universe. He was a former Cornell astrophysicist and NASA scientist who had worked on hydrogen bomb tests at Eniwetok and Bikini as a young Army man. His professorial background presupposed a devotion to academic freedom. But as the administrator of NASM, the most popular of the Smithsonian's sixteen museums, he had other constituencies including the Institution's Board of Regents, the veterans' lobby, and Congress. In an August 7 *Washington Post* op-ed piece timed for the 49th anniversary of the bombings, he granted homage to the brave veterans who beat a ruthless enemy in the Pacific, but he insisted that future generations deserved "the full story." Appearing firm, he ended the column with a pledge of fairness: "This is our responsibility, as a national museum in a democracy predicated on an informed citizenry. We have found no way to exhibit the *Enola Gay* and satisfy everyone. But a comprehensive and thoughtful discussion can help us learn from history. And that is what we aim to offer our visitors."

Behind closed doors, however, the Smithsonian was reeling from escalating hostility on Capitol Hill and in the press. In response to the first wave of bad publicity launched by the AFA,

Harwit alerted his curators in an April 16 memo that he, too, had reservations: "A second reading shows that we do have a lack of balance and much of the criticism that has been levied against us is understandable." Like Correll, Harwit wanted more emphasis on Hitler's and Tojo's atrocities and less on our own. Specifically, he recommended retooling the "emotional center" of the exhibit, the searing section on Ground Zero: "Take out all but about one third of the explicit pictures of death and suffering in section 400. Add to section 400 pictures of prisoners just released from Japanese internment camps." As for the "intellectual heart" of the exhibit, in which Truman's decision was submitted to history, Harwit proposed pulling back: "The alternatives to the bomb are stated more as 'probabilities' than as 'speculations', and are dwelled on more than they should be....Reduce much of the speculative material about what might have been possible without the atomic bomb."

The curators attempted to accommodate Harwit and a rapid-response internal review by patching on an introductory unit to the exhibit the would catalogue at length Japan's infamies in the Pacific theater. They also inserted and subtracted photos, and altered the language in spots. But Script Two (dated May 31), delivered to the AFA for reaction, did not stop the flak. Probably hoping to neutralize the immovable air force lobby, Harwit performed an endrun by formally inviting the American Legion into the review process. The Legion, which had already rebuked the exhibit in solidarity with other veterans, was provided a copy of Script Three in September. "I am absolutely convinced that their idea was they would manipulate the American Legion into a position to fracture the veterans' opposition, but we were a little smarter than they thought," said Hubert Dagley, the AL's internal affairs director and a former Vietnam intelligence officer. "But we never attacked any individuals or called in question anybody's patriotism."

Emboldened by the Smithsonian's backpeddling, the soldierly AL vetters, led by Dagley, mounted a line-by-line, artifact-by-artifact inspection that chipped away the mind and the soul of the exhibit during three long sitdowns with the curators. Though more civil than the air force boys, the Legion was equally relentless in shooting down anything that, according to their National Executive Committee Resolution 22, "questions the moral and political wisdom involved in dropping the atomic bomb."

Shelving objectivity, a pack-prone press flew wing-to-wing with the veterans. Without checking the revised script for accuracy or context, reporters, columnists, and editorial writers across the country pounced on the "Western imperialism" quote that Correll and other interested parties had flogged to make the curators appear foolish.

For example, the ellipsis-prone editorialists at the *Wall Street Journal* opined unsportingly on August 29:

> The picture that emerges from the script is of besieged Japan yearning for peace. This Japan lies at the feet of an implacably violent enemy—the United States—hell-bent on total victory and the mass destruction of women and children. And why? "For most Americans, this war...was a war of vengeance. For most Japanese it was a war to defend their unique culture against Western imperialism."

Jeff Jacoby siezed the historical heights in his *Boston Globe* column of August 16:

> *Western imperialism?* It was not Westerners who proclaimed the Greater East Asia Co-Prosperity Sphere, invaded Manchuria, Malaya and the Philippines, devastated Nanking, mass-raped Korea's young women, bombed Pearl Harbor and conducted the Bataan Death March. The theme of "Japan as Victim" would be appalling in a 9th-grade term paper. In a Smithsonian Institution script, it is stupefying.

Neither the *Wall Street Journal* nor Jacoby had done sufficient homework. The offending sentences had been rewritten in May's

Script Two: e.g., "For most Americans, this war was different from the one waged against Germany and Italy: it was a war to defeat a vicious aggressor, but also a war to punish Japan for Pearl Harbor and for the brutal treatment of Allied prisoners. For most Japanese, what had begun as a war of imperial conquest had become a battle to save their nation from destruction." Although the passage was discarded once and for all in August's Script Three, the press would not let go of the bone. *The New York Times* reprinted it as late as February 5, 1995 without remarking on its dead duck status.

With the exception of Robert Reno in *Newsday*, the punditocracy scorned the Smithsonian's attempt to look under the hood of Hiroshima. George Will and Cokie Roberts (*This Week With David Brinkley*), Charles Krauthammer and Jonathan Yardley (*The Washington Post*) R. Emmett Tyrrell, Jr. (*The Washington Times*), John Leo (*U.S. News & World Report*), Eric Breindel (*The New York Post*), and Terry Golway (*The New York Observer*) were especially scathing. *Time* essayist Lance Morrow leaped over the top with the comment that the script "had the ring of a perverse generational upsidedownspeak and Oedipal lèse majesté worthy of a fraud like Oliver Stone." The nastiness of the columns often coincided with biased reporting. Ken Ringle's long roundup in the *Washington Post* (September 26, 1994) was the most egregious of the genre. Spreading the veterans' smear about the curators' lack of military service, Ringle baited Crouch and Neufeld on Vietnam:

> Exhibit curator Neufeld, born in 1951, is a Canadian citizen who spent his undergraduate years at the University of Calgary between 1970 and 1974, when Americans were fleeing to Canada to escape the Vietnam War....
>
> Project manager Crouch was born in 1944 in Dayton, Ohio. A social historian with an undergraduate degree from Ohio University, he took his graduate courses at Miami University and Ohio State during the Vietnam War, earning his PhD in 1976.

"The press was utterly irresponsible and engaged in McCarthyite discourse," said Ed Linenthal, a member of the Exhibition Advisory Board and professor of religion and American culture at the University of Wisconsin (Oshkosh). "They assumed that the grotesque caricature of script and curatorial motives that was presented by powerful interests was the whole truth, and never dug deeper. They even put words in the mouths of the curators to make them appear pro-Japanese. The *Washington Post* was among the worst."

In the wake of this multiple-front onslaught and fearing congressional wrath, the Smithsonian seemed to surrender unconditionally. "You have no idea of the forces opposing this exhibit, not in your wildest dreams—jobs are at stake, the Smithsonian is at stake," a demoralized Crouch told Father John Dear, a peace Jesuit who visited the museum in September to read the script. Recalling Mary McCarthy's remark about Hiroshima's being a "hole in human history," Crouch grumbled about the heavy-handed censorship that had robbed the script and display of its meaning.

"Crouch urged me to organize the media and get to Harwit, who he felt was being manipulated," said the 36-year-old protégé of Daniel and Philip Berrigan's. Dear was handicapped by house confinement, part of his punishment for hammering a F-15 fighter plane at North Carolina air force base with Philip Berrigan in a Ploughshares disarmament action. Nonetheless, the padre rounded up some colleagues from the peace community to powwow with Harwit and the curators on September 20. "We talked about conscience and morality, not just history, and appealed to their integrity," said Dear. "Crouch and the curators did not speak at the meeting, and Harwit seemed exasperated. He said to us: 'Where have you been? You're too late. Why haven't you been in before? Why haven't you talked to the media?' Without making any promises to restore or strengthen the script, he thanked us for coming in."

Though slow in arriving, the backlash in the academy was caustic. The executive board of the Organization of American

Historians issued resolutions in October, reproaching both the museum's dumbing-down posture and Congress's un-Americanism. Upping the ante, a group of nine Hiroshima experts including psychiatrist Robert Jay Lifton, McCloy biographer Kai Bird, and Bernstein of Stanford, challenged the bona fides of the Script Five in a jagged encounter with Harwitt and the curators on November 16. Bernstein was embarrassed for the besieged Director who seemed pained in defense of the indefensible, that is, allowing military censorship inside the Smithsonian. "He knew that we knew that he didn't believe his own arguments," said Bernstein. Harwit found himself in the sticky position of justifying the disappearance of Ike's *pensée* on the bomb. In 1963, the former president and Supreme Allied Commander in the European Theater uttered a much valued quote in the revisionist compendium. Interviewed in *Newsweek* (November 11) apropos his memoir, *The White House Years*, Ike alleged that he spoke against the bomb to War Secretary Stimson in July 1945 at Potsdam: "I told him I was against it on two counts. First, the Japanese were ready to surrender and it wasn't necessary to hit them with that awful thing. Second, I hated to see our country be the first to use such a weapon." Bernstein wondered how the Smithsonian could abide erasing a *president's* opinion in the script, and all Harwit could say was that Ike was merely expressing a "personal opinion," and therefore it was somehow irrelevant.

No doubt influenced by Bernstein's scholarship, the original script had been properly parsimonious on the invasion dead, saying: "It nonetheless appears likely that post-war estimates of a half million American deaths were too high, but many tens of thousands of dead were a real possibility" (see page 49 of *Crossroads*). But after the veterans massaged the text, the dubious million-man estimate had crept into the script along with Marshall's supposed June 18 estimate of 230,000 casualties for the first stage alone. Irritated by this anti-historical revisionism, Bernstein was determined to make Harwit see the light.

"I told him that I had gone back to read Admiral Leahy's diary for the June 18 White House meeting on the invasion and realized that Marshall had actually predicted casualties of 63,000, not 230,000, which was the highest pre-Hiroshima estimate available to Truman," Bernstein recalled. "I challenged him to show me his pre-bomb source for a million." Harwit could not—his shaky seven-figure claim came in 1946.

Apparently beyond appeal, Harwitt brushed off the expert delegation. He refused to budge on Script Five that had so completely adopted the military view that the first wall label (see page 3 of *Crossroads*) was shorn of the following statement: "To this day, controversy has raged about whether dropping this weapon on Japan was necessary to end the war quickly." The historical complexities of Harwit's curators had been supplanted by the simplicities of the political-military lobby.

"After the meeting, Michael Neufeld and Tom Crouch refused to answer questions but seem abashed, almost apologetic," averred Lifton and his co-author Greg Mitchell in their new book, *Hiroshima in America: Fifty Years of Denial.* "Harwit, who had to maintain the official line, appeared haunted, almost broken, by what had occurred. The clear impression one received was of three decent men caught in a bureaucratic and ethical vise."

Following this inauspicious exchange, the historians sent a letter, signed by fifty-plus professors including Chomsky of MIT and Alan Brinkley of Columbia, to Dr. I. Michael Heyman, the new Secretary of the Institution: "It is unfortunate that the Smithsonian is becoming associated with a transparent attempt at *historical cleansing.* That archival documents and artifacts have been removed from the exhibit under political pressure is an intellectual corruption."

Then, in January of 1995, an unexpected twist occurred. Director Harwit finally said no. After being kicked around for months by the insatiable, armchair Toynbees of the Air Force Association and American Legion, he decided upon a revision of his own regarding the much debated invasion casualties. On January 9, he wrote a tide-turning letter to Hubert Dagley, the internal affairs director of the American Legion:

Dear Hugh,

As you will remember, last fall we spent a good deal of time discussing one of the labels in the script for *The Last Act: The Atomic Bomb and the End of World War II* [the new title of *Crossroads*]. That label involved losses of lives that would have been expected in an invasion of Japan, and cited the casualty estimates given to President Truman by his most senior advisors on June 18, 1945. They were the last estimates given to him before the war's end in August.

The highest of the figures cited for the invasion of Kyushu at the June 18 meeting appeared to be those of Admiral Leahy, who said that he expected loss rates comparable to those suffered at Okinawa, or around 30%. Prof. Barton Bernstein of Stanford University, in a paper he had published some years ago, interpreted that figure to mean 30% of the 766,700 "total assault troops", Marshall had mentioned earlier in the meeting. On that basis, Bernstein thought Leahy's remarks meant casualty levels around a quarter of a million for the Kyushu invasion.

Our Museum accepted those figures, but in a more recent meeting with Bernstein, he took us to task for this, saying that he had, in the meantime, found Leahy's diary entry for that same day. We checked on that in the archives and found that Leahy's entry summarizes the entire June 18 meeting with these words,

"From 3:30 to 5:00 P.M. the President conferred with the Joint Chiefs of Staff, the Secretary of War, the Secretary of the Navy, and Assistant Secretary of War McCloy, in regard to the necessity and the practicability of an invasion of Japan. General Marshall and Admiral King both strongly advocated an invasion of Kyushu at the earliest practicable date.

General Marshall is of the opinion that such an effort will not cost us in casulaties more than 63,000 of the 190,000 combatant troops estimated as necessary for the operation."

As Bernstein pointed out to us, 63,000 represents 30% of 190,000, and that evidently is the figure that Leahy had

had in mind at the meeting that afternoon.

Seeing that our earlier label text had been based on a misapprehension, we needed to revise it. I am sending you the text of the label as it now reads. It does not alter the figures Truman cited after the war, but it gives a different interpretation of what he might have had in mind.

If you have any concerns or comments, I'd greatly appreciate you letting me know.

Sincerly yours,
Martin Harwit

Although the becalmed but still wary veterans were reserving final endorsement of the exhibition until they saw it with their own eyes, they went berserk at Harwit's last stand. Dagley said that he was incensed not so much by the new configuration of casualties as by an apparent breach in Harwit's October agreement not to make eleventh-hour alterations. Dagley and the AL's National Commander William M. Detweiler visited the Smithsonian's new Secretary, I. Michael Heyman on January 18, 1995, to report their lost confidence and cancel the truce. According to Dagley, the meeting was brief and charged.

"Heyman was visibly angry," Dagley recalled. "He told us that we made his job very difficult, saying that he didn't know how he was going to deal with the historians and the academic community. I replied that if it weren't for the men this exhibit was about, he wouldn't have historians or an academic community to worry about. At that, Heyman said we had nothing more to talk about. He literally stood up, walked around his desk and showed us the door."

All bets were off. Eighty-one Republican and Democratic members of the House of Representatives ungenerously called for Harwit's ouster for "defiance and disregard for needed improvements to the exhibit." William M. Detweiler, the AL's National Commander, took his case directly to the Oval Office with a letter of January 19:

Dear Mr. President:

After months of research and direct negotiations with officials of the National Air and Space Museum, The American Legion has reluctantly concluded that further efforts to correct the politically charged *Enola Gay* exhibit are futile. On behalf of all World War II veterans, I am asking your help to see this tragic episode in the life of the nation's most revered museum brought to a speedy conclusion.

National Air and Space Museum officials, despite an accord reached with our representatives in September 1994, and in defiance of their Smithsonian Institution superiors, have restored to the exhibit highly debatable information which calls into question the morality and motives of President Truman's decision to end World War II quickly and decisively by using the atomic bomb. The hundreds of thousands of American boys whose lives were thus spared and who lived to celebrate the 50th anniversary of their historic achievement are, by this exhibit, now to be told their lives were purchased at the price of treachery and revenge. This is an affront to all Americans.

We have informed the Secretary of the Smithsonian Institution, I. Micheal Heyman, of our decision. We ask that the exhibit be canceled, the Congress investigate the process by which it was developed, and that the historic B-29 be displayed outside any political or philosophical context by an institution willing and able to do so. We believe the National Air and Space Museum is the most appropriate museum to do so, but if and when officials there will do so in conformity to our request for a neutral display of the aircraft.

We are pressing our position with all who are concerned about this issue, including Members of the United States Senate and House of Representatives. We need your support, and America's veterans need your support. Please help.

Sincerely,
William M. Detweiler

The renewed outbreak of hostilities had reached critical mass. The radioactive core was ostensibly passed to the freshly ensconsed Secretary Heyman, an ex-Marine who came to the Institution via the University of California (Berkeley) where he had been chancellor for ten years. During his installation in September of 1994, Heyman had stood forthrightly behind his beleaguered curators and the museum's duty to history. "The Smithsonian could have avoided controversy by ignoring the anniversary, simply displaying the *Enola Gay* without comment, or setting forth only the justification for the use of atomic weapons without either reporting the contrary arguments or indicating the impact of the bombs on the ground," he said. "My view is that the Smithsonian has a broader role than simply displaying items in the so-called nation's attic or eschewing important topics because of the political difficulties created by an exhibition."

But in the intervening months politics had prevailed. Betraying his own words, Heyman handed the store to the soldiers at the gate. He chose to scrap the script, photos, artifacts, and videotapes in favor of a stand-alone show of the *Enola Gay*. "In this important anniversary year, veterans and their families were expecting, and rightly so, that the nation would honor and commemorate their valor and sacrifice," Heyman announced on January 29, 1995. "They were not looking for analysis and, frankly, we did not give enough thought to the intense feelings such analysis would evoke."

On the same day, Detweiler urged in a press release that the Smithsonian lock up its history of Hiroshima and Nagasaki permanently: "We will insist that no materials related to the exhibit that is now canceled will be disseminated. We understand that the Institution will not produce such materials, and we will hold them to that promise. That includes catalogues, descriptive narratives, and video tapes."

Detweiler's statement closed with a perplexing Jeffersonian flourish. "Freedom of thought and conscience are among those freedoms most cherished by our people. They are among the fundamental freedoms that our fathers and grandfathers took up arms to defend a half century ago. This has been a vigorous exercise, uniquely American, of those cherished freedoms. And I thank God they are alive and well in America."

Edward Linenthal, a professor of religion and American culture at the University of Wisconsin (Oshkosh), had a unique perspective on the *Enola Gay* affair. A member of the Exhibition Advisory Board, he had recently experienced a similarly sensitive situation in Washington while researching his book, *Preserving Memory: The Struggle To Create America's Holocaust Museum*. His dismay with events at the Smithsonian was tempered by a sense of inevitability.

"In hindsight, the exhibition was doomed," Linenthal wrote to this writer. "Trying to make more complex a sacred narrative of the dropping of the bomb at a museum long considered a shrine to the celebration of American airpower, on the occasion of the fiftieth anniversary of World War II, when many expected the commemorative voice to be the privileged one, ignored, perhaps, the political realities of the time. Except for some historians— who were quickly and contemptuously distanced—there was no interest group willing to stand up and say that some kind of exhibit that blended the historical voice and the commemorative voice could and should be created."

"In the end, we have all lost a great deal. We have lost a chance to offer a commemorative thanks to veterans. We have lost the chance to remind each other that irony, ambiguity, and complexity are part of every human story. We have lost a chance to remind a new generation of the horror of nuclear war. We have lost a chance to remind ourselves that tragedy lurks even within stories that many believe have 'happy endings.' And, we have allowed the arrogance and ignorance of members of Congress— acting as if they were commissars in a totalitarian state—to threaten a public institution, in effect, to press for the regulation of public memory. This is a precedent that will come back to haunt the integrity of history and memory in this country for a long time."

It must be supposed that retired Brigadier General Paul W. Tibbets, the 80-year-old pilot of the *Enola Gay*, was happy with the outcome. Tibbets got what he wanted from the Smithsonian commemoration—his plane, a plaque and no questions asked. "I am not a museum director, a curator, or politician," said Tibbets at the Airmen Memorial Museum in Suitland, Maryland, on June 8, 1994. "I am a military man trained to carry out the orders of a duly elected commander-in-chief....Today, on the eve of the 50th Anniversary of the end of World War II, many are second-guessing the decision to use the atomic weapons. To them, I would say STOP."

TWO

Truman Meets the Devil's Advocate: A Moral Inquiry

"We thank God that [the atom bomb] has come to us instead of to our enemies; and we pray that He may guide us to use it in His ways and for His purpose."
President Harry S. Truman, radio address, August 9

World War II was engorged with atrocities. From Nanking to Guernica, from the Bataan Death March to Malmedy, from the "comfort women" of southeast Asia to the Jews and Gypsies of Auschwitz, the trail of innocent blood was so long and so thick that extraordinary international tribunals were convened in Nuremberg and Tokyo. For the first time in history war criminals were prosecuted and hanged.

Yet some mass killings, even ones involving tens of thousands of women and children, were hailed as famous victories. These "good" atrocities were committed by Great Britain and the United States in saturation bombing campaign against more than one hundred German and Japanese urban centers with names like Hamburg, Berlin, Dresden, Tokyo, Hiroshima and Nagasaki.

"The hideous process of bombarding open cities from the air, once started by the Germans, was repaid twentyfold by the ever-mounting power of the Allies and found its culmination in the use of the atomic bombs which obliterated Hiroshima and Nagasaki." Churchill boasted in his memoir, *The Second World War*. Far surpassing the *Luftwaffe* in the carnival of death, Allied planes killed approximately 900,000 German civilians and injured as many more. This bloody chapter in American history has been largely sanitized—though it paved the way for the inferno of Japan where approximately 500,000 Japanese non-combatants were burned to death in incendiary raids before Hiroshima. "In peacetime Americans had agreed that bombing civilians was murder," Rutgers University historian William O'Neill commented in *War and Democracy*. "...Some coarsening of its moral fiber must be expected of a nation fighting a terrible foe. But the United States had never previously made war against women and children, and should not have done so then. Even a war for democracy must have limits."

Apart from the horror of it all, the bombing of Germany was a military catastrophe. Postwar studies showed that targeting Hitler's cities was strategically futile and cost treasonous numbers of battle dead: one in ten U.S. soldiers who perished under fire during the war—29,000 of 292,000—flew with the Army Air Force in the European theater. Despite the documented madness of massacring civilians from the sky, American statesmen who ordered such attacks and the servicemen who carried them out were honored as patriots and heroes, and still are.

Victor's justice protected suspected war criminals on our side. Stalin had no legal concerns about the liquidation of 20,000 Polish officers in the Katyn Forest in 1940; Churchill was not hounded for personally ordering the Dresden bombing in February of 1945; nor did Truman fear judicial review of his atomic decision.

The matter of Allied city bombing might have surfaced at Nuremberg if embarrassment had not determined otherwise. Count One of the Indictment involved a criminal conspiracy to engage in "the indiscriminate destruction of cities, towns, and villages, and devastation not justified by military necessity," yet aerial bombardment was omitted from the list of Nazi crimes. Why were the murderous raids on Rotterdam, Warsaw, Coventry and London exempted, especially when German air minister Hermann Goering was in the dock? Because the prosecution did not relish the prospect of defense lawyers' bringing up worse sky-crimes by the Allies. In similar fashion, the Tokyo trial of Japanese Jodls and von Ribbentrops dismissed evidence concerning the atomic bombs.

Unquestionably, Churchill and Truman would have fared badly in any Nuremberg-style proceeding. You do not have to be Dorothy Day to perceive a family resemblance between the SS's slaughter of 640 villagers in Oradour, France, which became part of the prosecution's case at Nuremberg, and the larger reprisal of Operation Gomorrah that consumed 45,000 dwellers of Hamburg thanks to the British Bomber Command. Although the genocide camps of the Third Reich warped moral comparisons, Allied massacres were in a nearby ballpark. "If Dachau was a crime, Hiroshima is a crime," observed the sainted pacifist A.J. Muste in *Not By Might* in 1947.

Israeli Foreign Minister Shimon Peres, who knows one or two things about crimes against humanity, recently invoked the equivalence concept. While ringing a Japanese peace bell at the United Nations in the summer of 1994, the Nobel Peace Laureate spoke of "two holocausts—the Jewish holocaust and the Japanese holocaust," adding that "nuclear bombs are like flying holocausts."

On the Judeo-Christian scale, city-cide appears to be an infallible call. The Roman Catholic Church, hardly an anti-war organization, annointed the Nuremberg view at the Second Vatican Council. In the final conciliar document, *Gaudium et spes* (December 7, 1965), which was expressly composed without traditional anathemas, the Roman hierarchy, singled out events like Hiroshima and Nagasaki for lone condemnation:

> The mere fact that war has regrettably broken out does not mean that everything becomes licit.
>
> Every act of war directed to the indiscriminate destruction of whole cities or vast areas with their inhabitants is a crime against God and man.

This statement, which was repeated in the new *Catechism of the Catholic Church*, carries heavy theological weight and must be taken by Catholics as a matter of faith.

The Vatican does not speak for everybody on peace and spoke barely at all about Allied atrocities while World War II was hot in Europe. Except for heretical articles in *Commonweal, America, Catholic World*, and *Theological Studies*, the American branch of the Church, which did not fear government firing squads, was shamefully silent. But since 1945, religious leaders of every stripe have cursed the Bombs of August. Fulton J. Sheen, then a Monsignor, preached against them at St. Patrick's Cathedral in New York City in April 1946. Responding to Truman's war-shortening, life-saving rationale for the slaughters, Sheen said: "That was precisely the argument Hitler used in bombing Holland." Even Father George Zabelka, the chaplain who blessed the crew of the *Enola Gay* on Tinian Island, repented in Stud Terkel's *The Good War*:

> Instead of a feeling of horror, which I should have felt as a Christian, as a priest, it just went by me. We had heard from other pilots who came back from raids how they saw firestorms in Tokyo, hundreds of thousands burned to death. We should have felt horror then that these were civilians. We had gone through the "just war" theory of Saint Augustine: civilians were not to be harmed. Yet it never occurred to us.
>
> I think the reason it went by us is that no voices were

raised by the hierarchy, by any religious leaders. The immorality of indiscriminate bombing. It happened in Dresden, it happened in Japan.

Putting a cap on Fr. Zabelka's contrition, the American bishops declared in their 1983 peace pastoral that "we must shape the climate of opinion which will make it possible for our country to express profound sorrow over the atomic bombing in 1945. Without that sorrow, there is no possibility of finding a way to repudiate future use of nuclear weapons."

Historians are typically wary of the moral realm. "...[T]he historian is not God," observed Henry Steele Commager in an *American Heritage* essay titled "Should Historians Make Moral Judgments?" "... Alas! If the reader does not know that Hitler was a moral monster and that the murder of six million Jews was a moral outrage, nothing the historian can say will set him right...."

Harking strictly to Commager's rule, the curators at the National Air and Space Museum danced nimbly around the rights and wrongs of Truman's decision. It seemed that in their hearts they knew that Hiroshima and Nagasaki were Nuremberg material, but in their text they remained casuistically evenhanded to all but the military-minded.

Nevertheless, on the surface at least, the demon of morality eventually did in the grand commemoration. Although the pro-bomb bunch at the Air Force Association and American Legion had purged almost every shred of moral ambiguity from script, in the end they preferred to crash the ship rather than allow a hint of treachery regarding the invasion estimates. Acting as if history was riding on the righteousness of Truman's six or seven-figure alibi, the AL's Detweiler hit the roof when Harwit's January fix "question[ed] the morality and motives of President Truman's decision to end the war quickly and decisively by using the atomic bomb."

Lacking the horizon of Shimon Peres, Detweiler did not appreciate the offense-against-humanity angle. Yet Peres' equation of

Auschwitz and Hiroshima, a shocking *j'accuse* from a ranking ally and Nobel Peace Laureate, deserves serious reflection. As *New York Post* editorial page editor Eric Breindel noted in his column on June 2, 1994: "After all, 'Holocausts' have perpetrators: If Nazi Germany bears responsibility for what Shimon Peres terms the 'Jewish holocaust,' doesn't this circumstance render the U.S. guilty of what he describes as the 'Japanese holocaust'?" The question Breindel was getting at is this: *Was Harry Truman an American hero for ordering a final solution to the Pacific war or, stripped of patriotic illusion and viewed through the lens of Nuremberg, was he less the plainspeaking, buck-stops-here American legend who told Stalin, MacArthur and Congress to go to hell, and more a moral scoundrel, a reverse Otto Schindler, who needlessly sent 200,000 Japanese people, as well as twenty-three American POWs, to grotesque skin-melting deaths in August 1945?*

Whether for Hiroshima and Nagasaki, or Nagasaki alone, Truman deserves to be tried posthumously for war crimes. Although Telford Taylor said that Truman's accuser could not be of this world, perhaps a prosecutor from hell would fill the job. This devil's advocate would rip the defendant for nuking two cities of a beaten and blockaded enemy without heeding the advice of Secretary of War Stimson, Assistant Secretary of War John McCloy, Navy Under Secretary Ralph Bard, and former ambassador to Japan Joseph Grew who suggested alternatives like a warning, a demonstration, and a negotiated surrender. The prosecutor would expose the lies behind the million-man claim, and Hiroshima as a military target; he would browbeat him on the instant Hirohito flip-flop *after* the bombs were dropped. Regarding this hypocrisy, McGeorge Bundy cracked in *Danger and Survival*: "…in a single day it proved possible to reconcile the concept of unconditional surrender with the retention of the emperor."

Truman's prosecutor would ask the defendant to read aloud the following passage from his August 9 statement:

Having found the bomb we have used it. We have used it against those who attacked us without warning at Pearl

Harbor, against those who have starved and beaten and executed American prisoners of war, against those who have abandoned all pretense of obeying international laws of warfare. We have used it in order to shorten the agony of war, in order to save the lives of thousands and thousands of young Americans.

Then the prosecutor would wade in acidly: "Mr. President, exactly whom did you mean by 'those who attacked us without warning at Pearl Harbor'? Hirohito, Tojo, Admiral Yamamoto, their top henchmen? How did you know that they were in Hiroshima and Nagasaki the days the bombs were dropped? Oh, excuse me, Kokura was the prime target on the 9th. So whom were you aiming at in Nagasaki?"

"Surely, you were joking with your reference to international law, unless international law permits burning down undefended cities as the Allies did in Germany and Japan."

"You told your Cabinet meeting on August 10 that you stopped a *third* bomb because you hated killing 'all those kids.' Why didn't the dead kids of Hiroshima give you pause about the soon-to-be-dead kids of Nagasaki?"

"As for the U.S. soldiers allegedly saved by the bombs, how come the number kept going up? The 'thousands and thousands' you mentioned in August jumped to 250,000 at the Gridiron Dinner in December, then leapt to a million 'casualties' in a draft of your memoirs before falling back to 500,000 'lives' in the published version. But you don't expect this court to believe that you were faced with an either/or choice, that is, either drop the A-bomb on enemy cities or send a half-million American boys to die in an invasion, do you?"

"May I refresh your recollection, Mr. President? As you said in *Years of Decision,* you told Ambassador Grew in late May that you liked his idea of promoting surrender by letting Japan know that Hirohito could retain his throne. Furthermore, you strongly implied in the text that if the A-bomb had fizzled in New Mexico, you would have implemented Grew's peace initiative prior to risking an invasion. You stated on page 417 of the first volume of *Decision* 'If the test should fail, then it would be even more important to us to bring about a surrender before we had to make a physical conquest of Japan.'"

"So it wasn't the bomb or the boys, was it? You were planning all along to prevent another 'Okinawa from one end of Japan the other.' Perhaps, then, you could explain to this court and to history why you didn't try out Grew's suggestion *before* killing 200,000 Japanese with those terror weapons. If you were willing to give up unconditional surrender on August 10, why not on August 5?"

"The simplest explanation is the best explanation. There was nothing complicated about your criminal decision, Mr. President, was there? Despite the advice of Grew, Stimson, McCloy and Bard who urged you to change the surrender terms and/or warn the Japanese about the bomb and/or demonstrate it first, you simply *wanted* to nuke the Japanese, and *fast*. You and your assistant James Byrnes rejected any contrary counsel, including Leo Szilard's conscientious objection. Your motives entailed money and the Soviets. The Manhattan Project cost $2 billion, and you desired to impress the rapacious Stalin with a show of American might, and end the war before he invaded Japan."

"These charges are not innuendoes. Byrnes himself is the source. 'How would you get Congress to appropriate money for atomic energy research if you did not show results for the money which has been spent already?' Byrnes told Szilard in May when the scientist implored him to stop the bomb. 'You come from Hungary,' Byrnes added, 'you would not want Russia to stay in Hungary indefinitely.'"

"Byrnes was interviewed in the August 15, 1960 issue of *U.S. News & World Report*. He was asked: 'Was there a feeling of urgency to end the war in the Pacific before the Russians became too deeply involved?' And he gave the following incriminating answer: 'There certainly was on my part, and I'm sure that, whatever views President Truman may have had of it earlier in the year, that in the days immediately preceding the dropping of the bomb his views were the same as mine—we wanted to get through the Japanese phase of the war before the Russians came in.'"

"That's beautiful, Mr. President, really beautiful."

In the public remorse department, Truman would be his own worst witness. "If [Japanese leaders] do not now accept our terms, they may expect a rain of ruin from the air, the like of which has never been seen on this earth," Truman threatened on the day after Hiroshima. "When you have to deal with a beast you have to treat him as a beast," Truman wrote to the Federal Council of the Churches of Christ on the day after Nagasaki. "It occurred to me that a quarter of a million of the flower of our young manhood were worth a couple of Japanese cities, and I still think they were and are," he said at the White House Gridiron Dinner on December 15, 1945. Rude and unashamed in retirement, he resolutely snapped at bomb critics. His state of mind was revealed in an unmailed 1962 letter to historian Herbert Feis. "It ended the Jap war. That was the objective. Now if you can think of any other ... egghead contemplations." Truman was more profane in 1961 when asked about going to Hiroshima for a television documentary. "I'll go to Japan, if that's what you want, but I won't kiss their ass," he is quoted saying in Merle Miller's *Plain Speaking: An Oral Biography of Harry S. Truman*.

The prosecutor might dip into Dwight Macdonald's September 1945 *Politics* article "The Bomb," and quote his corrosive debunking of Truman's bad faith:

> Such moral defenses are offered [by Truman] as: the war was shortened and many lives, Japanese as well as American, saved; "we" had to invent and use The Bomb against "them" lest "they" invent and use it against "us"; the Japanese deserved it because they started the war, treated prisoners barbarously, etc., or because they refused to surrender. The flimsiness of these justifications is apparent; *any* atrocious action, absolutely *any* one, could be

excused on such grounds. [But] there is only really one possible answer to the problem posed by Dostoyevsky's Grand Inquisitor: if all mankind could realize eternal and complete happiness by torturing to death a single child, would this act be morally justified? (emphasis in original)

As for the ultimate haymaker, kept in reserve for maximum effect, the devil's advocate would rest his case by pulling out a piece of paper, and reading the following condemnation of the A-bomb into the record: "You have got to understand that this isn't a military weapon. It is used to wipe out women and children and unarmed people, and not for military uses."

Turning to the defendant, the prosecutor would say: "Those words were addressed to Army Secretary Kenneth Royall during the 1948 Berlin Blockade to squelch the idea of preemptive nuclear strike against the Soviets. Do you recognize those words, Mr. President? (*pause*) They are yours."

Despite the preponderance of historical evidence hanging HST, there is a pocket of white American male intellectuals who have attempted to make (or state) a moral argument for the twin massacres. Prominent among these Hiroshima deniers are David McCullough, George Will, William Manchester, William Styron, Paul Fussell, Charles Krauthammer, Lance Morrow, Martin Peretz, and honorary Yankee, Paul Johnson of Great Britain. None of these deniers has provided a sustained apologia, not even McCullough in his 3.6-pound, 1117-page biography, *Truman*. As one might imagine, logical backup for mass killings of enemy civilians tends to peter out after a few sentences or paragraphs. Among this pantheon of intellects the degree of *trahison*, both historical and moral, is astounding.

For instance, during the heyday of the Smithsonian controversy, George Will threw nothing but spitters. "If the question is, was the bomb necessary and moral," Will said on *This Week With David Brinkley*, "the answer is emphatically yes." Though the anti-Smithsonian John Leo conceded that the atrocities were "morally ambiguous" in *U.S. News & World Report*, Will's scorecard was based strictly on the numbers. He said that Army Chief of Staff General George C. Marshall had informed Truman that an invasion would take some 250,000 American lives. So buzz off.

Indeed, Truman alleged in the first volume of his memoirs, that "General Marshall told me that it might cost half a million American lives to force the enemy's surrender on his home grounds." However, Truman's citation was wobbly. According to Dr. Larry Bland, editor of the George Marshall papers, there is nothing in Marshall's archives that supports Truman's number. As detailed above, Marshall signed off on a War Department memo that stated, "an estimated loss of 500,000 lives due to carrying the war to conclusion *under our present plan of campaign*, is considered entirely too high" (emphasis in original).

Perhaps Will did not realize that Truman was blowing smoke with the Marshall reference, but he is smart enough to know that alternatives existed and that moral principles do not come out of the barrel of a bomb bay.

Paul Fussell, University of Pennsylvania English Professor and renowned literary critic, became the Robert Faurisson of Hiroshima denial in 1981 when he published a 36th anniversary essay in *New Republic* with the outré title of "'Thank God for the Atom Bomb'—Hiroshima: A Soldier's View." Fussell's approach broke new ground in the ethics of warfare. Appointing World War II infantrymen like James Jones, William Manchester and himself as the best and brightest ombudsmans, he skewered non-uniformed skeptics like John Kenneth Galbraith, who contended that the atomic hits had been gratuitous. "In general, the principle is, the farther from the scene of horror, the easier it is to talk," asserted the former Army second lieutenant whose rifle platoon was slated for the invasion of Japan. "...The degree to which Americans register shock and extraordinary shame about the Hiroshima bomb correlates closely with lack of information about the Pacific war."

Fussell's view emanated from Pacific island foxholes where brave G.I.'s fought a ferociously cruel foe under diabolical conditions. Whatever these long-suffering combat soldiers wanted—

"by any means"—was good. He quoted from Manchester's *Goodbye Darkness: A Memoir of the Pacific War*:

> After Biak the enemy withdrew to deep caverns. Rooting them out became a bloody business which reached its ultimate horrors in the last months of the war. You think of lives which would have been lost in an invasion of Japan's home islands—a staggering number of Americans but millions more of Japanese—and you thank God for the atomic bomb.

Fussell's amoral broadside caused a memorable stir at *New Republic*. "[N]o division of the magazine in years was as deep as the one which followed the article's publication," recalled editor-in-chief Martin Peretz in a recent diary column. "No, not even *The Bell Curve*."

Michael Walzer, author of *Just and Unjust Wars: A Moral Argument With Historical Illustrations*, lodged an objection in a letter-to-the-editor: "With Fussell, it seems, there are no limits at all; anything goes, so long as it helps bring the boys home." But Fussell remained unfazed, and brandished his unorthodoxy anew in reply: "My aim in writing the article on Hiroshima was to complicate, even mess up, the moral picture."

As if jinxed by the untenability of their stance, Hiroshima deniers cannot write their history straight. Every moral argument for using the bomb seems to contain a poison-pill of misinformation or missing information. Take Fussell's scorn for Galbraith's let's-wait-for-the-Japanese-to-surrender attitude. "Allied casualties were running to over 7,000 per week," Fussell claimed in his article. "'Two or three weeks,' says Galbraith. Two weeks more means 14,000 more killed and wounded, three weeks more, 21,000. Those weeks mean the world if you're one of those thousands or related to one of them."

The 7,000-a-week casualty rate caught the eye of Richard H. Minear, professor of history at the University of Massachusetts (Amherst) and author of *Victor's Justice: The Tokyo War Crimes*

Trial. Minear checked U.S. battle statistics without luck. Finding no American land fighting or major naval operations in the Pacific in the month prior to Hiroshima, he queried Fussell about the nebulous statistic. "Do you have a source for that figure?" he asked by letter on October 15, 1993.

"No, I don't know where I got the figure of 7,000, but it would not be inaccurate if we went back a few months before August, and noted the date the drop[s] were *planned,*" Fussell responded inaccurately (brackets and emphasis in original). The first A-bomb was not tested until July 16, and there were no drop dates scheduled until July 25.

The quality of Fussell's Deo Gratia has not been strained by the years. "I'm delighted the bomb was dropped," Fussell told *The Washington City Paper* in April of 1994. "It saved my life and the lives of many others. I saw no reason to be nice to the Japanese then, and I don't see any reason now. They started the war, we did not."

Paul Johnson is a British journalist-historian with a reputation for rigorous (conservative) thought. Johnson's interest in faith and morals has produced weighty histories of Christians and Jews as well as a lofty assault on the foibles of lefty mandarins from Rousseau to Chomsky in *The Intellectuals.* His meditation on Hiroshima and Nagasaki could be expected to contain criticism in the key of Jacob Bronowski who pondered in *Science and Human Values* that "Nothing happened in 1945 except that we changed the scale of our indifference to man." But not so. Despite Johnson's heavy God background, he rendered completely to Caesar on the atom bomb in his 20th century history, *Modern Times*:

> Truman promptly signed an order to use the bomb as soon as possible and there did not seem to have been any prolonged discussion about the wisdom or morality of using it, at any rate at the top political and military level.
>
> As General Groves put it: "The Upper Crust wanted it as soon as possible." America and Britain were already hurl-

ing at Japan every ounce of conventional explosive they could deliver, daily augmented new technology and resources; *to decline to use the super-bomb would have been illogical, indeed irresponsible,* since its novelty might have an impact on Japan's so far inflexible resolve to continue resistance [emphasis added].

Having absolved Truman of guilt, Johnson blamed the massacres on the Japanese:

> Those who died in Hiroshima and Nagasaki were the victims not so much of Anglo-American technology as of a paralyzed system of government made possible by an evil ideology which had expelled not only absolute moral values but reason itself.

Johnson's disregard for basic historical facts and baseline moral principles was paralytic as well. Truman's willful indifference to alternatives to the super-bomb, which he said was "the most terrible thing in history," and his sacrifice of Nagasaki just 76 hours later, which historians excepting perhaps only McCullough, have rebuked, was illogic in excelsis. For Johnson to argue that *failing* to kill 200,000 Japanese was "irresponsible"—a neglect that a *New York Post* editorial, probably executed by Breindel, said would have constituted a "criminal act"—was irresponsibility elevated to depravity.

Just a few pages later, without retracting his anti-ethical imperative, Johnson suddenly went revisionist by quoting Captain Adolph Feel Jr., an American defense counsel at the Tokyo Tribunal who criticized the shooting of surrendering Japanese soldiers. With a refined sense of military honor, the captain exclaimed: "We have defeated our enemies on the battlefield but we have let their spirit triumph in our hearts." Johnson commented:

> That was an exaggeration; but it contained an element of

truth. The small scale bombing of Chinese cities in 1937-8 had been condemned by the entire liberal establishment in America. When the time came to suggest the first target for the atom bomb, it was the President of Harvard, James Conant, representing the interests of civilization on the National Defense Research Committee, who made the decisive suggestion "that the most desirable target would be a vital war plant employing large numbers of workers and closely surrounded by workers houses."

Like Johnson, *Time* essayist Lance Morrow put aside ordinary moral restraints about killing women and babies. Dragging Primo Levi into his argument for the Japanese holocaust, which was akin to citing Anne Frank in favor of the Rape of Nanking, Morrow dared to write in *Time* (September 19, 1994):

> When the Italian author Primo Levi was in Auschwitz, a guard told him, *"Hier ist kein warum."* (Here is no why.) He was right. That was the terror, the mystery, the evil.
> But you have to make distinctions, even—or especially—when using the vocabulary of seeming absolutes. At Hiroshima there was, precisely, a *warum*, an excellent why.

Morrow meant the big bang. Reprising the damned-if-we-don't position, he said: "To have possessed a weapon that would end such a war almost instantly and not to have used it would have been inexplicable and, to those who would have died in a longer war, inexcusable." Yet nobody in Washington *knew* a priori that the bomb would have the desired effect, and besides, Morrow's criterion would permit poison gas, plague bombs, and other fiendish measures as long as they promised to stop the fighting.

In deference to history Morrow opened the door an inch to the alternatives, and then swiftly slammed it shut:

> It is possible in hindsight to entertain hypothetical doubt about whether an invasion of the Japanese home islands

would have been absolutely necessary at that stage of the war. Perhaps the Japanese would have submitted, although nothing in experience predicted that. One may argue whether the nuclear bombs really saved a million or two or more lives, Japanese and American, that might have been lost in a protracted endgame. But sometimes hindsight is decadent and a little fatuous.

Skipping over the *foresight* of Truman advisers who proposed *tertiae viae*, what about the hindsight of War Secretary Stimson? In *On Active Service*, a third-person memoir written largely by McGeorge Bundy, Stimson made the stunning, unheralded admission that Truman's reluctance to alter the surrender terms to preserve Hirohito's throne prior to Hiroshima may have wasted 200,000 Japanese lives: "Only on the question of the Emperor did Stimson take, in 1945, a conciliatory view; only on this question did he later believe that history might find that the United States, by its delay in stating its position, had prolonged the war".

David McCullough—patrician, dignified, Yale '55—is the dean of deniers. Ironically, he abandoned a life of Picasso, the painter of *Guernica*, to do a biography of Truman, the shatterer of Hiroshima and Nagasaki. "I'm very interested in art, and painting in particular," McCullough said. "The idea was to write a book about Picasso as the Krakatoa of modern painting, to treat him as an historic event as well as a biographical subject with a great deal of stress on how he forced the century to see differently. But I very soon found that I didn't care to spend the next three years with him. I really did find him terribly obnoxious. It was a false start. I've only had one in my writing life and that was it. I'm very glad I didn't do it because it led me to the best subject I've ever had—Truman."

McCullough seemed to worship the president who pulled the nuclear trigger. "God was good to us when he gave us Harry Truman," he said to Richard Hefner on the latter's PBS program *The Open Mind*. Wearing affection on his sleeve,

McCullough gave his cherished subject an astonishingly free ride on Hiroshima *and* Nagasaki. Unwilling to wrestle with Truman's most momentous act even in the epilogue, he handed off judgment to Eric Severeid. "I am not sure he was right about the atomic bomb, or even Korea," said the late sage of CBS News, swimming close to the revisionist shore. "But remembering him reminds people what a man in that office ought to be like. It's character, just character. He stands like a rock in memory now."

Why would McCullough spend enormous professional capital whitewashing Truman in the body of the text only to close with Severeid's ambivalent epitaph? Where was McCullough on the moral quotient? "All of the bombing of all of the cities was immoral," he said shortly after *Truman* was published. "The fire-raids were immoral. World war is immoral. I think that whether you are slaughtering someone with an ax or with a rifle, murder and god-awful destruction of civilization, societies, human beings, old, young, civilian and the rest is horrible in the extreme. But it was war. These were decisions made in the heat and the hatred and the limited knowledge of the moment of war."

McCullough described himself as "essentially pacifist," yet he, too, embraced the massacre option. "Truman was commander-in-chief during a war that was savage in the extreme," he said. "I'm not suggesting that the bombings were not a god-awful moment in history. But given the atmosphere of the time, when atrocities were the standard business of the day, Truman dropped the bombs to stop the killing and I think he made the right decision. It would have taken a different kind of man to say no to Marshall and [presidential advisor James] Byrnes."

"A more moral man?" McCullough was asked.

"I don't like going back into history and imposing a superior morality," he replied.

When asked where Truman expressed *any* moral concern for the folks living in Ground Zero, McCullough broke off the dialogue.

According to Churchill, Truman showed no scruples at Potsdam about snuffing out two Japanese cities. "There was unanimous, automatic, unquestioned agreement around our table; nor did I hear the slightest suggestion that we should do otherwise," Churchill wrote in his memoir.

A year later, after McCullough gained the Pulitzer Prize for biography and a second Francis Parkman Prize from his compatriots in the Society of American Historians, the colloquy on the bomb was renewed. "I have no intention and had none of ever protecting or glorifying anyone involved in the decision," McCullough said. "That's not my responsibility, it's not my business." Still tense in defense of Hiroshima, he was more vexed about Nagasaki, which earned a single, matter-of-fact paragraph in *Truman*. "[Truman's] mistake was signing an initial order that gave release of the go-ahead of both bombs at once," he remarked tersely and technically about the deaths of an estimated 70,000. "Look, I will make a very flat statement to you, and I really don't want to continue this interview. My statement: The decision to drop the atomic bomb is one that people will examine and debate for years to come, for hundreds of years to come, and should. New information may come to light which will change what we know. I have given this subject my attention and I have done what I think is a fair appraisal of the situation at the time. I have stressed those influences on the president and those around him, and the book stands for itself. And if these people don't agree with it, that's their prerogative."

Though working on a giant canvas, McCullough took the same shortcuts as his fellow deniers. In order to acquit Truman of Nuremberg crimes he wrote out major bomb dissenters like Navy Under Secretary Ralph Bard and former Japanese Ambassador Joseph Grew, unforgettable characters in every forthright account of Hiroshima. (Both Truman and Stimson gave Grew his due in their reminiscences; and Bundy rendered homage to Bard in *Danger and Survival*.) McCullough also rid his hagiographic landscape of thirty years of revisionist lit. Neither the term revisionism, nor any derivative, appeared in the book or the voluminous backnotes. "Conscience" does not appear in the index under Truman. But "morals and integrity of" has five brief entries (fifteen less than "piano playing of"), though none related to incinerating cities. (N.B. James David Barber's chapter on Truman in *The Presidential Character* devoted merely a sentence to the bomb decision.)

McCullough escaped recrimination for his contorted narrative of Hiroshima and Nagasaki the first time around. Except for Ronald Steel in *New Republic*, reviewers revered *Truman* as the crowning achievement of a much honored popular historian in the autumn of a splendid career. They marveled at the glory of his style and the grandeur of his range, and politely forgave the bend in his knee.

Yet history may not be gentle to McCullough. Revisionism is gaining on him already. Not only did his account of the bomb cost him a National Book Critics Circle Award, but two of his original champions—Columbia professor Alan Brinkley, who launched the *Truman* boom with an extravagant frontpage notice in the *New York Times Book Review*, and Catherine Clinton, who chaired the friendly Pulitzer biography jury—have expressed profound second thoughts about his atomic scholarship. "The people who gave McCullough prizes should be embarrassed," said Bernstein. "We learn who the butler was, but the book is unencumbered by critical analysis, and in many places by deep archival research."

Brinkley, a professor of modern American history at Columbia, said that he had detoured around his reservations. Though he asserted in the *Times* that *Truman* was an "honest and revealing portrait" containing "intelligent, straightforward accounts of [HST's] most controversial moments," the passages on the bomb were privately bothersome. "The last thing I wanted to do was an academic review of a non-academic book in the *Times*," Brinkley explained. "I would have raised different questions and used different standards on some points had I been writing for the *American Historical Review*. *Truman* is not the kind of book I would have written. It's very difficult to defend McCullough's treatment of the decision to drop the bomb. His scholarship on Hiroshima is not considered one of the great moments in the book. But I don't think he is being dishonest as much as he is not being engaged. If he's dishonest, then much of the revisionist scholarship is equally dishonest in making use of the partial record."

Clinton, whose specialty is 19th century America, is a former research associate at Harvard's W.E.B. DuBois Institute. Describing the Pulitzer jury process, Clinton said: "Unless the book is in one's field, we're more expert readers than experts." Although she felt that McCullough's treatment of Hiroshima was skimpy, the issue was not uppermost in her mind during deliberations.

According to Pulitzer protocol, the biography jury nominated three books for the consideration of the ultimate judges on the Pulitzer Board: *Truman, Kissinger* by Walter Isaacson, and *Genius: The Life and Science of Richard Feynman* by James Gleick. "The finalists were not ranked in order and superlative adjectives were used to describe all three," said Clinton. "I especially liked McCullough's writing about the mythic epic of the American Century of which Truman was a tailor-made icon. I was not unhappy that *Truman* eventually won."

But soon after the award was announced, Clinton heard murmurs from colleagues about a seriously botched job on the bomb, and she began wondering. "In all frankness, it didn't occur to me that McCullough was being dishonest," she remarked. "As writers and biographers, we all come across material that doesn't fit. But I am willing to say that I may have been mistaken. *Truman* was a great book, but if McCullough ignored information, consciously and deliberately, simply because it worked against his thesis, I would call that fabricating history."

In contrast to the Pulitzer Board that graced *Truman* with the prize of prizes, the board of the National Book Critics Circle revolted against the biography. As the only title listed on twenty-five percent or more of the memberships' ballots, *Truman* was an automatic finalist and the grassroots favorite in its category. But when the inner circle of the NBCC met to choose the winners, some raised doubts about *Truman*'s authenticity on the bomb and it faded from contention. "A biographer of Truman who does not face Hiroshima with analytical skepticism, especially since Truman never expressed any reservations himself, abdicates his responsibility to the historical record," said Herb Leibowitz, editor of *Parnassus* and president of NBCC.

Although McCullough had a personal stake in the Smithsonian morality play, he has, perhaps prudently, recused himself. "I know nothing about the Smithsonian's 'Enola Gay' exhibit, beyond what I've seen in the papers," he wrote to Capaccio of *Defense Week* last October when he publicly admitted the snafu about the "Handy" memo. Far out on the grassy knoll of Hiroshima denial, the president of the Society of American Historians seemed to know when to fade away.

William Manchester, however, did not hesitate to enter the contretemps. Although immersed in the third volume of his Churchill biography in the Florida Keys, Manchester spoke to *New York Observer* columnist Terry Golway about his Smithsonian discontents in February of 1995. Golway was a sympathetic listener. His "Wise Guys" column began:

> William Manchester carries a photocopy of his heart x-ray when he travels by air. "There's a Japanese bullet in the right ventricle, and it sets off metal detectors," the ex-Marine said. It is a reminder of his youthful days spent on a South Pacific beach called Okinawa.
>
> Mr. Manchester, historian and veteran, watched the debate over the Smithsonian Institution's infamous Hiroshima exhibition with the fury of an eyewitness whose credibility is under attack. "I don't understand these revisionists at all," he told Wise Guys. "You'd think the museum would give credence to those of us who were there. I guess we just don't count any more."

Initially snookered by his military sources, Golway wrote that the Smithsonian's script was a "politically correct wartime story" that "tarnished the sterling legacy of Mr. Manchester's generation." "Wise Guys" continued:

"I resent being put on the defensive by all of this," Mr. Manchester said. "I hitched a ride from Amherst to Springfield and signed up to defend my country. I didn't do it because I was a racist who wanted to exterminate the Japanese race." He said he "would not have been offended" by a discussion of whether or not the bombing of Hiroshima was justified. But, he added, there was a context to the atomic bomb attacks only those who lived through the war can appreciate.

Manchester's sentiments are owed respect. His courage and that of his fallen comrades must be honored. That goes without saying. But veterans wear their trunks too high when they link their march across the Pacific with criminal decisions made in Washington. Baldur von Shirach, leader of Hitler Jugend, was tried at Nuremberg, not the jugend. Nonetheless, the Fussellian assumption in Manchester's argument (paraphrased by Golway) —that you had to be there to understand the massacres of Hiroshima and Nagasaki—is weak. Douglas MacArthur lived through the war, and *he* deplored the bomb. Manchester himself conveyed MacArthur's strong feelings in his biography, *American Caesar*. In a passage that tended to tarnish Truman, Manchester relayed the general's displeasure with the Potsdam ultimatum:

> MacArthur was appalled. He knew that the Japanese would never renounce their emperor, and without him an orderly transition to peace would be impossible anyhow, because his people would never submit to Allied occupation unless he ordered it. Ironically, when surrender did come, it was conditional, and the condition was a continuation of the imperial reign. Had the general's advice been followed, the resort to atomic weapons at Hiroshima and Nagasaki might have been unnecessary.

Manchester was reminded of this passage in light of his

Hiroshima kiss. But his written reply on March 23, 1995, side-stepped MacArthur's revisionism. While conceding the inculpability of the atomic victims, Manchester chastised the messengers with unworthy anti-intellectualism:

> Because the bombings of Hiroshima and Nagasaki had led to the surrender, they can fairly be said to have prevented an invasion and the horrors which would have followed. That, however, does not alter the fact that both were appalling tragedies. How else can the slaughter of over 140,000 innocents be described? Moreover, the bombers had set loose the genie of nuclear weaponry, which has haunted the world for fifty years and may eventually lead to its total destruction.

I do, however, wonder about the motives of those who dwell upon the atomic bombings to the exclusion of all other World War II calamities. During the years which ended in 1945 some 55,000,000 people perished, 99 percent of whom did *not* die in Hiroshima and Nagasaki. The grim total includes the victims of Hitler's terror bombings of England, the U.S. terror bombings of Japan, the rape of Nanking, the destruction of Dresden, the Hamburg firestorm, the Japanese massacre of 100,000 Filipinos in Manila, the Nazi slaughter of 6,000,000 Jews in Eastern Europe, and the starvation of 3,000,000 Indians in the great Bengali famine of 1943, a direct consequence of the struggle for Assam.

They must be remembered with grief, and it seems to me, with grief alone. Any exploitation of their memory to advance sophistic reasoning—to argue, for example, that the United States was waging a racist war in the Pacific—is a further violation of them. If it weren't ghoulish, that bizarre contention would be ironic, for afterward we found that there had, in fact, been racism out there—on the other side. The Japanese, like the Aryans, had believed that theirs was the superior race.

Manchester's letter, which reacted to several correspondents on the *Enola Gay* exhibit, was addressed to Bernstein and copied to this writer. Bernstein had requested a reference for an unfootnoted quote in *American Caesar* connecting MacArthur to the discredited million-man invasion figure. The quote read: "[MacArthur] had no illusions about the savagery that lay ahead—he told Stimson that Downfall [the codeword for the overall invasion] would 'cost over a million casualties to American forces alone'—but he was confident that with the tanks from Europe he could outmaneuver the defenders of the great Kanto Plain before Tokyo." But unlike his friend McCullough, who begrudgingly admitted using a bad number, Manchester ducked an accounting of MacArthur's alleged seven-figure estimate—for the third time according to Bernstein.

Another old soldier, William Styron, was gratified by the bomb. His benediction was softer and more eloquent than Fussell's and Manchester's, though almost as wrongheaded. In 1945, Styron was a young Marine officer preparing for the invasion. Naturally, he was scared about landing on the beaches of Japan. The atom bomb arrived as a pleasant relief. "I cannot say, from this distance in time, what is more firmly lodged in my memory—the desperate fatalism and sadness that pervaded, beneath our nervous bravado, the days and nights of us young boys, or the joy we felt when we heard of the bomb, of Hiroshima and Nagasaki, and of the thrilling turnaround of our destiny," he observed in a *Newsweek* essay (January 11, 1993). "It was a war we all believed in and I wanted to test my manhood; part of me mourned that I never got near the combat zone. But Hiroshima removed from my shoulders an almost tactile burden of insecurity and dread. Later I often used the word ecstatic to describe my reaction."

So far, so good. Styron's animal instinct was all too human. As a young medical student, Robert Jay Lifton, author of the classic *Death in Life: Survivors of Hiroshima*, had similar feelings. "I remember telling a friend that, if a single American life were saved, dropping the bomb was the right thing to do," Lifton recalled. Although Styron put aside the ecstasy defense in his maturity, he revived the "good" atrocity argument popularized by *Reader's Digest*. ("Never in all the long history of human slaughter have lives been lost to greater purposes," the *Digest* stated in November, 1945.) So at odds with his own *non viva el muerte* politics, he found a ray of sunshine amid the black rain:

> ...it might be said that the sacrifice of its victims represented an object lesson and perhaps a priceless warning, preventing the future use of the weapon that achieved such destruction. If so, the many deaths and the suffering—the same that assured my probable survival and that of my Tokyo comrade in arms, along with legions of others—may be justified, if we who have lived so long afterward are fit to justify such a fathomless event.

Styron's "larger meaning" dodge is the last resort of a Hiroshima denier. This kind of morally macabre reasoning helped the bomb-makers of the Manhattan Project to salve their conscience. "I was a susceptible young scientist and an admirer of [J. Robert] Oppenheimer's and [Niels] Bohr's," said Philip Morrison, the physicist who assisted in the design and arming of the Nagasaki device, in the *Village Voice*. "I more or less followed their lead. Bohr's view was that the bomb should be manifested to the world in a believable way so as to prevent this terrible catastrophe from happening on a thousandfold larger scale in the future. Hard as it was, his view persuaded me. Maybe it was wrong. But look, this was a very high stakes game. Two hundred thousand lives was not the stake. The stake was the next war. It was not a terror bomb, it was the bomb of the future, as the world has shown by building 50,000 of the damn things."

Obviously, Morrison is not an ethical primitive. After surveying the ashes of Ground Zero in Hiroshima, he returned home to write the anti-nuke constitution of the Federation of Atomic Scientists. A witty polymath with a distinguished academic career at Cornell and MIT, he has labored tirelessly against the bomb.

However, Morrison's illumination was weirdly shortcircuited.

"I don't think the bombs were used *entirely* unwisely, *entirely* thoughtlessly," he added. "In the light of history, it may be that a demonstration more than a test was necessary. But then you say, 'But why two bombs?' And there you have a strong case." When asked pointblank if he would do it all over again, he replied: "You raise an interesting question about individual responsibility, but my concern was with the event. Were there a time when I could have changed the event, I would have. But just washing my hands as Pontius Pilate did on that famous occasion, I'm not sure that's right either. The bible is full of all kinds of lessons.... What I say is to some degree self-serving. I have a great moral dilemma about this thing. I'm not a pacifist, but I think I ought to be. But I'm not a vegetarian, either."

Something there is that blocks the moral sensibility of thinking Hiroshima deniers. "The most demonic success of Hitler was his ability to Hitlerize his enemies," German Lutheran theologian Dieter Georgi remarked in *Harvard Magazine* (March–April 1985). While Peretz deemed the Allies morally superior because the Axis "elevated atrocities from an occasional tactic to an intrinsic strategy," the cyclopian Morrison saw a parallel. "When we beat the Nazis, we emulated them," he told Studs Terkel in *The Good War*. "I include myself. I became callous to death. I became willing to risk everything on war and peace. I followed my leaders enthusiastically and rather blindly."

If there is some kind of equivalence between the "Jewish holocaust and the Japanese holocaust" as Shimon Peres asserted, and if "'Holocausts' have perpetrators," as Eric Breindel contended, perhaps the parallel statements of two soldiers, one German and one American, one judged, one unjudged, can elucidate the original sin:

"Don't you see, we SS men were not supposed to think about these things; it never even occurred to us.... We were all so trained to obey orders without even thinking that the thought of disobeying an order would never have occurred to anybody."
Rudolf Franz Ferdinand Hoess, Commandant at Auschwitz (1940-1943), at the Nuremberg Tribunal, 1946

"I am an airman, a pilot. In 1945, I was wearing the uniform of the US following the orders of our commander-in-chief. I was, to the best of my ability, doing what I could to bring the war to a victorious conclusion—just as millions of people were doing here at home and around the world. Each of us—friend and foe alike—were doing the dictates of our respective governments."

Brigadier General Paul Tibbets (Ret.), pilot of the Enola Gay, *in 1994*

THREE

Apologia Pro Hiroshima and Nagasaki

"What better moment than the fiftieth anniversary of the end of World War II for us unequivocally to say of Hiroshima and Nagasaki, Never Again."
Doug Ireland

John Paul II has confessed the Church's sinful attachment to the African slave trade.

Germany has bowed its head in repeated shame for the Six Million.

The bishop of Coventry has expressed sorrow for Britain's leading part in the burning of Dresden.

Emperor Akihito has voiced "deep sadness" for Japan's atrocities in China.

But two presidents of the United States have declined to say sorry for the Bombs of August.

George Bush was stone cold to the idea of exchanging mutual regrets on the fiftieth anniversary of Pearl Harbor. Mentioning legions of American soldiers saved by the bomb, Bush sneered at the remorse thing on *This Week With David Brinkley*: "Not from this president....There should be no apology requested, and that in my view, is rank revisionism."

President Clinton brusquely refused to answer a reporter's apology inquiry after a ceremony at the Marine Corps Memorial commemorating the Battle of Iwo Jima on February 19, 1995. When the question was broached again at the annual convention of the American Society of Newspaper Editors in Dallas on April 7, Clinton simply said, "No," noting that Truman had made the right decision "based on the facts that he had before him."

Clinton's personal attitude toward the atomic massacres remained unuttered until his April 18 press conference when he was asked about his apparent lack of sympathy for the victims. Though gentler than Bush, Clinton did not bend on a half-century of American denial: "Do I wish none of it had happened? Of course I do. But that does not mean that President Truman in the moment of decision made the wrong decision. Or that the United States can now apologize for a decision that we did not believe then, and I don't believe now, was the wrong one."

A low contrition streak runs deep in a country that enslaved Africans for two hundred and fifty years, exterminated most of its native population, and recently killed some three million Indochinese. If we waited forty years merely to make reparations for the unconstitutional roundup of Japanese-Americans during the war, time is not on the side of Hiroshima and Nagasaki.

Philip Morrison, Edward Teller, David McCullough, William Styron, William Manchester, Martin Peretz, Arthur Schlesinger, Paul Nitze, Paul Tsongas, Barney Frank, and seventy-one percent of Americans polled by Gallup in June 1994 feel unapologetic about dropping the bomb.

Jerry Brown and Michael Kinsley, standing for three percent of the population, are neutral.

Hans Bethe and George McGovern, representing another

three percent, have mixed emotions.

But Garry Wills, Nat Hentoff, Edward Sorel, John Kenneth Galbraith, Richard Rhodes, Tom Hayden, Curtis Sliwa, Jonathan Demme, Daniel Ellsberg, the late, great Linus Pauling, and twenty-three percent of Americans believe that the United States should apologize to Japan.

"The notion of facing up to the sins of one's culture, whether it's about slavery or the incarceration of the Nisei, is a good thing," said Wills on the 47th anniversary of the bombing. "A conservative likes to take credit for tradition when it flatters him or her. So you should take the blame as well. Demanding that Japan apologize first for Pearl Harbor only trivializes the matter."

Styron esteems Wills, the author of acclaimed books on Washington, Jefferson, Lincoln and Nixon, but not his apology concept. In a letter responding to this writer's query, Styron wrote on April 10:

> I think I have tried to face up to the sins of our culture, to use Garry Wills's term, as well as any American writer.
>
> But there are so many pious and hypocritical points of view suggested in your letter—from those of the Pope and the Church to that of the ignorant and misinformed Eisenhower to that of the admirable Garry Wills—that I find it hard to adequately express my contempt for the idea of apologizing to Japan, much less explaining the many reasons why such an apology would be outrageous—the most important being that the lives of thousands of the potential invading troops on the mainland of Japan (myself included) were almost certainly saved by the dropping of the atomic bomb.
>
> Despite the Emperor's sanctimonious "deep sadness," the Japanese have never officially apologized for their appalling atrocities against civilians in Asia and against Allied prisoners of war, scores of thousands of whom died in conditions approaching those of Nazi concentration camps, and whose ordeal has recently been definitively

chronicled in *Prisoners of the Japanese* by Gavan Daws. By contrast, the Germans have admirably confronted their Nazi past, and Americans have dealt soul-searchingly not only with slavery and our sins against Native Americans but also with our criminal war in Vietnam, culminating at this very moment with the remarkable confessions of Robert McNamara.

The Japanese have steadfastly refused, as a nation, to accept guilt for their recent history (this has been scathingly documented by Ian Buruma in the *New York Review of Books*), but until they do, our future, and theirs, will be in danger. I am convinced by the evidence that the Japanese were *not* ready to surrender, and that, tragic as it was, the dropping of the atomic bomb was an historical necessity. But even if this were not so, there would be a need for Japan to accept blame for its atrocious past (of which Pearl Harbor was only a small component), and that they have not done so remains a moral outrage and an offense to humanity.

Styron's blast was echoed more painfully, almost nihilistically, by William Manchester whose heart was hardened on Okinawa. Responding to the same letter, he wrote on March 23:

Demands that nations apologize to one another are equally preposterous. The warlords of the early 1940s have long been in their graves. Most of the leaders of today's governments have no recollection of the war; many, including our incumbent President, weren't even born when it ended. What would be accomplished by a Japanese apology for the attack on Pearl Harbor? It would merely taunt the 2,000 American sailors entombed in the rusting hulk of the *Arizona*. Great crimes cannot be absolved by contrition. And the weary *lieux commun*—pledges that we must never let it happen again—mock every evening's news telecast. It *is* happening again, every day, in Chechnya, in Bosnia-Herzegovina, in Algeria, in Pakistan, in Ulster, in

Palestine, in the subways of Tokyo. And nothing—and no one—will stop it.

The martyrs of World War II have been dead for half a century. Many, if not most, belonged to my generation, and each year my awareness of them, and my sense of loss, grows stronger. In the name of Almighty God, let them alone.

Arthur Schlesinger, Albert Schweitzer Professor of the Humanities at City University of New York, was un-Schweitzerian on the issue. "The Japanese have not only never apologized for Pearl Harbor, but to this day the few Japanese historians who have tried to write honestly about the Pacific war have encountered a very tough time in Japan," Schlesinger said. "Japanese textbooks contain the most sanitized account of their invasion of China and their claim that they were forced into the Second World War and so on. Somebody must be kidding if they expect we should apologize to Japan, for Christ's sake....Even if the Japanese apologized for Pearl Harbor, I would not alter my position."

Paul Nitze, former vice-chairman of the U.S. Strategic Bombing Survey and arms negotiator for Ronald Reagan, claimed that the destruction of Hiroshima and Nagasaki was gratuitous. "The Japanese were in such bad shape that we concluded they would surrender by November 1945, whether or not the Russians came in, whether or not we invaded the home islands, whether or not we dropped the bomb," said Nitze, paraphrasing the Survey's judgment. Nevertheless, Nitze shed not a tear and gnashed not a tooth for the unlucky denizens of Ground Zero. Despite the Hague Conventions, the Nuremberg and Tokyo tribunals, and the just war tradition, he regretted nothing. "The whole idea of apology is insane. There are no rules of morality in war that I know of."

The most bizarre naysayer was Edward Teller, the father of the hydrogen bomb and Reagan's Strategic Defense Initiative. In a perverse moral calculus, Teller might apologize to the

Japanese, yet not for our nuking tens of thousands of women and children, which he admitted was a blunder, but rather for prosecuting the enemy's arch criminals in Tokyo. "I think the bombings were a mistake," Teller said. "We had been at war. I think it would have been much better if we did not use the atomic bomb prior to demonstrating it and having the chance to end the war without killing people. Had that happened, there would have been a better understanding among the American people about what was going on and the strong anti-nuclear sentiments would not have developed. The war had been started by the Japanese, and while I think the bombing was a mistake, an apology is not needed or logical. It is essentially an improper question to ask."

"...While I am uncomfortable about the Nuremberg procedure, I feel even more uncomfortable about the Tokyo procedure where Prince Fuminaro Konoye, who tried to make peace in July on a mission to Russia, he was completely unjustly arrested as a war criminal and committed suicide. ...And for *that* I would apologize to the Japanese. It is one thing to apply a weapon when it probably was unnecessary. That was a mistake. But if, after people have been defeated, you then treat them improperly, for that an apology might be in order."

New Republic editor-in-chief Martin Peretz, softer than Teller on the bomb but equally obdurate about apologizing, maintained that it was not "unreasonable" to cremate two Japanese metropolises. Prompted by this writer's letter, he devoted a column to the subject in the April 17 *New Republic*:

I've been reading *The Wages of Guilt: Memories of War in Germany and Japan* by the journalist and *TNR* contributor Ian Buruma. Full of stunningly textured insights, the book was published in late 1994 and so should still be in the bookstores. It will certainly be relevant to the debate which will rage as we get closer to August 6. This is a macabre travel book, a journey to places in which the memories of war are vivid and haunt both conscience and consciousness.

It is a comparative book, and the comparisons are stark. Let me put this a little crudely: the Germans have kept their diaries of the past, worked on them, reconsidered them, worked on them again, not to obscure but to reveal. Any serious person you meet in Germany has wrestled with the war, the Holocaust and the war. This is not the case at the other end of the Axis which, to be sure, did not enact a genocide. By and large, the Japanese are deniers, and they use the two atomic bombings to nullify the evidence of that about which they do not want to know themselves. See how far you will get in conversation, for example, if you raise the Nanking Massacre with most Japanese, even very thoughtful ones. More likely, you will not, upon further consideration, raise the matter at all. You know it will offend and don't want to be impolite.

All this came to mind when I read the recent front-page *New York Times* story about Japanese atrocities— specifically the use of Chinese prisoners for brutal experiments involving chemical and biological agents—during the war. It's not clear what provoked this attention just now. What the *Times* detailed surely is already well known although not quite absorbed. Of course, there had been war crimes proceedings after the war. And, then, beginning some fifteen years ago, random individuals began to speak out: a film maker, a novelist, a veteran of the invasion of China, among others. The secrets could not be suppressed forever. In 1981 and 1982, the Japanese press was suddenly full of the grim truths.

What is surprising, in fact, is that while the Japanese were learning, however reluctantly, about what their soldiers did during the war, the information was not passed on to American readers by American journalists stationed in Japan. Quick to pick up leads, American scholars have mined the materials ever since. But American knowledge of the most barbaric practices by the Japanese goes back at least to 1945. Japan's Unit 731 performed vast medical experiments whose cruelties rivaled Dr. Mengele's. These apparently did not quite shock American officials when they discovered this line of research right after the war, or did not shock them enough. Buruma tells us that guilty Japanese doctors were let free in exchange for their data.

Maybe this big play given by the *Times* to the evidence, at once shrouded but public, of Japanese crimes against humanity will mute the call for American remorse about the bomb. If anything, in fact, this evidence bolsters the case for why dropping the bomb seemed reasonable to Harry Truman and the men around him and why it still doesn't seem unreasonable to some of us. Had the bomb not been dropped many more thousands of Allied and Japanese troops would have been felled in combat. Prisoners of war would have been tortured and killed. And, as the Allied victory became surer, the subjects of the soon-to-be-vanquished Japanese empire would have had wreaked on them the savagery which only a religious "banzai" army in defeat could imagine inflicting.

In any case, who could be certain, when (or that) Japan would have actually surrendered? Some Japanese believe that, instead of a war crimes tribunal imposed by the victors, there should have been a war crimes trial initiated by the Japanese themselves. But with what crimes would the indicted be charged? One Japanese historian answers: "For starting a war which they knew they would lose." Could rulers who had started such a war be counted on to end it just because it had been lost on the battlefield? He who is sure about that will be sure about everything.

Still mired in rationalization, the American who may have the most to feel sorry for in 1995, will not say *mea maxima culpa.* "I'm a consequential moralist, not an intentional one," said Philip Morrison. "Apologies seem a matter of good intentions."

The anti-apologists above tend to have either generation (World War II) or politics (rightist) in common. The two exceptions, Paul Tsongas and Barney Frank, liberals' liberals from the "Don't Blame Me" state of Massachusetts, and might be expected to exercise a Pauling on Nagasaki, if not Hiroshima. Not close. Like Clinton, Tsongas had faith in Truman. "I don't believe we dropped the bomb for the hell of it," said the former Democratic presidential aspirant. "Truman wouldn't drop bombs for the sake of dropping bombs. He would have to have a good reason. You do not go about apologizing for actions that were warranted, although any large loss of civilian life is to be lamented."

Frank held the lamentation in check. Seeming affronted by the apology question, he snapped at this writer's daughter, Caitlin, at the Radio & Television Correspondents Association Dinner in Washington on March 16.

"I don't think it's appropriate at all," said the congressman. "I don't think we should apologize. The war was largely started by the Japanese. The apology is due from them to the victims of their aggressions. Should everybody apologize? Why for Hiroshima and Nagasaki, and not for the firebombing of Dresden or the bombing of Tokyo or any civilian bombings? Are there a minimum number of people killed before you apologize?"

"The bombs killed two-hundred-thousand," she replied.

"What's the minimum number?" he asked.

"There is none."

"Then how do you make a rational decision?" he shot back.

Jerry Brown straddled the fence. "I'll have to think about an apology," Brown said while campaigning for the Democratic presidential nomination in New York in 1992. "You know any kind of destruction like that is a moral evil. You're in the middle of a war—the bombing of Dresden—I don't know where this jesuitical discussion would end."

Michael Kinsley usually leans *a gauche* on genocide and weapons of mass destruction in *New Republic*, but he was not moved to make amends for Truman's bombs. "Have the Japanese apologized for Pearl Harbor?"

George McGovern was a bomber pilot in Europe during World War II, but he spontaneously consented to an apology. "Yeah sure," McGovern said, "but at that time I thought it was great. I was 22 years old and it meant the end of the war." However, when the conversation moved to war crimes, McGovern suddenly reversed course: "No, I wouldn't apologize. I think the bombs were the greatest thing in the world, and I still do."

Hans Bethe, a German émigré and Nobel Laureate who labored on the Nagasaki weapon, is one of many tortured A-bomb creators who have suffered post-Ground-Zero syndrome. "If you ask me if I have known sin, yes," Bethe said in the *Village Voice*. "Not specifically for the bombing of Hiroshima and Nagasaki, but for generally bringing this weapon into the world." As for an apology, Bethe remarked: "Well, I don't think that is an important problem, but I see no harm if there is an apology from both sides, on our side for the atomic bombing and from Japan on Pearl Harbor. That would be a fair thing to do."

What separates the pro-apologists from the anti-apologists is a sensitive genocide-detector, one that flutters at the sound of Truman's biblical threat to leave no stone upon a stone in Japan. The chilling words of the Potsdam ultimatum, joined by Churchill and Chiang Kai-shek, will resound forever in the annals of vengeance: "The full application of our military power, backed by our resolve, will mean the inevitable and complete destruction of the Japanese forces, *and just as inevitably the utter devastation of the Japanese homeland*....We call upon the Government of Japan to proclaim now the unconditional surrender of all the Japanese armed forces, and to provide proper and adequate assurances of their good faith in such action. *The alternative to Japan is complete and utter destruction*" (emphasis added).

Nat Hentoff, the *Village Voice*'s searcher of hard cases, ranks Hiroshima and Nagasaki with history's all-time atrocities including the destruction of European Jews. "Not so much because Japan was defeated but because of the peculiar terror of the weapon," Hentoff said. "That's why Paul VI called the bombing 'butchery of untold magnitude.'"

"These bombings were totally unrelated to strategic objectives and broke a moral barrier by ushering in an age of nuclear terror," said Tom Hayden. "We have yet to acknowledge their immorality. But we haven't apologized to Native Americans either. I'd start there."

"I can't help thinking that there's little difference between Mylai and the atomic bombings," said Richard Rhodes, author of *The Making of the Atomic Bomb.* "They both involved the wanton destruction of non-combatants—old men, women, and children."

Michael Tomasky, a political columnist for *The Villiage Voice,* has a master apology plan:

Well, Hiroshima and Nagasaki would be a decent enough place to start. Next perhaps could come Vietnam, Nicaragua, El Salvador, the Philippines, the Dominican Republic, Chile, Zaire, Angola… In other words, if the United States ever wants truly to set a moral example among nations, it can start doing so by acknowledging the terror it has spread and financed in the name of democracy. Were it not for the unique nature of the horror of the atomic bombs, I'd consider what the United States did to all the other countries listed above far, far worse; at least in Japan we were fighting a genuinely fascist country whose threat to world stability existed in point of fact, rather than in the minds of a few dishonest hacks who happened to be in charge of national security policy.

What's past is past, some will say. But this temptation to let lying dogs sleep must be overcome if the next century is to stand a chance of improvement over the one limping toward its grave. In fact, here's my suggestion for a good way to start the next one: America, Russia, and the dark century's other imperial powers (including, of course, Japan), all get together and confess to the world the extent of their crimes, all of which were committed in the name of making the world safe for something or other. Once the extent to which the world was made unsafe by all of them is fully known, then can the world's citizens imagine and demand a new way. I suspect, though, that, as usual, people will die trying.

ALBERT EINSTEIN once called NATIONALISM "THE CHILDHOOD DISEASE OF MANKIND". THE INABILITY OF SUPER-PATRIOTS TO CRITICIZE THE DEPLORABLE ACTS OF THEIR OWN COUNTRY SHOULD BE REGARDED, THEREFORE, AS A CASE OF ARRESTED DEVELOPMENT.

Edward Sorel

Curtis Sliwa, founder of the Guardian Angels and now a conservative talk show host on New York City's WABC radio, drew on his streetwise background. "Absolutely, we should apologize," Sliwa said. "The bombings were racist. We dropped on them on yellow people after all those 'yellow peril' propaganda films by Frank Capra." Contrasting the strategy of his Angels with that of the criminals of World War II, he said: "We go after drug dealers, but we leave their wives and children alone."

"I'd be just as anxious to apologize for Dresden," said John Kenneth Galbraith who worked on the European Strategic Bombing Survey. "...I was given the task of establishing the economic justification for bombing cities, which was extremely limited."

Doug Ireland, veteran radical journalist who is covering the '96 presidential race for *The Nation*, was revolted by the indifference of liberals, but not surprised:

Liberalism's greatest flaw is its moral relativity, which has made it so easily recouperable by nationalism. When

"Dr. New Deal" was replaced by "Dr. Win the War," thereby ushering in the birth of the national security state, a host of crimes suddenly became justifiable on the grounds of the greatest good. The incineration of Dresden's civilian population, which had no material effect on the German war effort, was made even more terrible by the simultaneous decision *not* to bomb the Nazi death camps as the World Jewish Congress had urged the United States to do.

By playing the numbers game, Barney Frank and company overlook the principle that the Nuremberg trials had helped establish: the taking of a single innocent human life is as great a horror as taking of a thousand, or ten thousand, or six million. If that were not so, why would we still be pursuing Nazi war criminals of minor grade fifty years later?

Dresden was destroyed at a time when the outcome of the European war was no longer in doubt, but it was an Allied crime inspired by the British and carried out under the command of the notorious "Butcher" Harris. The war in the Pacific, however, was uniquely American, and the decision to drop the bomb was solely ours. Liberal defenders of that decision conveniently overlook the fact that, at that moment in time, Japanese capitulation could have been secured if Japan had simply been assured that they would keep their Emperor, something that Truman admittedly *knew*.

This makes a mockery of the idea that bombing Hiroshima was somehow necessary to save the lives of American troops. Not only did we allow the Japanese to keep their Emperor, in the service of the cold war we recruited their biological warfare experiments and reinstalled at the command of the Japanese economy the industrial criminals who had begun the war and reaped enormous profits from slave labor (one of the reasons Japan's corporate life today has a neo-militarist culture of organization).

From Breckinridge Long (architect of the anti-Semitic

plot in FDR's State Department) and James Byrnes (the right hand who counseled Truman's left hand to drop the bombs) to Robert McNamara and Henry Kissinger, from the turning away of Jews from American shores and the internment of Japanese-Americans to the carpet-bombing of Vietnam and Cambodia and the Gulf War's careless extinction of huge numbers of Iraqi women and children, America has a great deal for which to apologize. In the case of Japanese-Americans, it already has. How much more urgent, then, to apologize for Hiroshima, when America became Moloch, Destroyer of Worlds, in the phrase made famous by Oppenheimer.

And contrary to the position taken by Bill Clinton—who uses MacNamara to justify his own tortured draft evasions, but simultaneously says, it's not the right time to discuss America's war in the Pacific—what better moment than the fiftieth anniversary of the end of World War II for us unequivocally to say of Hiroshima and Nagasaki, Never Again.

In the certain absence of an official government apology, the pacifist Fellowship of Reconciliation, directed by Jo Becker and headquartered in Nyack, New York (914-358-4601), has embarked on a grassroots campaign to gather signatures for an open letter— A Call for Repentance and Reconciliation—that apologizes for August 6 and 9, 1945. The text of the letter reads:

The image of the atomic mushroom cloud is etched forever in human memory as we commemorate the fiftieth anniversary of the bombings of Hiroshima and Nagasaki. We, the undersigned citizens of the United States, express our profound sorrow to the Japanese people as we recall the suffering and death left in the wake of the destruction of the two cities. On behalf of those peace-loving people of our country who grieve over the decision of our government to drop the bombs and the unimaginable pain inflicted upon the families and survivors of the doomed cities, we extend a heartfelt apology. We are deeply sorry for the agony caused by these actions, and we ask for your forgiveness.

This apology does not ignore the atrocities committed by Japanese forces in their march across Asia, nor does it forget the suffering and death of those in the occupied countries, among the Allies, and those in the armed forces. But we reject mass killing and obliteration bombings as acceptable policies, then or now. Means and ends are inextricably related, as the seed is to the tree. We feel it necessary to acknowledge and atone for the decision of our nation to introduce the use of atomic weapons and for the subsequent nuclear arms race which still hangs over the head of civilization.

In the fifty years since the war ended, many in the United States and Japan have worked tirelessly to promote reconciliation and friendship between our two peoples. With our signatures below, we solemnly pledge to continue these efforts. We promise to work with our Japanese friends and with others around the world for universal disarmament and the creation of a global culture of peace.

FOR's statement has been signed by Daniel Ellsberg, Jonathan Demme, the Berrigan brothers, David Dellinger, Howard Fast, Pete Seeger, and a number of religious leaders. An interfaith delegation will present the signatures at fiftieth anniversary commemorations in Japan.

Although it takes only one party to apologize, the Japanese government has discouraged American compassion by wantonly ignoring its own war crimes. An amoral axis seems to obtain between Japanese and American officialdom and veteran groups. A resolution calling for an apology to Asian nations has gotten nowhere in Japan's Parliament. Four and a half million Japanese have signed a petition against the proposal.

Their Newt Gingrich, the 81-year-old Seisuke Okuno, said in the *New York Times* (March 6, 1995) that the shoe was on our foot: "Incendiary bombs fell on Japan like rain and atomic bombs were dropped on Hiroshima and Nagasaki. And the

Russian Army committed mind-boggling atrocities against Japanese. So we think that there were war crimes more serious than any committed by Japan."

Their American Legion commander, Masao Horie, chairman of the Japan Veterans Association, told the *Times*: "I think World War II was one in which Japan was cornered and forced to fight for its self defense."

As a people, however, the Japanese are ahead of their elite. Four out of five believe that the state owes more compensation to the Asian victims of the Emperor's troops.

Clearly, a unilateral U.S. apology could serve the militarist element in Japan. "An American apology is very tricky," observed MIT history professor John Dower, author of *War Without Mercy* "What is considered a radical idea over here is conservative in Japan."

The memory of holocausts, however, is too important to be left to generals and politicians. Ed Linenthal, the religious studies professor from the University of Wisconsin (Oshkosh) who sat on the Smithsonian's Exhibition Advisory Board, has reflected on the apology puzzle, and suggested a way out:

> Japan and the United States have been doing an awkward and distasteful dance since shortly before the 50th anniversary ceremonies of the attack on Pearl Harbor regarding whether apologies were due to the United States for the attack, whether, in turn, apologies were due for the use of atomic weapons, which nation would be the first to offer such apologies, and from whom such expressions of remorse would come.
>
> An apology is a significant act of memory, remembering one's role in past injustice, offering an expression of sincere remorse for damage or injury inflicted, in the hopes that such an expression can heal the enduring wound. It is, perhaps, much easier for individuals to apologize than a nation. And yet, as we end the era of commemoration of World War II, questions of unspoken apologies persist,

from many Asian nations and the United States.

Germany's many acts of official contrition after the war and its continuing sense of responsibility for the Holocaust has been viewed as an official apology—although *no* act of contrition will heal this particular wound—but questions endure in Europe as well. Is Austria's sense of self as a victim nation a way of conveniently ignoring its role as enthusiastic murderer of Jews? Does Poland continue to murder the memory of Jews by forgetting the particular Holocaust of the Jews in their own nation? The question rages with particular anger in the Pacific. Perhaps it is because of continuing official Japanese resistance to owning up to the barbarities perpetrated on so many Asian nations and Allied prisoners of war. Perhaps it is because of the widespread Japanese perception that they were the victims of the conflict, as if the war started on August 6, 1945. This breeds only lingering resentment fanned by Japanese economic success.

As the 50th anniversary of the use of atomic weapons approaches, many Americans angrily and bitterly reject any idea of apology for Hiroshima and Nagasaki. "They deserved it" and "it ended the war and saved American and Japanese lives." Interestingly, however, polling data suggest that were the Japanese to apologize for Pearl Harbor, 50 percent of Americans would be willing to apologize for Hiroshima and Nagasaki.

If the function of national apologies is to make political points, to attempt to gain the moral highground, if it is an attempt to use such memory as a weapon, then I am not in favor of such insidious acts. If, however, acts of apology by the Japanese can help them officially engage their conduct in the war, and help bring closure to this horrific period in our history, then I am in favor of it.

If an American apology can serve to remind us all that immense human tragedy accompanies war—even a war celebrated as just, and an act remembered by so many of us as grimly necessary—if an apology can remind us of the human cost of war, then perhaps such an apology could be read as a humble and sobering reflection on the tens of millions of innocents lost in the last "good" war, and may strengthen what may be a universal resolve not to let this horror happen again.

Nevertheless, the remorseless pilot of the *Enola Gay* will not dip his wing in sorrow or pity. Following the no-can-do spirit of the current and immediate past commanders-in-chief, Tibbets hangs tough fifty years after unleashing the first nuclear holocaust. "Those of us who gained that victory have nothing to be ashamed of," he said at the Airmen Memorial Museum, "nor do we offer any apology."

FOUR

SATANIC RAPTURES

"The atomic bomb is shit."
J. Robert Oppenheimer

Tom Crouch, the man who mistook Hiroshima for a nuclear holocaust, remarked at an April symposium at the University of Michigan in Ann Arbor that his exhibit was gunned down because it "challenged an article of national faith," which is that nuking two Japanese cities was the most merciful way to assure surrender.

Harry S. Truman, of course, was the Baptist of this uncanny creed. Not only did he salute Divine Providence for delivering the weapon into American hands, but he invoked Him as Divine

Targeter, saying that "we pray that He may guide us to use it in His ways and for His purpose."

Winston Churchill espoused the same holy hell doctrine. "To avert a vast indefinite butchery," he wrote in his memoirs, "to bring the war to an end, to give peace to the world, to lay healing hands upon its tortured peoples by a manifestation of overwhelming power at the cost of a few explosions, seemed, after all our toils and perils, a miracle of deliverance."

Henry Stimson fortified the nobility of the city-sized pentecosts by paraphrasing *King Lear* in *On Active Service* ("He hates them who would upon the rack of this tough war would stretch them out longer."), suggesting, too, that Somebody up there liked the Bombs of August.

Yet this beatific vision has a black hole—it excludes the ultra-Dante scenes from Ground Zero as recorded by Dr. Michihiko Hachiya in *Hiroshima Diary:*

I saw several people plunging their heads into a half-broken water tank and drinking the water.... When I was close enough to see inside the tank I said "Oh!" out loud and instinctively drew back. What I has seen in the tank were the faces of monsters reflected from the water dyed red with blood. They had clung to the side of the tank and plunged their heads in to drink and there in that position they had died. From their burned and tattered middy blouses I could tell that they were high school girls, but there was not a hair left on their heads; the broken skin of their burned faces was stained bright red with blood. I could hardly believe that these were human faces.

I saw fire reservoirs filled to the brim with dead people who looked as though they had been boiled alive. In one reservoir I saw a man, horribly burned, crouching beside another man who was in one reservoir. He was drinking blood-stained water out of the reservoir.... In one reservoir there were so many dead people that there wasn't enough room for them to fall over. They must have died sitting in the water.

There were so many burned that the odor was like drying squid. They looked like boiled octopuses.... I saw a man whose eye had been torn out by an injury, and there he stood with his eye resting in the palm of his hand. What made my blood run cold was that it looked like the eye was staring at me.

Men whose whole bodies were covered with blood, and women whose skin hung from them like a kimono, plunged shrieking into the river. All these become corpses and their bodies are carried by the current toward the sea.

Survivors began to notice in themselves and others a strange form of illness. It consisted of nausea, vomiting, and loss of appetite; diarrhea with large amounts of blood in the stools; fever and weakness; purple spots on various parts of the body from bleeding into the skin...inflammation and ulceration of the mouth, throat, and gums... bleeding from the mouth, gums, throat, rectum, and urinary tract...loss of hair from the scalp and other parts of the body...extremely low white blood cell counts when those were taken...and in many cases a progressive course until death.

Some miracle. Some deliverance. Factoring in the brethren of Ground Zero—the burned, the poisoned, the vaporized—defenses of Truman's order have become satanic raptures, faith in Hiroshima and Nagasaki sheer apostasy.

For example, Hubert Dagley, the American Legion's internal affairs director, said that the schoolgirls of Hiroshima got what was coming to them: "It was a horrible thing, of course, but they weren't in school. They had been conscripted into the military and put in the street to build firebreaks. They were put in harm's way by their government....Maybe Truman considered children as combatants."

The Legion's callousness toward death originated at the national commander level. In September of 1994, as the Legion commenced its review of the Smithsonian script, William Detweiler pooh-poohed the high-low dispute over the invasion casualties. It did not matter to him whether a half-million American boys or 18 times fewer were rescued by the bombs. Deserting Truman's masquerade of proportionality, Detweiler implied that 200,000 Japanese, mostly women and children, were a suitable sacrifice regardless of the number of U.S. dead. "The use of a weapon against a brutal and ruthless aggressor to save 30,000 American lives was as morally justifiable as to use it to save 500,000," he said at the first meeting between the curators and the legionnaires. (But four months later, Detweiler would sabotage the exhibit after Harwit said the he would replace the higher figure with the lower, complaining to the White House that Truman's "morality" was being challenged.)

Contradicting the entire World War II canon as well as former chief Navy chaplain John Cardinal O'Connor, who condemned the saturation-bombing of Germany, Richard Hallion, the air force's historian-in-chief, absolved his employer of any wrongdoing. "There was no indiscriminate city bombing in World War II," said Hallion with a spin worthy of the Tobacco Institute. "The Allied bombing campaign was driven by ethical considerations." He repeated the tenet that Hiroshima, headquarters of Japan's 2nd Army and billet for 40,000 troops, was a vital military target, pure and simple. Yet if this were the case, why did the U.S., which had torched sixty-plus Japanese cities between February and June 1945, wait until August 6 to take out Hiroshima? Any reader of history knows the answer—the Army Air Force laid off Hiroshima, Nagasaki, Kokura and Niigata because the Target Committee wanted pristine test tubes for its $2 billion experiment. But Hallion said, none too frankly: "It was Hiroshima's time."

Presumably, it was Dresden's time on February 12, 1945. But casting out the evil spirits of Churchill, Simon Barrington-Ward, the Bishop of Coventry, went to Dresden on the fiftieth anniversary of the Allied bombing to make a confession. "Hitler's war had unleashed a whirlwind into which we were swept," the Bishop announced from the pulpit of Dresden's Cathedral. "The dynamic of war swept away our inhibitions. When the British and American air forces destroyed Dresden we had suppressed our moral principles."

Since Dresden was supposedly bombed in reprisal for the Luftwaffe's raid on Coventry, Bishop Barrington-Ward, who is also a member of the House of Lords, was a natural repenter for the British people. Although the Good Shepherd of Coventry has no equivalent over here, perhaps Major General Donald Harlin, the Protestant chief chaplain of the U.S. Air Force, and his Catholic deputy, Brigadier General Arthur Thomas, are best suited for this Samaritan's mission. However, both vicars forsook comment on the bombs mala fides and an American apology when approached via letter last April, and both refused to come to the telephone when called at Bolling Air Force Base in May.

"They don't think it would be constructive to talk," said Colonel Tom Boyd of the Air Force Office of Public Affairs, a media relations op of the sort never available to Christ.

"Our sworn duty was to God, country and victory," said Tibbets, apparently not in that order, and not without Chaplain Harlin's and Thomas's silent blessing.

However, there was one retired chaplain willing to come in from Caesarean cold. In 1946, Father Francis X. Murphy, a Redemptorist, was a chaplain at the United States Naval Academy. Feeling sympathy for his military flock and commander-in-chief, he wrote in *Catholic World* that Truman's decision was "in accordance with the divine plan."

Under the pseudonym of Xavier Rynne, Father Murphy went on to fame in the 60s as the author of *Letters From Vatican City*, a series of bestselling books on the intrigues of Vatican II that were excerpted with fanfare in *The New Yorker*.

Eighty-years-old and living in St. Mary's Parish in Annapolis, the priest had not thought much about his heretical stance of fifty years ago. "For crying out loud," he said when reminded of his dusty "divine" scenario for the Bombs of August. "Of course, I'd rewrite that today. It was wrong to bomb those two cities."

Sources

References not indicated in the text are listed below.

ONE: How the Smithsonian Was Forced To Stop Worrying and
Love the Bomb

Crouch quotation is from author interview with Father John Dear.

Taylor quotations are from author article in *The New York Observer,* November 9, 1992.

Conant, Bundy, and Stimson quotations are from James Hershberg's *James Conant:
Harvard To Hiroshima And the Making of the Nuclear Age* (1993).

Pauling quotation is from author interview.

Morrison quotations are from author article, "Apologia Pro Hiroshima and Nagasaki,"
in *The Village Voice,* August 11, 1992.

Hoover memo to Truman is from *Herbert Hoover and Harry S. Truman: A Documentary
History* (1992), edited by Timothy Walch and Dwight M. Miller. Hoover's memo
to Stimson is from the National Archives in Washington, D.C. (Bruce Lee revived
the Hoover memo as a justification for the bomb in *Marching Orders* (1995).
Unlike McCullough, Lee cited the War Department's refutation of Hoover's numbers. Even so, without presenting any supportive evidence, Lee argued that
Hoover's officially dismissed guesswork was indeed influential in Washington and
thus Truman was not lying in his postwar claims about 500,000 invasion dead.
Lee's case was weakened by his failure to explain (1) why Hoover's out-of-the-loop
speculation would be taken seriously by anybody in high places, especially after
War Department planners had disparaged it; and (2) why neither Truman nor his
men ever mentioned Hoover's importance in their memoirs. After all, Truman was
under great pressure to justify his decision. If Hoover's memo had any credibility,
surely Truman would have cited it. Ironically, Hoover was a strong critic of the
bombing of Hiroshima and Nagasaki.

All direct McCullough quotations are from two interviews with author, except for
remark made at Sarah Lawrence which is from a
videotape of his appearance at the college on November 9, 1994.

Capaccio article is from *Defense Week,* October 11, 1994.

Sherwin quotation is from *The Nation,* May 15, 1995.

Crouch planning document and memo to Harwit, and Adams memo to Harwit was
released by the Air Force Association. Papers made available to author by AFA
will be referred to as AFA Documents.

Gingrich quotation is from *New Republic,* March 13, 1995.

Hallion note was provided by anonymous source to author. Hallion memo to curators was sent to author from Hallion. Hallion quotation is from the November 1994 *American Legion.*

Hatch letter is from AFA Documents.

Humphreys memo is from AFA Documents.

Harwit memo is from AFA Documents.

Dagley quotation is from author interview.

Quotation from May script was provided to author by Greg Mitchell.

Linenthal quotation is from personal communication with author.

Dear quotation is from author interview.

McCarthy quotation is from Paul Boyer's *By The Bomb's Early Light (*1994).

Bernstein quotation is from author interview.

Letter to Heyman from historians was released by Physicians For Social Responsibility, Washington, D.C.

Harwit letter to Dagley was released by the American Legion.

Dagley quotation is from author interview.

Quotation from congressional letter is from *The New York Times,* January 26, 1995.

Detweiler letter to President was released by the American Legion.

Heyman's first quotation is from *Smithsonian Magazine,* November, 1994; the second is from *The New York Times,* January 30, 1995.

Linenthal quotation is from personal communication with author.

All Tibbets quotations are from his statement at the Airmen Memorial Museum in Suitland, Maryland, on June 8, 1994, which is included in AFA Documents.

TWO: Truman Meets the Devil's Advocate: A Moral Inquiry

Truman quotation is from Boyer's *By The Bomb's Early Light* (1994).

The Nuremberg Indictment is from Telford Taylor's *The Anatomy of the Nuremberg Trials: A Personal Memoir* (1992).
Peres quotation is from *The New York Post,* July 2, 1994.

Sheen quotation is from *Bulletin of the Atomic Scientists*, May 1, 1946.

The Catholic Bishops peace pastoral and Truman's August 9 statement are from Boyer.

Commager article is reprinted in *A Sense of History: The Best Writing from the Pages of American Heritage* (1985), edited by Byron Dobell.

Detweiler quotation is from his letter to President.

Regarding Truman's cross-examination: Truman quotation by Wallace is from McCullough's *Truman*. Truman remarks on August 6 and 9, 1945 and shifting casualty estimates are from Boyer; Byrnes quotation is from William Lanouette's *Genius in the Shadows: A Biography of Leo Szilard, the Man Behind the Bomb* (1992); Truman Gridiron quotation is from McCullough; Truman letter to Feis is from *Hiroshima in America: Fifty Years of Denial* (1995) by Robert Jay Lifton and Greg Mitchell; Truman remark to Royall is from Gregg Herken's *The Winning Weapon: The Atomic Bomb and the Cold War, 1945–1950* (1980).

Leo quotation is from *U.S. News & World Report*, October 10, 1994.

Fussell article is from *New Republic*, August 22 & 29, 1981.

Peretz quotation is from *New Republic*, April 17, 1995.

Walzer exchange with Fussell is from *New Republic*, September 23, 1981.

Fussell quotation is from the *Washington City Paper*, April 7, 1994.

Fussell response to Minear is dated October 28, 1993; correspondence was provided to author by Minear.

New York Post editorial quotation is from *The New York Post*, August 8, 1992. The full quotation reads: "*Not* using the bomb, given the circumstances, would have been a criminal act."

Steel review is from *New Republic*, August 10, 1992.

Brinkley review is from *The New York Times Book Review*, June 21, 1992.

All direct Bernstein quotations and Brinkley quotation are from author interviews.

Clinton and Leibowitz quotations are from author interview.

McCullough quotation is from letter to Capaccio, dated September 24, 1994; correspondence was provided to author by Capaccio.

Golway column is from *The New York Observer*, February 13, 1995.

Lifton quotation is from Boyer.

Hoess is quoted in Taylor.

THREE: Apologia Pro Hiroshima and Nagasaki

Ireland quotation is from personal communication with author.

Wills quotation is from author interview.

Schlesinger, Nitze, Teller, Tsongas, McGovern, Hentoff, Hayden and Sliwa quotations are from author article, "Candid Conversations About the Bomb: Should America Apologize?," *The Scarsdale Inquirer,* August 14, 1992.

Brown, Kinsley and Rhodes quotations are from author interviews.

Bethe quotation is from author article in *The Village Voice.*

Tomasky quotation is from personal communication with author.

Full Ireland quotation is from personal communication with author.

Dower quotation is from author interview.

FOUR: Satanic Raptures

Oppenheimer quotation is from Lanouette.

Crouch quotation is from the *Washington Post,* April 20, 1995.

Truman quotation is from his radio address of August 9, 1945.

Quotation from Hachiya generally follow Richard Rhodes's excerpting in *The Making of the Atomic Bomb* (1987).

Dagley quotation is from author interview.

Detweiler quotation is from American Legion press release, September 22, 1994.

O'Connor reference is from his sermon on Desert Storm delivered at St. Patrick's Cathedral in New York City on January 20, 1991. His statement was: "But never, never would there be justification for direct bombing, direct killing of innocent civilians as was done over Germany during World War II."

Hallion, Barrington-Ward, and Boyd quotations are from author interviews.

Murphy quotation in *Catholic World* is from Boyer and second Murphy quotation is from author interview.

The Crossroads: The End of World War II, The Atomic Bomb and the Origins of the Cold War

This exhibit contains graphic photographs of the horrors of war. Parental discretion is advised.

[*Editor's Note*: The following is the verbatim text of the original Smithsonian script including a few parenthetical indications of material that was to come. This reproduction omits all photographs and their captions, but retains an illustration, a chart and a few facsimiles of documents from the planned exhibition.]

"TODAY IS V-E DAY"

May 8, 1945, was "Victory in Europe Day." Allied soldiers, sailors and airmen had brought the European War to a close by forcing complete and unconditional surrender on the Nazi Reich. They had won total victory in a just cause.

For one moment the Allies could celebrate—the war was not over. In the Pacific, the battle with Japan was becoming increasingly bitter. Allied losses continued to mount. It seemed quite possible that the fighting could go on into 1946. Unbeknownst to all but a small number of decision-makers and scientists, however, the Western Allies were preparing a revolutionary new weapon: the atomic bomb. To this day, controversy has raged about whether dropping this weapon on Japan was necessary to end the war quickly. But one thing is clear. The Pacific War would end in a way that few could anticipate on V-E Day.

UNIT 1: A FIGHT TO THE FINISH

In 1931 the Japanese Army occupied Manchuria; six years later it invaded the rest of China. From 1937 to 1945, the Japanese Empire would be constantly at war.

Japanese expansionism was marked by naked aggression and extreme brutality. The slaughter of tens of thousands of Chinese in Nanking in 1937 shocked the world. Atrocities by Japanese troops included brutal mistreatment of civilians, forced laborers and prisoners of war, and biological experiments on human victims.

In December 1941, Japan attacked U.S. bases at Pearl Harbor, Hawaii, and launched other surprise assaults against Allied territories in the Pacific. Thus began a wider conflict marked by extreme bitterness. For most Americans, this war was fundamentally different than the one waged against Germany and Italy—it was a war of vengeance. For most Japanese, it was a war to defend their unique culture against Western imperialism. As the war approached its end in 1945, it appeared to both sides that it was a fight to the finish.

Combat in the Pacific — 1945

As the Pacific War entered its final climactic stage during the first half of 1945, the fighting reached unprecedented levels of ferocity and destructiveness. Fearing that unconditional surrender would mean the annihilation of their culture, Japanese forces fought on tenaciously.

To many on the Allied side, the suicidal resistance of the Japanese military justified the harshest possible measures. The appalling casualties suffered by both sides seemed to foreshadow what could be expected during an invasion of Japan. Allied victory was assured, but its final cost in lives remained disturbingly uncertain.

THE STRATEGIC SITUATION, SPRING 1945

By the time of the German surrender, the Allies had reversed Japan's dramatic 1941-42 sweep into the Pacific and southeast Asia. U.S. forces advancing through the southwest Pacific had reconquered most of the Philippine Islands. The U.S. Pacific Fleet had destroyed the bulk of Japan's navy, had blockaded the Japanese home islands with submarines and had either cut off or captured most of Japan's southern and central Pacific island outposts. British forces had advanced into Burma.

Although disorganized resistance continued in the Philippines and Japanese armies remained intact in Southeast Asia, China, and Manchuria, the Allies began to execute their strategy for the final destruction of the Japanese Empire. The cost proved shockingly high, however, as Japanese forces used suicidal tactics in the air and on the ground to defend islands close to their homeland.

NO HOLDS BARRED — IWO JIMA AND OKINAWA

American war plans for the first half of 1945 centered on landings on the islands of Iwo Jima and Okinawa, combined with an aerial bombing campaign against Japanese cities. Planners selected Iwo Jima to provide an emergency airfield for B-29s

4

returning from raids on Japan. They expected massive U.S. firepower to annihilate the enemy garrison there in a matter of days. Okinawa, only 640 kilometers (400 miles) from the southern tip of Japan, was expected to provide a base for assaults on the Japanese home islands.

Instead of proving easy operations against an enemy on the verge of collapse, Iwo Jima and Okinawa became costly battles of attrition taking weeks longer than hoped. By the end of the fighting on the two islands, total U.S. casualties for the first half of 1945 had exceeded those suffered during the previous three years of the Pacific war. To those in combat, Iwo Jima and Okinawa were a terrible warning of what could be expected in the future.

"...a passionate hatred for the Japanese burned through all Marines...My experiences...made me believe that the Japanese had mutual feeling for us...This collective attitude, Marine and Japanese, resulted in savage, ferocious fighting with no holds barred...This was a brutish, primitive hatred, as characteristic of the horror of war in the Pacific as the palm trees and the islands."

Private First Class Eugene B. Sledge, 1st Marine Division, in "With the Old Breed at Peleliu and Okinawa"

IWO JIMA: A SLICE OF HELL

On Iwo Jima, the Japanese garrison controlled the island's high ground. They had constructed an interlaced network of underground fortifications in the side of Mt. Suribachi, a dormant volcano dominating the 29 square kilometer (11 square mile) island. Instead of leaving cover to attack the landing force on the beaches, the Japanese defenders remained in their dugouts and poured a deadly rain of fire on the U.S. Marines.

Rather than a few days, wresting control of the island from the dug-in defenders took nearly five weeks of bitter fighting that cost the Marine Corps over 6,800 dead and almost 20,000 wounded. Japanese losses were also horrendous. When fighting on Iwo Jima ended on March 26, only 200 of the Japanese garrison of 20,700 remained alive as prisoners.

OKINAWA: A BATTLE OF UNPRECEDENTED FEROCITY

As the first waves of the American assault force landed on April 1, 1945, Okinawa's Japanese defenders put up little resistance. Instead of engaging in a hopeless attempt to repel U.S. forces on the beaches, the Japanese 32nd Army largely abandoned the northern portion of the island. It withdrew to fortifications and caves in the hilly terrain near the ancient strongpoint of Shuri Castle to the south. Such positions offered excellent fields of fire, allowing the Japanese defenders to exact a heavy toll for every piece of territory surrendered.

As the soldiers and Marines of the U.S. Tenth Army struggled to root out the island's 83,150 defenders from their underground shelters, American artillery and bombs transformed the island into a devastated wasteland of craters and corpses. In spite of vast American material superiority, Japanese resistance was not finally crushed until the end of June, at a cost of over 12,500 U.S. dead and 35,500 wounded.

WAR WITHOUT MERCY

"The Japs had to be killed anyway because of how they fought; there was no other way. But what made you want to do it was your friends. When you saw their corpses day after day, your hatred—oh God, hatred—built day after day. By June, I had no mercy for a single Jap who was trying to surrender."

Evan Regal, a U.S. Marine Corps flamethrower operator on Okinawa, 1945

By the third week of June, Okinawa's remaining defenders had withdrawn to the island's southernmost tip with no hope of evacuation. Surrender, even for those inclined to do so, proved extremely difficult. Americans were reluctant to take prisoners and Japanese officers and NCOs often shot those attempting to give up. Over 10,000 surrendered nonetheless, the largest number to do so during the war. But most chose suicide or battle to the death. In the end, the Japanese Army lost over 70,000 men.

Thousands of Okinawan refugees, their homes and villages

6

destroyed, also found themselves trapped by the fighting. Caught in crossfire, at least 80,000 civilians perished.

COMBAT FATIGUE

The protracted fighting on Iwo Jima and Okinawa and high U.S. casualties caused severe combat fatigue for many U.S. soldiers and marines. As the fighting on the islands dragged on far longer than initially expected, lack of opportunity for rotation out of the combat zone began to undercut the morale of some troops. Many believed that after eighteen months in the war zone they deserved to be shipped home. Instead, planners selected their units for the invasion of Japan, offering only the prospect of more bitter fighting to the survivors of Iwo Jima and Okinawa.

"Okinawa was a killing field. In the 82 days of battle for that island, an average of 2,500 people died every day. Under those conditions, with death everywhere, I seemed to have gone into a sort of trance. It was as if I had left my body and was looking at myself in a movie. I just did not feel anything."

Peter Milo, American soldier on Okinawa, 1945

PREPARATIONS FOR THE INVASION OF JAPAN

As the Okinawa battle reached its bloody climax during June, the United States began to gather the forces required to execute the largest amphibious operation in history. U.S. Planners believed that the assault would be met with formidable opposition, including suicide attacks by aircraft, midget submarines, piloted torpedoes, motor boats, and even explosives-laden swimmers. To those responsible for planning and executing the invasion of Japan, the potential for appalling casualties was clear.

THE *KAMIKAZE*

"Even if we are defeated, the noble spirit of this *kamikaze* attack corps will keep our homeland from ruin. Without this spirit, ruin would certainly follow defeat."

Vice-Admiral Takijiro Ohnishi, sponsor of the kamikaze *corps, 1945*

During October 1944 Japanese Navy and Army pilots began a desperate campaign of suicide crash dives against Allied ships. Called *kamikaze* or "divine wind," the attacks took their name from a typhoon that destroyed a 13th century Mongol invasion fleet before it could reach Japan. Vice Admiral Takijiro Ohnishi, who orchestrated the formation of the *kamikaze* corps, hoped that the suicide attacks would enable Japan to overcome the material superiority of the Allies or at least salvage a spiritual victory for Japan. The *kamikaze* campaign proved enormously costly to the Allies, particularly in the invasion fleet off Okinawa, but failed to reverse Japan's decline toward defeat.

THE WAY OF THE SAMURAI

"Without regard for life or name, a samurai will defend his homeland."

From a letter by kamikaze *pilot Teruo Yamaguchi, 1945*

Proponents of suicide attacks appealed to pilots' patriotism and to their belief that death in battle would insure their afterlife as spirit-guardians of Japan. *Kamikaze* pilots who endorsed such sentiments often considered themselves the embodiment of the samurai values of self-sacrifice and devotion to the Emperor. To demonstrate their commitment, many wore samurai-style *hachimaki* (headbands) and swords during their final flights.

THE RITUAL OF DEATH

"Please do not grieve for me, Mother. It will be glorious to die in action. I am grateful to be able to die in a battle to determine the destiny of our country."

From the last letter of kamikaze *pilot Ichizo Hayashi, April 1945.*

Ritual and mysticism accompanied *kamikaze* pilots' preparations for suicide attacks. Before climbing into their aircraft on the day of a mission, the flyers received a ceremonial toast of sake or water, which signified spiritual purification. As another symbol of purity, pilots often flew their final missions in clean uniforms or even burial robes.

8

For good luck, many wore *senninbari* (thousand stitch wrappers), a cloth belt for which a pilot's mother had solicited contributions of a single stitch each from women in her community. Others carried small dolls belonging to daughters or family photographs as charms to insure the success of their crash dives.

FLOATING CHRYSANTHEMUMS

The invasion of Okinawa for the first time placed a large part of the U.S. Pacific Fleet within range of aircraft attacking from bases in Japan. From April to June 1945 Imperial Navy and Army pilots flew over 1,800 individual suicide sorties as part of ten mass assaults of up to 400 aircraft against U.S. ships. Called Kikusui or "floating chrysanthemum" operations after the emblem of 14th-century samurai hero Masashige Kusonoki, these *kamikaze* attacks sank 28 ships and damaged 176.

The scale of the *kamikaze* operations off Okinawa expended pilots at an alarming rate. To make up these losses, replacement pilot training became severely abbreviated, causing the already poor quality of Japanese flyers to deteriorate further. Some reached their units barely able to take off and land. In spite of these problems, advocates of suicide operations hoped to meet Allied landings in Japan with over 5,000 *kamikaze* aircraft.

FIGHTING THE *KAMIKAZE*

While supporting the invasion of Okinawa, the U.S. Navy suffered its heaviest losses of the entire war, primarily from *kamikaze* attacks. Although the *kamikaze* campaign failed to drive the U.S. fleet away from the island, the mass suicide attacks proved a severe shock to the Allies. U.S. military and naval commanders, fearing the psychological effect of the *kamikaze*, ordered a news blackout on reports of the suicide attacks that lasted until the end of the Okinawa fighting. To the ships' crews, the experience seemed to confirm Japanese fanaticism and offer a grim foreboding of what they would endure in future operations.

"Jap planes and bombs were hitting all around us. Some of our

9

ships were being hit by suicide planes, bombs, and machine gun fire. It was a fight to the finish...How long will our luck hold out?"

Seaman First Class James J. Fahey, aboard the light cruiser Montpelier, 1945 (from "Pacific War Diary")

A PILOTED BOMB: THE YOKOSUKA MXY7 OHKA

Proponents of the *kamikaze* corps expected the *Ohka* (Cherry Blossom) piloted suicide bomb to prove even more destructive than conventional *kamikaze* airplanes. Conceived by Navy Lieutenant Ota during 1944, the *Ohka* was carried aloft by a mother plane and released up to 96 km (60 mi) away from its target. Solid-propellant rockets in the rear boosted the bomb's speed to over 800 kph (500 mph) during the final dive to the target, making it nearly impossible to shoot down with anti-aircraft fire. Its 1,200 kg (2,600 lb) warhead was sufficient to sink or severely damage any ship unlucky enough to be hit.

In practice, the *Ohka* proved far less formidable than hoped, leading U.S. sailors to nickname it the *Baka* (foolish) bomb. The lumbering mother planes, usually Mitsubishi G4M "Betty" bombers, were often shot down before flying close enough to the U.S. fleet to release their payloads. Over 750 *Ohka* Model 11s were produced, of which several hundred were used against the U.S. fleet off Okinawa. Only a handful of *Ohka* pilots succeeded in hitting ships and they sank only one.

THE NATIONAL AIR AND SPACE MUSEUM'S *OHKA*

The National Air and Space Museum's *Ohka* is a Model 22, the successor to the Model 11 used at Okinawa. Unlike the rocket-powered *Ohka* Model 11, the Model 22 was powered by an early type of jet engine, which was expected to double the bomb's range. Although it had only begun flight testing during early 1945, proponents of the *Ohka* Model 22 hoped to meet the expected Allied invasion fleet with hundreds of the new type. Nearly sixty had been produced before the end of the war terminated further development.

The wartime history of the National Air and Space Museum's *Ohka* remains obscure. The museum's *Ohka* was brought from Japan to the U.S. after its capture by the Navy, spending a short time at Alameda, California, during 1946. The Navy then transferred the suicide bomb to the Smithsonian in 1948. After years in display storage at the museum's Paul E. Garber Facility in Suitland, Maryland, the *Ohka* Model 22 was restored for this exhibit during 1993 and 1994.

A Torch to the Enemy: The Strategic Bombing of Japan

While the Allies struggled to destroy the remaining Japanese forces in the Pacific during the first half of 1945, the U.S. strategic bombing campaign against Japan, begun the previous year, escalated dramatically. The raids flown after late February razed every major Japanese city and killed several hundred thousand civilians.

This campaign against Japanese urban centers represented not only the culmination of U.S. plans for the bombing of Japan, but also the ultimate demonstration of the destructiveness of strategic bombing as predicted by air power theorists before and during World War II. Although Germany, Italy and Japan had been widely condemned in the 1930s for attacks on civilian populations, during World War II civilians themselves had become the target.

"The American government and the American people have for some time pursued a policy of whole-heartedly condemning the unprovoked bombing and machine gunning of civilian populations from the air."

President Franklin D. Roosevelt, December 2, 1939

"I want no war against women and children, and I have given the Luftwaffe instructions to attack only military objectives."

Adolf Hitler, September 1939

"We can all strongly condemn any deliberate policy to try to win a war by the demoralization of the civilian population through the process of bombing from the air. This is absolutely contrary to international law..."

Neville Chamberlain, Prime Minister of Great Britain, September 14, 1939

FROM THE BLITZ TO THE FIRESTORM

In spite of early war statements condemning strategic air campaigns against civilians, all of the belligerent powers quickly succumbed to the temptation to strike at the enemy's heartland from the air. By the fall of 1940, catastrophic losses suffered in daylight attacks led the German Luftwaffe to undertake the first night area raids against British urban centers. Although extraordinarily destructive, this campaign failed to undermine British civilian morale. Instead, the attacks provoked a desire for massive retaliation against Germany.

Between 1940 and 1943, initial small-scale attacks by the Royal Air Force's Bomber Command escalated into massive "thousand bomber" raids aimed at the destruction of entire German cities. By 1945 incendiary (fire) bombs and high explosives had reduced great cities such as Berlin, Hamburg and Dresden to smoking ruins.

THE AMERICAN BOMBING CAMPAIGN IN EUROPE

The leaders of the U.S. Army Air Forces (USAAF) entered World War II determined to prove the value of daylight precision bombing against carefully selected targets. Their aim was to destroy Germany's ability to make war by attacking key factories, oil production facilities, transportation networks, and other strategic objectives.

American planners persisted in the face of British skepticism, heavy losses and difficulties in achieving accuracy. By mid-1944 the gradual erosion of German air defenses combined with a massive buildup of U.S. bomber forces enabled USAAF commanders to continue their policy of daylight attacks on industrial targets. But true precision bombing was difficult to achieve. Cloudy weather often resulted in less accurate drops by radar.

The desire to undermine civilian morale also caused USAAF leaders to expand the campaign to large-scale daylight attacks against German cities.

THE LONG ROAD TO TOKYO

"...we'll fight mercilessly. Flying Fortresses will be dispatched immediately to set the paper cities of Japan on fire. There won't be any hesitation about bombing civilians—it will be all-out."

U.S. Army Chief of Staff General George C. Marshall, November 15, 1941

During 1941, U.S. air planners began to formulate plans for bombing Japan as relations between the two countries deteriorated. Except for the daring April 1942 raid by aircraft-carrier-launched bombers led by Col. James H. Doolittle, the skies over the Japanese home islands would remain free of American aircraft until 1944.

Protected from air attack by the enormous distances separating it from Allied bases, Japan was not struck again until June 15, 1944, when small numbers of the new B-29 Superfortress began attacks from China. The stage for the final bombing campaign of World War II was not set, however, until the capture of the Marianas Islands, situated 1,300 miles from Tokyo.

TOKYO IN FLAMES

Dismayed with the results of early raids, General Curtis E. LeMay proposed a radical change in tactics after taking command of the Marianas-based bombers in January 1945. Instead of striking individual factories in daylight precision raids with high-explosive bombs, his B-29s would attack urban areas at night with incendiary (fire) bombs.

LeMay ordered a major test of his new tactics on the night of March 9–10, 1945. Flying in three 600-km (400 mi)-long streams, 334 B-29s struck Tokyo for nearly three hours. Within thirty minutes of the first bomb, fires were burning out of control. At the center of the ensuing firestorm, temperatures reached 1000 C (1,800 F). Water boiled in canals and cisterns.

Approximately 100,000 people perished and a million were made homeless. Fifty years later, the March 9–10 Tokyo raid remains the single most destructive nonnuclear attack in human history. "This blaze will haunt me forever. It's the most terrifying sight in the world, and, God forgive me, the best."

A B-29 pilot following the raid of March 9–10, 1945

"I couldn't tell if they were men or women. They weren't even full skeletons. Piled on top of each other. The bottom of the pile all stuck together..."

Kobayashi Hiroyasu, a survivor of the Tokyo firestorm, March 9–10, 1945

"Although Mother never expressed it in words, I think she had the most difficult time. She had let the child on her back die. We don't know if she left him somewhere, or if he just burned up and fell...She's now eighty-eight years old. When she could still get around, I used to take her to pray at the graves. She'd pour water on them and say: 'Hiroko-chan, you must have been hot. Teruko-chan, you must have been hot.'"

Funato Kazuyo, a survivor of the March 9–10, 1945, raid

UNPRECEDENTED DEVASTATION

The great Tokyo raid marked the beginning of a five-month period during which Japan would suffer incredible devastation. Moving from one city to another, B-29s destroyed one half the total area of 66 urban centers—burning 460 square kilometers (180 square miles) to the ground. Some cities, like the chemical and textile manufacturing center of Toyama, were completely destroyed. The five-month-long USAAF incendiary campaign against Japan probably took more civilian lives than the half million killed during the five years of Allied bombing of Germany.

"No matter how you slice it, you're going to kill an awful lot of civilians. Thousands and thousands...We're at war with Japan. Would you rather have Americans killed?" *Major General Curtis E. LeMay, 1945*

OPERATION STARVATION

In addition to the all-out air attacks on Japanese cities, the

14

USAAF and U.S. Navy took additional steps to bring Japan to its knees. By spring 1945, U.S. Submarines had succeeded in destroying the Japanese merchant marine. A B-29 campaign aptly code-named "Operation Starvation" completed the process of isolating the home islands by mining Japanese harbors and coastal waters. Carrier-based aircraft contributed to the operation by bombing and strafing a wide variety of targets. By early summer, shipping, manufacturing, transportation, and food distribution had largely ground to a halt.

Two Nations at War

The United States and Japan remained insulated from the harsh reality of total war longer than any other major belligerents of World War II. As the Pacific War entered its fourth year in 1945, both had nonetheless undergone profound change. For Japanese civilians, the horror of war had finally come home in the form of daily air raids, severe privation, and the threat of invasion. For many Americans, combat in the Pacific remained a distant series of events reported through a veil of censorship in newsreels, newspapers, magazines and radio. The cost of victory in American lives, however, represented a very real concern for all with loved ones in the Pacific.

The distance separating Japan and the United States underscored the cultural gulf separating the two societies. Ignorance about the other's culture, combined with racism, desire for revenge, and the strain of total war produced virulent hatred on both sides.

HOME FRONT, U.S.A.

World War II energized the United States as had few events in our national history. By the spring of 1945, government spending for weapons, munitions, vehicles, clothing, and thousands of other items had brought the Great Depression to an end. Wages soared and unemployment plummeted. Women and members of minority communities entered the work force in unprecedented numbers.

With consumer goods in short supply, and rationing in force, Americans saved as never before. They invested in war bond drives, lending the government the funds needed to finance the war effort. But after over three years of war, Americans were tired. They longed for peace, the return of their sons, brothers, husbands, and fathers, and the realization of their deferred dreams of material prosperity.

THE ARSENAL OF DEMOCRACY

By the spring of 1945, the United States had become, as President Franklin Roosevelt predicted, "the arsenal of democracy." The miracles achieved by wartime industry demonstrated the enormous untapped power of the American economy. During the course of World War II, U.S. industry produced 296,429 airplanes; 87,620 ships; 102,357 tanks and self-propelled guns; 372,431 artillery pieces; and 44 billion rounds of small-arms ammunition. At the 1943 Teheran Conference, Soviet leader Joseph Stalin, no admirer of capitalism, toasted: "American production, without which this war would have been lost."

THE ROOTS OF A NEW AMERICA

American society underwent fundamental change during the war years. "Rosie the Riveter" became a cultural heroine as women entered the labor force in unprecedented numbers, often employed in jobs previously held only by men. American youngsters, with time on their hands and money in their pockets, transformed a New Jersey band singer named Frank Sinatra into the first teen entertainment idol. Newspaper and magazine writers worried about the rise of juvenile delinquency, and wondered how many "quickie" wartime marriages would last. While Americans longed for a return to "normal," they sensed that things would never be the same.

THE LIMITS OF DEMOCRACY

"A viper is a viper, wherever the egg is hatched—so a Japanese-American, born of Japanese parents, grows up

Japanese, not an American."

Los Angeles Times, 1942

A sense of dedication and national purpose marked the American home front during World War II. But the pressures of wartime life and the desire to present a united front to the enemy had underscored the extent to which some Americans were not yet full citizens.

In the spring of 1945, tens of thousands of Americans of Japanese ancestry remained in the ten camps in which they had been summarily incarcerated since 1942. Black migrants moving from rural areas to higher paying jobs in American cities quickly discovered that they too had not left racism behind. Hispanics faced similar problems in Los Angeles and much of the Southwest.

The contrast between the actual treatment of minorities and the public expressions of an international fight for freedom and democracy would provide an important foundation for post-war movements for social equality.

"Probably in all our history, no foe has been so detested as were the Japanese. The infamy of Pearl Harbor was enough; but to it were soon added circumstantial accounts of Japanese atrocities at Hong Kong, Singapore, and finally and most appallingly, upon American prisoners in the Philippines...Emotions forgotten since our most savage Indian wars were reawakened..."

Allan Nevins, "While You Were Gone," 1946

THE YELLOW PERIL

With deep family roots in nations such as Germany and Italy, most Americans had little difficulty understanding their European enemies as good people misled by evil leaders. Anti-Asian racism, long a factor in American life, made it impossible to view the Japanese enemy in that fashion.

Plunged into war by the Japanese surprise attack on Pearl harbor, Hawaii, on December 7, 1941, and horrified by accounts of Japanese mistreatment of prisoners of war in the Philippines and elsewhere, Americans regarded their Pacific enemy as a

17

nation of treacherous and inhuman fanatics. Wartime advertising and propaganda portrayed the Japanese as sub-human "monkey-men," vicious rodents, or venomous insects.

Louseous Japanicas

The first serious outbreak of this lice epidemic was officially noted on December 7, 1941, at Honolulu, T. H. To the Marine Corps, especially trained in combating this type of pestilence, was assigned the gigantic task of extermination. Extensive experiments on Guadalcanal, Tarawa, and Saipan have shown that this louse inhabits coral atolls in the South Pacific, particularly pill boxes, palm trees, caves, swamps and jungles.

Flame throwers, mortars, grenades and bayonets have proven to be an effective remedy. But before a complete cure may be effected the origin of the plague. the breeding grounds around the Tokyo area, must be completely annihilated.

Cartoon from the U.S. Marine Corps monthly Leatherneck, *March 1945.*

FINISHING THE JOB

Americans celebrated the victory in Europe in May 1945, then went back to work, determined to achieve total victory over Japan. The job was far from over, and looming on the horizon was the prospect of the losses that might be suffered in an invasion.

THE JAPANESE HOME FRONT AT WAR

By the summer of 1945, Japan was a nation on the brink of collapse. American land, air, and naval forces had finally arrived on the doorstep of the home islands. B-29s of the 20th Air Force were systematically burning Japanese cities to the ground. The submarine campaign and aerial mine laying operations had cut lines of supply and communication. After the fall of Okinawa, the Japanese people waited in their island fortress, prepared to repulse the enemy on the beaches. But their conditions would increasingly undermine their power to resist.

HARDSHIP ON THE HOMEFRONT

"Everything goes to the military, the black marketeers, and the big shots. Only fools queue up."

Kiyosawa Kiyoshi, diary entry, April 30, 1943

By fall, 1944, the Japanese people could no longer adequately feed or clothe themselves. The shortage of farm workers and lack of chemical fertilizers drastically cut domestic agricultural production. The Allied blockade had cut the supply of vital rice and soy products once imported from Korea and China.

Although silk remained available, cotton and other imported fibers had vanished. Clothes were now manufactured of *sufu*, a cloth in which small amounts of cotton were woven with wood pulp, goat hair, and tree bark.

Dwindling supplies of food and clothing led to rationing, price controls, and long lines outside those stores where goods were available. In spite of stiff penalties, prices soared and the black market became a fact of life. As early as the spring of 1944, rice was 14 times the official price.

LABOR

"On the night shift, after standing up for hours, we were marched into a dining hall where we had our supper. Supper was a bowl of weak, hot broth, usually with one string of a noodle in it and a few soybeans on the bottom. We would gulp it down, then go back to work in the factory."

Hirako Nakamono, a school girl employed in a Hiroshima aircraft factory, 1945

Japanese industry suffered from a severe labor shortage throughout the war years. By 1944 the situation had become critical. Farm workers judged unsuitable for military service were conscripted for factory labor. Women went out to work in

19

unprecedented numbers. Junior and senior high schools closed as students were assigned to industry, public transport and the construction of roads and fire-breaks.

SLAVE LABOR

The Japanese government turned to slave labor to ease the severe manpower shortages. Some 667,000 Koreans and 38,000 Chinese who had labor contracts to work in Japan ultimately became slave laborers. Forced to work under armed guard at difficult and dangerous tasks during the day, they were housed behind electrified fences at night. Protests were punished by beatings, floggings and execution. During the course of the war, an estimated 67,000 Korean and Chinese slave laborers would die in Japanese custody.

By 1945, most Allied prisoners of war being held in Japan were also treated in a manner indistinguishable from slave laborers. Like their compatriots in Japanese camps overseas, they were often starved, beaten and tortured.

THE COMING OF THE "B-SAN"

The first B-29 raids were directed against industrial targets and took few lives. "We went through those early bombings in a spirit of excitement and suspense," one journalist recalled. "There was even a spirit of adventure, a sense of exultation in sharing the dangers of war even though bound to a civilian existence." People joked about the "regularly scheduled service" of the "honorable visitors." The B-29s, lovely silver specks glittering in the sun as they flew at altitudes of over 30,000 feet, became popularly known as the "B-San," or "Mr. B."

Long insulated from the personal experience of war, Japanese civilians were ill-prepared for the incendiary raids of 1945. With most men absent in military service, the burden of civil defense fell on women and the elderly, who were organized into neighborhood associations. The only equipment they had were primitive, hand-operated pumps supplemented by bucket brigades and wet mops.

"Air raid. Air raid. Here comes an air raid!
Red! Red! Incendiary bomb!
Run! Run! Get mattress and sand!
Air raid! Air raid! Here comes an air raid!
Black! Black! Here come the bombs!
Cover your ears! Cover your eyes!"
Song designed to teach the basics of civil defense to Japanese children, 1944

"Proper air raid clothing as recommended by the government to the civilian population consisted of a heavily padded hood over the head and shoulders...to protect...from explosives...The hoods flamed under the rain of sparks; people who did not burn from the feet up burned from the head down. Mothers who carried their babies strapped to their backs, Japanese-style, would discover too late that the padding that enveloped the infant had caught fire."
Robert Guillian, "I saw Tokyo Burning" (1981)

THE DEMONIC OTHER

"It has gradually become clear that the American enemy, driven by its ambition to conquer the world, is coming to attack us...the barbaric tribe of Americans are devils in human skin...Western Barbarian Demons."
From an article published in "Manga Nippon," a popular magazine, October 1944

Like Americans, the Japanese people viewed their enemies in racist terms. Allied people and leaders were pictured as inhuman demons, lice, insects, and vermin. Wartime propaganda made frequent reference to the "Jewish" nature of the Allied cause. Japanese soldiers and civilians alike were convinced that American troops were waging a "war of extermination" against Japan. The mass suicides on Saipan and Okinawa demonstrated that Japanese mothers would kill themselves and their children rather than allow themselves to fall into the hands of the "devilish" U.S. Marines.

"100 MILLION HEARTS BEATING AS ONE"

By the summer of 1945, every man and woman in Japan over the age of 13 was a member of the People's Volunteer Army, and subject to military discipline. All across Japan, the subject-soldiers of the Emperor drilled with spears and other makeshift weapons in preparation for the final battles on the beaches. If the invasion came, the Japanese people were prepared, as one of them later recalled, to "match our training against their numbers, our flesh against their steel." But the ability of the Japanese people to fight was increasingly undermined by blockade, starvation, overwhelming Allied air power and the collapse of industrial production.

UNIT 2: THE DECISION TO DROP THE BOMB

"That was not any decision you had to worry about."
President Harry S. Truman

While Americans and Japanese alike expected the war to end after a bloody invasion of Japan, the U.S. government was readying a secret weapon that would dramatically affect the war's outcome: the atomic bomb. In the spring and summer of 1945, American leaders would have to decide whether to use this new weapon without warning against Japanese cities.

According to British Prime Minister Winston Churchill, however, "the decision whether or not to use the atomic bomb…was never even an issue." Upon becoming President in April 1945, Harry Truman inherited a very expensive bomb project that had always aimed at producing a military weapon. Furthermore, he was faced with the prospect of an invasion and he was told that the bomb would be useful for impressing the Soviet Union. He therefore saw no reason to avoid using the bomb. Alternatives for ending the Pacific war other than an invasion of atomic-bombing were available, but are more obvious in hindsight than they were at the time.

DECIDING TO BUILD THE BOMB

The atomic bomb was ultimately used against Japan, but it was built as a weapon against Germany. In late 1938, German scientists accidentally discovered how to split ("fission") the uranium atom, releasing nuclear energy. When physicists in the United States learned of this discovery, many immediately realized that Hitler might acquire a fearsome new weapon: an atomic bomb. Refugees from the Nazis, most notably the Hungarian physicists Leo Szilard and Eugene Wigner, feared this possibility so much that they began to search for a way to warn Western governments.

THE EINSTEIN LETTER

Szilard and Wigner, in their search for a way to warn the U.S. government, eventually hit on the idea of asking the famous physicist Albert Einstein, himself a refugee from Nazi Germany, to sign a letter to President Franklin Delano Roosevelt. In August 1939, Einstein put his signature on the letter at his summer home in Long Island, New York. It was conveyed to President Roosevelt in October.

The letter may have initiated the American atomic-bomb project, but its effect has often been exaggerated. The United States did not immediately begin a crash program to build nuclear weapons. Until 1941, efforts went ahead rather slowly.

Albert Einstein
Old Grove Rd.
Nassau Point
Peconic. Long Island

August 2nd, 1939

F. D. Roosevelt
President of the United States,
White House
Washington, D.C.

Sir:

Recent work in nuclear physics made it probable that uranium may be turned into a new and important source of energy. New experiments performed by E.Fermi and L.Szilard, which have been communicated to me in manuscript, make it now appear likely that it will be possible to set up a chain reaction in a large mass of uranium and thereby to liberate considerable quantities of energy. Less certain, but to be kept in mind, is the possibility of making use of such chain reactions for the construction of extremely powerful bombs. Such bombs may be too heavy for transportation by air plane, but not too heavy for being carried by boat, and a single bomb exploded in a port might very well destroy the port together with the surrounding territory.

This being the situation, you may find it desirable that some contact be established between the Administration and the group of physicists who are working in this country on the subject of chain reactions. One possible way of achieving this would be for you to entrust a person who has your confidence, and who could perhaps act in an inofficial capacity, with this task.

I understand that Germany has stopped the sale of uranium. That she should have taken such early action might perhaps be understood on the ground that the son of the German Under-Secretary of State, von Weizsäcker, is attached to the Kaiser-Wilhelm-Institut in Berlin where some of the American work on uranium is now being repeated.

The United States has only poor ores of uranium. Better ores in moderate quantities are mined in the former Czechoslovakia and in Canada, while the most important source of uranium is Belgian Congo.

Yours very truly,

A. Einstein .

(Albert Einstein)

This is the original letter from Albert Einstein to President Roosevelt. Lent by the Franklin Delano Roosevelt Library.

LEO SZILARD (1898–1964)

No one was more central to both the origins of the atomic bomb, and to protest against its use on Japanese cities, than this exiled Hungarian physicist. Born in Budapest of a wealthy Jewish family, Szilard was a brilliant student and the winner of the Hungarian national mathematics prize at the age of eighteen. He received his Ph.D. in physics from the University of Berlin in 1922, but was forced to leave Germany in 1933 when Hitler came to power. In that same year he first conceived of a nuclear chain reaction as the means of liberating atomic energy—and of making an atomic bomb. He came to the United States in January 1938.

During the war, Szilard worked at the Chicago Laboratory of the atomic bomb project. But after the defeat of Germany, he feared that using the bomb on Japan would start a nuclear arms race with the Soviet Union. He was a key figure in the scientists' movement against using the bomb in the spring and summer of 1945. After the war, he devoted his life to warning the world about the dangers of the nuclear arms race.

A CRASH PROGRAM BEGINS

In 1941, even before the Japanese attack on Pearl Harbor, the American atomic-bomb program was greatly accelerated. Independent research in Britain strongly supported the feasibility of a bomb. Furthermore, Vannevar Bush, the head of American civilian scientific research for the military, received a report that German scientists were pushing ahead on their own bomb project. On October 9, 1941, President Roosevelt approved intensified research into the feasibility of an atomic bomb.

THE GERMANS DECIDE NOT TO BUILD A BOMB

Soon after the American decision, the German authorities (unaware of the American deliberations) decided not to build a nuclear bomb. The huge investment required in industrial and research facilities was judged—correctly—to be too large for the

German war economy to bear. Some historians and scientists have also asserted that German physicists were uncooperative with Nazi authorities because they were afraid of giving Hitler the bomb, but this assertion remains questionable.

In June 1942, Armaments Minister Albert Speer made the final decision not to proceed with a bomb, although research on nuclear reactors continued. The Western Allies, however, did not know this fact. The United States and Britain had to continue on the assumption that the Nazis would acquire the atomic bomb, possibly before they did.

THE MANHATTAN PROJECT: A GIGANTIC ENGINEERING ENTERPRISE

In June 1942, President Roosevelt transferred that atomic-bomb project to the War Department's Army Corps of Engineers. In order to disguise this ultra-secret project, the Corps created a Manhattan Engineer District to direct the effort, with a shadow headquarters in New York City. Appointed as head of the Manhattan Project, as it came to be called, was General Leslie Groves.

Groves' major task was to build the huge industrial facilities that would be required to separate the small quantities of fissionable uranium and plutonium needed for a bomb. Although the Manhattan Project is best remembered for its brilliant scientific leadership, it was more than anything else a massive engineering enterprise. At the height of construction in mid-1944, the Project employed nearly 129,000 people.

A MOST SECRET PLACE

In late 1942, Manhattan Project chief Gen. Groves chose physicist J. Robert Oppenheimer to head a new laboratory devoted to the final design of atomic bombs. Oppenheimer recommended a remote site in New Mexico for the facility, which gathered many famous scientists together in complete secrecy. Los Alamos Laboratory was opened in April 1943.

During the last two years of World War II, the Los Alamos

staff made a crash effort to design two different bombs. A nuclear explosion could be triggered in uranium 235 by employing a gun to fire one piece of U235 at another. It was found, however, that the more-easily-made plutonium 239 could only be successfully exploded by first compressing it into a smaller sphere with high explosives. This "implosion bomb" proved to be Los Alamos' most difficult challenge.

LESLIE GROVES (1896–1970)

General Groves was the central organizer of the Manhattan Project. The son of a military chaplain, he graduated from the U.S. Military Academy at West Point in 1918 with a degree in civil engineering. During the military buildup that began in 1940, Groves served as the deputy commander of all Army construction projects. He was responsible for building the Pentagon, which was finished just as the war began.

Groves wished to be assigned overseas to command combat engineers, but on September 17, 1942, he was told that he would take over the Manhattan Project, which was in need of a strong leader. Some eminent scientists within the Project found him authoritarian and arrogant. Groves was, however, indispensable to the success of the massive construction program that began in 1942. His technical competence and decisive leadership were also essential.

J. ROBERT OPPENHEIMER (1904–1967)

At the instigation of Groves, Dr. Robert Oppenheimer became a key scientific leader in the Manhattan Project. Oppenheimer was born into a wealthy New York Jewish family and was a brilliant student who mastered exotic Oriental languages as well as theoretical physics. He graduated with a Ph.D. in physics from the University of Goettingen, Germany, in 1927 and became a professor at the University of California, Berkeley. In the late 1930s the Nazi persecution of the Jews and the Spanish civil war turned the formerly apolitical physicist into a leftist with personal ties to a number of Communists.

In 1942, Oppenheimer was Groves' inspired and unexpected choice to head the Los Alamos Laboratory. The relatively young physicist proved to be a superb leader and scientific manager. After the war, Oppenheimer played an important role in advising the U.S. government about nuclear weapons. In 1954, as a result of the McCarthy-era "witchhunts," he was stripped of his security clearances after a controversial investigation into his earlier political history.

AN EXPECTATION OF MILITARY USE

"At no time, from 1941 to 1945 did I ever hear it suggested by the President, or any other responsible member of the government, that atomic energy should not be used in the war."
Henry Stimson, Secretary of War (1940–1945)

"If this weapon fizzles, each of you can look forward to a lifetime of testifying before congressional investigating committees."
Gen. Groves to his staff, December 24, 1944

The small number of decision-makers who knew about the ultra-secret Manhattan Project always assumed that the bomb would be used, either against Germany or Japan. The United States' huge investment in the atomic bomb—two billion 1940s dollars, or roughly forty billion 1990s dollars—also drove Gen. Groves and his project leaders to demonstrate that the money had not been wasted. In the spring of 1945, production of fissionable materials was accelerated, because Groves was afraid that the war would be over before an atomic bomb could be dropped.

Historical Controversies:
Would the Bomb Have Been Dropped on the Germans?
Some have argued that the atomic bomb would never have been dropped on the Germans, because it was much easier for Americans to bomb Asians than "white people." The racial character of the Pacific conflict has been cited to support this view.

29

During 1943 and 1944, Gen. Groves and others discussed employing the atomic bomb in the Pacific first because the Japanese were judged to be less capable of analyzing a bomb that failed to explode. Racial stereotypes may have had a role in this attitude, but the consensus of most, if not all, historians is that President Roosevelt would have used the bomb on Germany if such an attack would have been useful in the European war. The point became moot because sufficient uranium and plutonium to make bombs could not be produced until the summer of 1945, after the German surrender.

THE "FAT MAN" ATOMIC BOMB

The Manhattan Project produced two different types of atomic fission bombs: the "Fat Man" plutonium implosion bomb and the "Little Boy" uranium gun bomb. The "Fat Man" type, one of which was eventually dropped on Nagasaki, Japan, was based on the principle that a sphere of the metal plutonium 239, when compressed suddenly, would reach a critical density sufficient to create a nuclear chain-reaction. Around the plutonium sphere were arrayed blocks of high explosives, which were specially designed to produce a highly accurate and symmetric implosion to compress the sphere.

The design of this bomb was very difficult and scientists at Los Alamos were not entirely confident of success. A test of the "Fat Man" would therefore be needed. In the spring of 1945, that test was scheduled for July.

ATOMIC FISSION BOMBS: HOW DO THEY WORK?

The nuclei of atoms are primarily composed of two elementary particles: protons and neutrons. Protons have a positive charge, while neutrons have no such charge. Certain very heavy nuclei, when hit by a neutron, have the tendency to split ("fission") into two smaller nuclei, resulting in the release of energy and more neutrons. If a "critical mass" of these elements are brought together, neutrons released by fission will run into other nuclei, causing more fission. If the conditions are right, this nuclear chain reaction can run out of control in millionths of a second, producing gigantic quantities of energy.

All nuclear weapons today use fission as the basic process for creating a nuclear explosion. Many current weapons, however, are "thermonuclear" bombs, which employ a fission explosion to create the extreme heat and pressure conditions needed to trigger the "fusion" of nuclei of the light element hydrogen. This "hydrogen bomb," to use the popular term, is far more efficient and destructive than an atomic bomb.

The principle of nuclear fission.

"The Most Terrible Weapon Ever Known in Human History"

On April 12, 1945, President Roosevelt died in Warm Springs, Georgia, to the shock and surprise of many Americans. Vice-President Harry S. Truman, who had only been in office since January 20, was immediately sworn in. Truman was quickly confronted with the need to approve the use of the atomic bomb, which could be ready by August.

The President also confronted a complicated situation in both Europe and in the Far East. Japan had effectively lost the war, but its government did not appear to be willing to surrender. The atomic bomb was one way to change that. Truman's advisers also told him that the bomb would be useful as a diplomatic lever in growing disagreements with the Soviet Union. On the other hand, Soviet entry into the Pacific conflict was another possible way of shocking the Japanese into surrender. An invasion of Japan loomed on the horizon if neither atomic bombs nor Soviet entry worked. For the new President, the situation was complex and difficult.

TRUMAN AND THE ATOMIC BOMB

President Truman "was like a little boy on a toboggan. He

31

never had the opportunity to say 'we *will* drop the bomb.' All he could do was say 'no.'"

General Leslie Groves

President Truman came into office with no knowledge of the atomic bomb, because Roosevelt had never revealed to him the secret at the heart of the Manhattan Project. Shortly after Truman's swearing-in on April 12, Secretary of War Henry Stimson mentioned it to him briefly. On April 25, Stimson gave him a more extensive briefing, accompanied by General Groves.

The President had inherited a project that had always aimed at making a usable weapon. In the following months, he never saw a compelling reason to question that assumption. As a result, Truman's role in the "decision to drop the bomb" was largely confined to verbally confirming proposals by his advisers.

1. Within four months we shall in all probability have completed the most terrible weapon ever known in human history, one bomb of which could destroy a whole city.

2. Although we have shared its development with the UK, physically the US is at present in the position of controlling the resources with which to construct and use it and no other nation could reach this position for some years.

3. Nevertheless it is practically certain that we could not remain in this position indefinitely.

a. Various segments of its discovery and production are widely known among many scientists in many countries, although few scientists are now acquainted with the whole process which we have developed.

b. Although its construction under present methods requires great scientific and industrial effort and raw materials, which are temporarily mainly within the possession and knowledge of US and UK, it is extremely probable that much easier and cheaper methods of production will be discovered by scientists in the future, together with the use of materials of much wider distribution. As a result, it is extremely probable that the future will make it possible to be constructed by smaller nations or even groups, or at least by a large nation in a much shorter time.

An original copy of the memorandum Stimson presented to Truman on April 25, 1945. It opens: "1. Within four months we shall in all probability have completed the most terrible weapon ever know in human history, one bomb of which could destroy a whole city."

HARRY S. TRUMAN (1884–1972)

Rising from humble origins in the Kansas City area, Truman was a veteran of World War I and a successful Missouri politician. He achieved prominence in the Second World War as a U.S. Senator and Chairman of the so-called Truman Committee, which acted as a watchdog over the huge industrial and military build-up during the war. In the fall of 1944, he was elected as Roosevelt's third Vice-President.

Truman was aware of the existence of the Manhattan Project while a Senator, but respected the Administration's request that he not inquire into its nature. As President, he held ultimate responsibility for the decision to use the atomic bomb. After the war, he claimed that he never once had moral qualms about the bombings, but his own diaries and letters indicate that this was not entirely the case. He was reelected in 1948 and was noteworthy for his role in the early Cold War, the Marshall Plan, the Berlin airlift and the Korean War.

HENRY L. STIMSON (1867–1950)

Born into a privileged northeastern family, Stimson was a prominent figure in the American political establishment for over four decades. He had been Secretary of War for President William Howard Taft, Governor-General of the Philippines for President Calvin Coolidge, and Secretary of State for President Herbert Hoover. Although Stimson was a lifelong Republican, President Roosevelt asked him to take over as Secretary of War in 1940 because of the urgent military buildup that began after Nazi victories in Europe.

Stimson was drawn into atomic-bomb decision-making in October 1941 when Roosevelt gave the program top priority. During the war, he remained a key policy adviser on nuclear energy. In spite of poor health and advance age, Stimson continued to play the same role under President Truman, although he was increasingly displaced by Truman's choice for Secretary of State, James Byrnes. Stimson went into a well-deserved retirement shortly after the surrender of Japan.

Japan Looks for a Way Out of the War

On April 5, 1945, one week before Roosevelt's death, Japanese Prime Minister Koiso and his Cabinet resigned because of the increasingly disastrous course of the war. It was the second such resignation in less than a year. Even the military-dominated Japanese political establishment was beginning to realize that a way had to be found to negotiate an end to the war. The Allied demand for "unconditional surrender" was, however, regarded as intolerable.

Emperor Hirohito approved the appointment of the aged Admiral Kantaro Suzuki as the new Prime Minister. But Suzuki's government was hobbled by severe tensions between civilian politicians interested in peace and die-hard military leaders who wished to fight a last battle in Japan. Surrender could not be openly discussed, nor could direct negotiations with the United States be undertaken, because hawkish Army generals dominated the government. As a result, opportunities to end the war early were greatly limited.

PEACE THROUGH MOSCOW?

Throughout the Pacific War, the Soviet Union and Japan had remained at peace, although they were allied with opposite sides in the European war. In the fall of 1944, the growing desperation of the Japanese government drove it to approach Joseph Stalin's communist regime for help in fending off defeat. After the appointment of the Suzuki cabinet in April 1945, these initiatives were renewed.

Two key civilian politicians—Marquis Kido, the Emperor's closest adviser, and Shigenori Togo, the new Foreign Minister—hoped to use the renewed approach to Moscow as a way to negotiate some kind of conditional surrender with the Allies. But they had to conceal their true intentions from the die-hard militarists who wished to fight on. As a result, the initiative remained weak and indecisive.

EMPEROR HIROHITO (1901–1989)

Crowned as the Showa ("Enlightened Peace") Emperor in 1926, Hirohito played a controversial role in World War II. A retiring and bookish man who was traditionally restricted from exercising much influence over the government, he was simultaneously worshipped as a god by the Japanese people and military. To the outside world he became a symbol of Japanese aggression and barbarism, yet he occasionally expressed his reservations to the military leadership about the course of the war. He nonetheless showed much enthusiasm for the armed forces and their conquests.

In the spring of 1945, Hirohito was aware that the war was lost and gave tentative encouragement to the peace feelers of Marquis Kido and Foreign Minister Togo. But he failed to take more decisive action until August, when the atomic bombs were dropped and Soviets declared war. Following the surrender, the Allies allowed Hirohito to remain on the throne. He presided over the renaissance of modern Japan.

Historical Controversies:
Did the United States Ignore the Japanese Peace Initiative?

In 1940, American intelligence experts succeeded in cracking the Japanese diplomatic code. "Operation Magic" allowed the U.S. government to decipher messages between Tokyo and the Japanese Embassy in Moscow, giving the United States knowledge of the Japanese peace initiative in the spring of 1945.

Some historians have claimed that the Truman Administration ignored the signs of a Japanese readiness to negotiate because of a desire to drop the atomic bomb on Japan in order to intimidate the Soviet Union. Other scholars have argued that the Japanese initiative was far from clear in its intentions. It is nonetheless possible to assert, at least in hindsight, that the United States should have paid closer attention to these signals from Japan. Like so many aspects of the "decision to drop the bomb," this matter will remain forever speculative and controversial.

"THE EMPEROR REMAINS AS THE SOLE STABILIZING FORCE"

A key stumbling block to any Japanese surrender was the position of the Emperor. To Japanese leaders, the Allied demand for "unconditional surrender" meant a destruction of the whole Japanese political system, including the monarchy. To many Americans, Hirohito was a hated symbol of Japanese military aggression. A poll taken in the spring of 1945 showed that a third of those surveyed wanted Hirohito executed immediately and another thirty-seven percent thought that he should be tried, imprisoned or exiled.

This public hostility greatly restricted the maneuvering room of President Truman and his advisers. Some Japanese experts, most notably the Undersecretary of State, Joseph Grew, nonetheless argued that the Emperor should be left on the throne as "the sole stabilizing force" capable of making the Japanese armed forces surrender. Truman listened, but did not accept Grew's arguments.

JOSEPH G. GREW (1880–1965)

Grew was the last United States Ambassador to Tokyo before the war. Although sympathetic to Japan, he supported stronger diplomatic action in 1940 as a warning against further Japanese aggression. Grew was interned in Japan for some months after Pearl Harbor, became deputy head of the State Department in 1944 and was often Acting Secretary of State in 1945.

Beginning in May 1945, Grew urged President Truman to make an offer of surrender, conditional upon the retention of Emperor Hirohito on the throne. Grew understood the mentality of the Japanese leadership, and he wished to end the war early to minimize Soviet influence in Asia. But Grew was unable to convince Truman and many of his key advisers, because such a move was considered too politically risky. Most Americans despised the Japanese and it was difficult to back away from the policy of "unconditional surrender" laid down by Allied leaders in 1943.

Historical Controversies:
Would the War Have Ended Sooner if the United States Had Guaranteed the Emperor's Position?

This is one of the most difficult "what if" questions in the "decision to drop the bomb" debate among scholars. In hindsight, it is clear that American and Japanese leaders might have reached an agreement on Japanese surrender, if the United States had made such an offer and if the Suzuki government had been willing to communicate directly with President Truman through a neutral power. In effect, that is what happened after the atomic bombings.

Some scholars have argued, however, that it took the shock of the atomic bombings and the Soviet declaration of war, which took place at about the same time, to give Hirohito a facesaving way to force a surrender on his hard-liners. A question like this can never be settled, but it is possible that there was a lost opportunity to end the war without either atomic bombings or an invasion of Japan, if Grew's advice had been accepted.

The Soviet Factor

Joseph Stalin's Union of Soviet Socialist Republics (USSR) was a critical factor in all American diplomatic and military calculations regarding the bomb and the Japanese, although Truman and Stimson later downplayed that sensitive fact. The Grand Alliance of the United States, the British Commonwealth and the Soviet Union, which was forged only after Nazi Germany attacked Russia in 1941, was an alliance of convenience. Suspicion between the capitalist West and the communist East remained high, in spite of positive feelings evoked by the common struggle against the Nazis.

In the spring of 1945, new tensions arose over the Soviet occupation of Eastern Europe that resulted from the German defeat. Moreover, the Truman administration had to consider how to tell Stalin about the atomic bomb and whether the bomb would be a useful diplomatic weapon in post-war struggles with Stalin. The President and his advisers also began to question the desirability of a Soviet entry into the Pacific war. Although the Cold War did not start until 1947, some of its roots can be seen during the war.

THE SOVIET UNION AND THE PACIFIC WAR

While the USSR was preoccupied with battling Germany, and the Japanese Empire was tied down fighting the Western Allies and China, neither power had an interest in disturbing their mutual peace. But as the defeat of the Nazis approached, the United States wanted the Soviets to attack and pin down the huge Japanese Army in China, so that it would be unavailable for transfer to the defense of the home islands. At the Yalta conference in February 1945, Stalin promised to enter the Pacific war two to three months after the surrender of Germany.

During the spring of 1945, some American leaders began to doubt the wisdom of this policy. The U.S. Navy's blockade of Japan was complete by about April, making a troop transfer from China almost impossible. Key advisers to President Truman also began to worry about the power of Communism in post-war Asia. But Stalin was determined to join the Pacific war in any case so that he could gain more influence in China, Korea and Japan.

THE SOVIET UNION AND THE ATOMIC SECRET

The Manhattan Project was a joint undertaking of the United States, Great Britain and Canada, although dominated by American resources and personnel. President Roosevelt and British Prime Minister Churchill had decided not to tell Stalin about the project, however, because they wished to delay the

Soviets' acquisition of nuclear weapons. Spies working for the Russians, including at least two scientists at Los Alamos, nonetheless sent atomic secrets back to Moscow.

As the bomb approached testing and use, the Western Allies had to decide whether to tell Stalin before dropping it on Japan, and what post-war nuclear policy should be. Some scientists and advisers urged that atomic weapons be given to the United Nations under a policy of "international control" so that a nuclear arms race might be avoided. Others did not trust the Soviets and saw advantages in an American or Anglo-American nuclear monopoly.

"PERSUADING RUSSIA TO PLAY BALL"

From the very beginning of Harry Truman's Presidency, Secretary of War Stimson advised him that the atomic bomb might be useful in post-war diplomatic disagreements with the Soviets. As tensions grew over the Soviet domination of Poland and other Eastern European countries, Stimson hoped that American possession of this spectacular new military power might help make the Russians "play ball" in Europe and elsewhere.

But it was Truman's choice for Secretary of State, James "Jimmy" Byrnes, who, more than anyone else inside the Administration, recommended a hard line against Soviet demands. Byrnes hoped that "the bomb...might well put us in a position to dictate our own terms at the end of the war."

JAMES F. BYRNES (1879–1972)

A South Carolina Democratic politician, "Jimmy" Byrnes rose to become one of the most powerful figures in the Roosevelt and Truman Administrations. As a U.S. Senator, he proved instrumental in the passage of Roosevelt's "New Deal" legislation. The President made him a Justice of the U.S. Supreme Court in 1941, but Byrnes only served about a year before resigning to take a leading position in war mobilization after Pearl Harbor. He became so influential in domestic policy that the press nicknamed him "Assistant President." Byrnes was widely expected to become Roosevelt's running-mate in 1944, but the Democratic convention picked Truman instead.

When Truman suddenly became President, he had had almost no foreign policy experience. He immediately sought out Byrnes as an adviser. The South Carolinian served as Secretary of State from July 1945 to January 1947.

Historical Controversies:
How Important Was the Soviet Factor in the "Decision to Drop the Bomb"?

Some historians have argued that the real reason why Truman, Stimson and Byrnes decided to use the bomb on Japan was because they hoped to intimidate Stalin and the Soviet Union. According to this argument, Truman and his advisers knew there were alternative ways of ending the Pacific war, but deliberately went ahead with the bombing of Japanese cities anyway because of the perceived diplomatic advantage.

Most scholars have rejected this argument, because they believe that Truman and his advisers saw the bomb first and foremost as a way to shorten the war. These historians also believe that the Manhattan Project had so much momentum in the spring of 1945, that it was difficult for Truman to stop the bombing. Still, virtually all now agree that the bomb's usefulness for "atomic diplomacy" against the Soviets provided one more reason for Truman not to halt the dropping of the bomb.

Selecting the Target

While American leaders considered what to do about Japan and the Soviet Union, planning went ahead for the military deployment of the atomic bomb. Target selection was put in the hands of a Target Committee controlled by General Groves and his Manhattan Project staff, although Army Air Forces personnel participated as well.

The Target Committee first met on April 27, 1945. Its primary concerns were showing off the bomb's power to the maximum effect and making the greatest impression possible on the Japanese. For accuracy, the Committee insisted that the bomb should be dropped in daylight and clear weather. The target should be a city undamaged by conventional bombing and possessing a geographical layout suitable for maximizing damage from the bomb's blast wave. Radiation effects were not thought to be important.

By the end of May, the Committee selected the following cities, in order of priority: Kyoto, Hiroshima, Kokura and Niigata. The Army Air Forces were asked to protect these cities from future firebombing raids.

STIMSON, GROVES AND THE SAVING OF KYOTO

The Target Committee's number one priority, Kyoto, was never bombed. On May 30, 1945, Groves visited the Secretary of War in his offices. Stimson asked for the target list and immediately vetoed Kyoto because it "was the ancient capital of Japan, a historical city, and one that was of great religious significance to the Japanese." Stimson had visited the city at least three times and was "very much impressed by its ancient culture." Stimson was particularly concerned that the destruction of this historic city would permanently embitter the Japanese against the United States after the war, resulting in an increase in Soviet influence.

Groves objected that Kyoto had a population of over one million, did much war work and had a geography highly suitable for the bomb. Stimson continued to refuse. Groves fought for two more months to reinstate the city to the target list, but never succeeded in overruling Stimson. Eventually the port city of Nagasaki was put on the list instead.

"WE COULD NOT GIVE THE JAPANESE ANY WARNING"

Discussion as to how the atomic bomb was to be used first was left to a second body, the Interim Committee on post-war nuclear policy. On May 31, 1945, Secretary Stimson chaired a meeting of this group of high-level policymakers, including James Byrnes as Truman's personal representative. Also attending were the Committee's scientific advisers, headed by Dr. Robert Oppenheimer.

Over lunch, Committee members briefly discussed whether the Japanese should be given a warning before the atomic bomb was dropped, and whether a bomb demonstration should be held first in the presence of delegates from Japan or neutral countries. These ideas were rejected on the grounds that a warning might cause the Japanese to try to shoot down the bomb-carrying plane or move prisoners-of-war into the target area, and a demonstration would be difficult to arrange and might be a failure.

An original copy of the official minutes of the interim committee meeting of May 31, 1945. The marked passage gives the committee's recommendation regarding the use of the bomb:

..."Secretary [Stimson] expressed the conclusion, on which there was general agreement, that we could not give the Japanese any warning, that we could not concentrate on a civilian area; but that we should seek to make a profound psychological impression on as many inhabitants as possible. At the suggestion of Dr. Conant the Secretary agreed that the most desirable target would be a vital war plant employing a large number of workers and closely surrounded by workers' houses."

Lent by the National Archives and Records Administration.

43

NUCLEAR WEAPONS AND THE BOMBING OF CIVILIANS

Throughout the discussions of the Interim and Target Committees, the escalation of bombing attacks on civilians in World War II was an important precedent and context. When Oppenheimer suggested on May 31 that several atomic attacks be carried out on the same day to shock the Japanese, Groves opposed the idea on the grounds that "the effect would not be sufficiently distinct from our regular air force [bombing] program." At that time, the firebombing of Japanese cities had already killed around two hundred thousand people.

The yield of the first atomic bombs also estimated at only one-tenth to one-half of what they turned out to be, and, until after the July atomic test, no one had a clear impression of what the heat and radiation effects would be like. As a result, many of those knowledgeable about the bomb did not see it as being drastically different than conventional strategic bombing, nor did they expect that the bomb would automatically end the war.

At the end of the war little remained standing in the firebombed sections of Tokyo.

"SUCH ATTACKS ON JAPAN COULD NOT BE JUSTIFIED"

Not everyone inside the small group privy to the atomic secret agreed that the bomb should be used without warning on Japanese cities. The strongest base of protest was in the Manhattan Project laboratory at the University of Chicago. Leo Szilard and other scientists there felt that the bomb project had been primarily a response to a threat from Germany. Attacking Japan, they felt, would not be fair without an opportunity being given to surrender first. They were equally concerned that using the bomb without warning the Japanese or telling the Soviets would increase the chances of an uncontrolled nuclear arms race with the USSR after the war.

The Chicago group tried writing a report, sending petitions to President Truman, and approaching Truman's adviser and

44

choice for Secretary of State, "Jimmy" Byrnes. The President never received the petitions and all the scientists' initiatives were frustrated because of the opposition of Byrnes, Groves, Oppenheimer, and other policymakers and scientists in control of the nuclear program.

MILITARY OPPOSITION TO THE BOMBING

Opposition to dropping the atomic bomb on Japan without warning also came from inside the military establishment. The most famous cases are those of Admiral Leahy and General (later President) Eisenhower. Leahy said in 1950 that he had denounced the bombing as adopting "ethical standards common to barbarians in the dark ages, " but 1945 documents only suggest that he was skeptical that the atomic bomb would ever work. Eisenhower claimed in 1948, and in his later memoirs, to have opposed the use of the bomb in conversations with President Truman at the Potsdam Conference in July 1945. But corroborating evidence for these assertions is weak.

We do know, however, that top civilian officials in the military departments, including Undersecretary of the Navy Ralph Bard and Assistant Secretary for War John McCloy, opposed the policy of use without warning.

SECRET ● July 17, 1945

A PETITION TO THE PRESIDENT OF THE UNITED STATES

Discoveries of which the people of the United States are not aware may affect the welfare of this nation in the near future. The liberation of atomic power which has been achieved places atomic bombs in the hands of the Army. It places in your hands, as Commander-in-Chief, the fateful decision whether or not to sanction the use of such bombs in the present phase of the war against Japan.

We, the undersigned scientists, have been working in the field of atomic power. Until recently we have had to fear that the United States might be attacked by atomic bombs during this war and that her only defense might lie in a counterattack by the same means. Today, with the defeat of Germany, this danger is averted and we feel impelled to say what follows:

The war has to be brought speedily to a successful conclusion and attacks by atomic bombs may very well be an effective method of warfare. We feel, however, that such attacks on Japan could not be justified, at least not unless the terms which will be imposed after the war on Japan were made public in detail and Japan were given an opportunity to surrender.

If such public announcement gave assurance to the Japanese that they could look forward to a life devoted to peaceful pursuits in their homeland and if Japan still refused to surrender our nation might then, in certain circumstances, find itself forced to resort to the use of atomic bombs. Such a step, however, ought not to be made at any time without seriously considering the moral responsibilities which are involved.

The development of atomic power will provide the nations with new means of destruction. The atomic bombs at our disposal represent only the first step in this direction, and there is almost no limit to the destructive power which will become available in the course of their future development. Thus a nation which sets the precedent of using these newly liberated forces of nature for purposes of destruction may have to bear the responsibility of opening the door to an era of devastation on an unimaginable scale.

If after this war a situation is allowed to develop in the world which permits rival powers to be in uncontrolled possession of these new means of destruction, the cities of the United States—as well as the cities of other nations will be in continuous danger of sudden annihilation. All the resources of the United States, moral and material, may have to be mobilized to prevent the advent of such a world situation. Its prevention is at present the solemn responsibility of the United States—singled out by virtue of her lead in the field of atomic power.

The added material strength which this lead gives to the United States brings with it the obligation of restraint and if we were to violate this obligation our moral position would be weakened in the eyes of the world and in our own eyes. It would then be more difficult for us to live up to our responsibility of bringing the unloosened forces of destruction under control.

In view of the foregoing, we, the undersigned, respectfully petition: first, that you exercise your power as Commander-in-Chief, to rule that the United States shall not resort to the use of atomic bombs in this war unless the terms which will be imposed upon Japan have been made public in detail and Japan knowing these terms has refused to surrender; second, that in such an event the question whether or not to use atomic bombs be decided by you in the light of the considerations presented in this petition as well as all the other moral responsibilities which are involved.

One of the original petitions to President Truman by Manhattan Project scientists, with the signature of Leo Szilard at lower left.
Lent by the National Archives and Records Administration.

Historical Controversies:
Was a Warning or Demonstration Possible?

The question as to whether there were feasible alternatives to dropping the atomic bomb without warning on civilians has been controversial from the outset. The Interim Committee raised valid concerns that a warning could endanger Allied servicemen and that a demonstration might be ineffective or a failure. The proposed alternatives were examined so briefly, however, that many scholars have argued that they did not get the attention they deserved. By this argument, Groves and the Manhattan Project set the agenda for using the bomb, and the already existing bombing of cities in Germany and Japan made it unlikely that President Truman's advisers would seriously question the dropping of the atomic bomb without warning. Other scholars have, however, defended the original decision that a warning or a demonstration was not a feasible alternative.

The Invasion of Japan: A Giant Okinawa?

American planning for an invasion of Japan continued in spring 1945 as if the atomic bomb did not exist. Not only was the Manhattan Project so secret that even many military planners were unaware of it, the effect of the new weapon on the Japanese was unknown. Under the leadership of Army Chief of Staff General George C. Marshall, the War Department continued to assume that an invasion would be necessary to force the Japanese government to surrender.

Not everyone in the U.S. military agreed with this strategy. The Navy believed that its blockade could force Japan to quit the war, while many Army Air Forces' generals thought firebombing could force surrender by itself or in conjunction with the blockade. Both groups pointed to the terrible casualties of the

Okinawa campaign in arguing against an invasion. General Marshall and his staff also feared heavy losses, but they argued that as in the case of Germany, only the occupation of the enemy's territory and capital would bring the war to an end.

"OPERATION DOWNFALL"—THE INVASION PLAN

On June 18, 1945, President Truman gave preliminary approval to the invasion plans presented by General Marshall. "Operation Downfall" would have two parts. On or about November 1, 1945, 767,000 Marines and Army soldiers would begin landing on the beaches of the southern island of Kyushu in "Operation Olympic." The invasion fleet would dwarf that of the landings in Normandy in June 1944. The objective of this operation was to occupy only the southern half of Kyushu and use it as an air base and staging area for a second invasion.

If the Japanese did not then surrender, the target date for "Operation Coronet"—the landings on the main island of Honshu—was March 1, 1946. A huge force of 28 divisions, twice the size of "Olympic," would land on beaches near Tokyo. Military planners assumed that it would take until about the end of 1946 to occupy the capital and enough of Honshu to force a final Japanese surrender.

GEORGE C. MARSHALL (1880–1959)

No American staff officer made a greater contribution to victory in World War II than General Marshall. A Virginian by birth, Marshall became Chief of Staff of the Army on September 1, 1939, the day Germany invaded Poland. He played an absolutely essential role in expanding the small, poorly armed U.S. Army of 1939 into the massive and effective force of 1943–1945. He was also a key strategist in Allied plans on all fronts.

Marshall was an important adviser to Presidents Roosevelt and Truman on the Manhattan Project. In June 1945, Marshall asked Truman whether it would be possible to give the Japanese a warning before dropping the bomb, but did not press his argument. He believed that an invasion of Japan was probably unavoidable in any case. After his retirement from the Army,

President Truman made him Secretary of State in 1947. He won the Nobel Peace Prize in 1953 for the Marshall Plan, which helped to revive the economies of Western Europe.

HALF A MILLION AMERICAN DEAD?

After the war, estimates of the number of casualties to be expected in an invasion of Japan were as high as half a million or more American dead—twice the number of U.S. servicemen killed on all fronts during World War II. In fact, military staff studies in the spring of 1945 estimated thirty to fifty thousand casualties—dead and wounded—in "Olympic," the invasion of Kyushu. Based on the Okinawa campaign, that would have meant perhaps ten thousand American dead. Military planners made no firm estimates for "Coronet," the second invasion, but losses clearly would have been higher.

Early U.S. studies, however, underestimated Japanese defenses. Moreover, the U.S. Navy leadership, who were unenthusiastic about the invasion, was skeptical of the studies. On June 18, 1945, Admiral Leahy pointed out that, if the "Olympic" invasion force took casualties at the same rate as Okinawa, that could mean 268,000 casualties (about 50,000 dead) on Kyushu. It nonetheless appears likely that post-war estimates of a half million American deaths were too high, but many tens of thousands of dead were a real possibility.

Historical Controversies:
Was an Invasion Inevitable If the Atomic Bomb Had Not Been Dropped?

The Japanese and American lives that would have been lost in an invasion have often been used to justify the atomic bombing of Japan. Scholars and analysts have questioned, however, whether an invasion was necessary. In 1946, the U.S. Strategic Bombing Survey said: "certainly prior to 31 December 1945, and in all probability prior to 1 November 1945, Japan would have surrendered, even if Russia had not entered the war, and even if no invasion had been planned or contemplated." Others are less confident that the Japanese rulers would have accepted defeat, especially if the Allies refused to guarantee the Emperor's position.

Some combination of blockade, firebombing, an Emperor guarantee, and a Soviet declaration of war would probably have forced a Japanese surrender, but to President Truman an invasion appeared to be a real possibility. Matters were not as clear in 1945 as they are in hindsight, because Truman and his advisers could not know how the war would actually end.

TRUMAN, STALIN, POTSDAM AND THE BOMB

In mid-July 1945, at a remote desert site in New Mexico, Manhattan Project scientists prepared for the world's first nuclear explosion—a test of the mechanism for the "Fat Man" bomb. Thousands of miles away, outside Berlin, Germany, the leaders of the major Allied powers were assembling for the Potsdam Conference. President Truman had delayed the Conference so that it would take place at the time the bomb was to be tested. Presumably he hoped to have the new weapon in hand at a time when tough negotiations with the Soviets were expected over the post-war settlement in Europe. The President also wanted to issue an ultimatum to Japan to surrender during the Conference. At Potsdam he in fact gave final verbal approval for dropping the atomic bomb on Japanese cities.

"I AM BECOME DEATH, DESTROYER OF WORLDS"

At 5:29:45 AM, July 16, 1945, a blinding flash and unbelievable heat seared the New Mexico desert—the first nuclear explosion in the history of the world. Codenamed "Trinity," the Manhattan Project's test of the plutonium implosion bomb was a stunning success. The explosion almost equaled that of 20,000 tons of TNT, many times what some had expected. General Groves and his Project leaders were jubilant and relieved. But for some, the spectacle also cast an ominous shadow over the world. Los Alamos scientific director Dr. Robert Oppenheimer thought of the lines from the Hindu scripture, the *Bhagavad Gita*, "I am become Death, Destroyer of Worlds."

"I was flabbergasted by the new spectacle. We saw the whole sky flash with unbelievable brightness in spite of the very dark glasses we wore...(F)or a moment I thought the explosion might set fire to the atmosphere and thus finish the earth, even though I knew that this was not possible."

Dr. Emilio Segré, Manhattan Project physicist and Nobel Prize winner

TRUMAN TELLS STALIN ABOUT THE BOMB

Coded telegrams about the successful atomic test reached Secretary of War Stimson at Potsdam within hours of the explosion. But it was only after General Groves' detailed report about Trinity was seen by President Truman on July 21, that he, Byrnes and Stimson really understood how powerful the new weapon was.

On July 24, Truman approached Soviet leader Stalin and mentioned as casually as possible that the U.S. now had "a new weapon of unusual destructive force." According to Truman, Stalin did not react, but merely stated that he hoped that the Americans would make "good use of it against the Japanese." The President and his entourage were not sure that the Soviet dictator had even understood, but Stalin knew that Truman was referring to the atomic bomb because of Soviet spying on the Manhattan Project.

July 25 1945

We met at 11 A.M. today. That is Stalin, Churchill and the US. President. But I had a most important session with Lord Mountbatten & General Marshall before that. We have discovered the most terrible bomb in the history of the world. It may be the fire distruction prophesied in the Euphrates Valley Era, after Noah and his fabulous Ark.

Anyway we think we have found the way to cause a disintegration of the atom. An experiment in the New Mexican desert was startling — to put it mildly. Thirteen pounds of the explosive caused the complete disintegration of a steel tower 60 feet high, created a crater 6 feet deep and 1200 feet in diameter, knocked over a steel tower ½ mile away and knocked men down 10,000 yards away. The explosion was visible for more than 200 miles and audible for 40 miles and more.

This weapon is to be used against Japan between now and August 10th. I have told the Sec. of War, Mr. Stimson, to use it so that military objectives and soldiers and sailors are the target and not women and children. Even if the Japs are savages, ruthless, merciless and fanatic, we as the leader of the world for the common welfare cannot drop this terrible bomb on the old Capitol or the new.

He & I are in accord. The target will be a purely military one and we will issue a warning statement asking the Japs to surrender and save lives. I'm sure they will not do that, but we will have given them the chance. It is certainly a good thing for the world that Hitler's crowd or Stalin's did not discover this atomic bomb. It seems to be the most terrible thing ever discovered, but it can be made the most useful.

HARRY S. TRUMAN LIBRARY
Papers of Harry S. Truman
President's Secretary's Files

President Truman's Potsdam diary for July 25, 1945, alludes to General Groves' report on the Trinity atomic bomb test and to Groves' continuing attempts to designate Kyoto ("the old capitol") as a target. Lent by the Harry S. Truman Library.

"FINI JAPS WHEN THAT COMES ABOUT"

During the Potsdam Conference, the American and Soviet leaders discussed the entry of the USSR into the war against Japan. After Stalin promised entry by August 15, Truman wrote in his diary on July 17, "Fini Japs when that comes about." But a day later he wrote, "Believe Japs will fold up before Russia comes in. I am sure they will when Manhattan appears over their homeland." Many of his advisers were now telling him that Soviet military intervention in the Far East was no longer desirable.

Stalin and Truman also discussed new diplomatic initiatives from Tokyo to Moscow in July. These messages more clearly expressed Emperor Hirohito's desire for a peace settlement. Since Stalin wished to enter the Pacific war, it was not in his interest to play up the new messages. President Truman and Secretary of State Byrnes, who knew about the messages from American intelligence reports, dismissed the Japanese diplomatic effort as nothing new.

AN ULTIMATUM TO JAPAN

On July 26, 1945, the three largest Allied powers already at war in the Pacific, the United States, Britain and China, issued the Potsdam Proclamation. This Proclamation was an ultimatum to the Japanese Empire to surrender immediately or face "prompt and utter destruction." Because of political opposition in America to concessions or modifications of "unconditional surrender," Secretary of State Byrnes eliminated any reference to the retention of Emperor Hirohito on the throne. Also eliminated were any direct references to the atomic bomb or Soviet entry into the war.

As a result of these changes, the Proclamation was not effective in changing the position of the Japanese government. The reaction of the military was especially hostile. On July 28, Prime Minister Suzuki announced that his government would ignore (*"mokusatsu"*) the Proclamation. This word was translated in the West as "treat with silent contempt," making the Japanese look even more arrogant. Nothing further stood in the way of using the atomic bomb on Japan.

THE OFFICIAL ORDER TO DROP THE BOMB

No written order from President Truman to drop the bomb on Japan exists. Throughout the spring and summer, the President had verbally confirmed proposals presented to him by Marshall, Stimson, Byrnes and Groves. "As far as I was concerned," said General Groves in his memoirs, "his [Truman's] decision was one of noninterference—basically a decision not to upset existing plans."

The actual order to drop resulted from a request of General Carl Spaatz, the commander of the newly created U.S. Army Strategic Air Forces. He reportedly said to General Thomas Handy, the Acting Army Chief of Staff in Washington, "Listen, Tom, if I'm going kill 100,000 people, I'm not going to do it on verbal orders. I want a piece of paper." After long-distance communications with General Marshall in Potsdam, Handy issued the order to Spaatz on July 25—before the Potsdam Proclamation was issued.

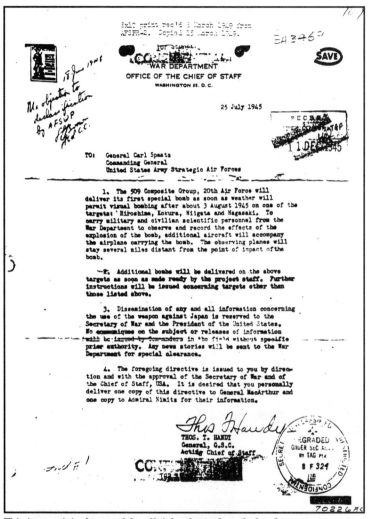

WAR DEPARTMENT
OFFICE OF THE CHIEF OF STAFF
WASHINGTON 25, D. C.

25 July 1945

TO: General Carl Spaatz
     Commanding General
     United States Army Strategic Air Forces

1. The 509 Composite Group, 20th Air Force will deliver its first special bomb as soon as weather will permit visual bombing after about 3 August 1945 on one of the targets: Hiroshima, Kokura, Niigata and Nagasaki. To carry military and civilian scientific personnel from the War Department to observe and record the effects of the explosion of the bomb, additional aircraft will accompany the airplane carrying the bomb. The observing planes will stay several miles distant from the point of impact of the bomb.

2. Additional bombs will be delivered on the above targets as soon as made ready by the project staff. Further instructions will be issued concerning targets other than those listed above.

3. Dissemination of any and all information concerning the use of the weapon against Japan is reserved to the Secretary of War and the President of the United States. No communiques on the subject or releases of information will be issued by commanders in the field without specific prior authority. Any news stories will be sent to the War Department for special clearance.

4. The foregoing directive is issued to you by direction and with the approval of the Secretary of War and of the Chief of Staff, USA. It is desired that you personally deliver one copy of this directive to General MacArthur and one copy to Admiral Nimitz for their information.

THOS. T. HANDY
General, G.S.C.
Acting Chief of Staff

*This is an original copy of the official order to drop the bomb.
Lent by the National Archives and Records Administration.*

Historical Controversies:
Was the Decision to Drop the Bomb Justified?

After fifty years, the controversy over this question remains heated. Many analysts continue to argue that the bomb ended the war quickly and saved lives—even if the American deaths in an invasion of Japan would have been significantly lower than the post-war estimates. On the other hand, other scholars have argued that the atomic bombings were unnecessary; a number of options were available to President Truman, but he decided to go ahead anyway because he wished to intimidate the Soviets.

The current consensus of most scholars is that the Soviets did play a role in the thinking of Truman and his advisers, but saving American lives and shortening the war were more important. Most historians also agree that there was scarcely any "decision to drop the bomb." Truman merely approved the preparations already underway; the Manhattan Project had a great deal of momentum and the strategic bombing of German and Japanese cities made atomic bombing easier to accept.

It is also clear that there were alternatives to both an invasion and dropping atomic bombs without warning—for example, guaranteeing the Emperor's position, staging a demonstration of the bomb's power, or waiting for blockade, firebombing and a Soviet declaration of war to take their toll on Japan. Since these alternatives are clearer in hindsight and it is speculative whether they would have induced the Japanese government to surrender quickly, the debate over "the decision to drop the bomb" will remain forever controversial.

UNIT 3: DELIVERING THE BOMB

August 6, 1945, 2:00 a.m., Tinian Island, the Central Pacific. Bathed in floodlights, the B-29 "Enola Gay" awaits take-off on an historic mission: dropping the first atomic bomb on Japan. The head of the Manhattan Project, Gen. Leslie Groves, had warned the "Enola Gay's" commander, Col. Paul Tibbets, to expect "a little publicity," but Tibbets and his crew are stunned by the scene on the tarmac. Movie cameramen, photographers and reporters surround the crew. Groves is determined that this is one moment in history that was not going to go unrecorded. Soon thereafter, at 2:45 a.m., the aircraft took off.

The beginning of the "Enola Gay's" mission was the culmination of over a year's work. The U.S. Army Air Forces had modified its most advanced bomber, the B-29, and had created a new, special military unit for delivering atomic bombs. This unit's mission was so secret that, with few exceptions, the nature of its weapons was concealed even from its members.

The B-29: A Three-Billion Dollar Gamble

Although ultimately chosen to deliver the first atomic bombs, the Boeing B-29 Superfortress was conceived, designed, and rushed into production as a very long-range conventional bomber. Of the total wartime production of over 2,000 aircraft, only 15 were sent to the Pacific as potential atomic bomb carriers before the war's end. Most of the rest formed the backbone of what was, by the spring of 1945, the most powerful and destructive bomber force of World War II.

The B-29 was the most technologically complex mass-production aircraft of World War II. The program to build it also represented the largest commitment of resources to a single military aircraft up to that time. Initiated in response to German victories in Europe during 1939 and 1940, the B-29 program eventually cost over 3 billion dollars—1 billion more than the Manhattan Project.

DESIGNING A SUPERBOMBER

In the wake of Nazi Germany's quick victory over Poland in 1939, Major General Henry H. "Hap" Arnold, Commander of the Army Air Corps, asked the War Department for authority to initiate design studies for a very long-range heavy bomber. After formulating its requirements for the new bomber, in January 1940 the Air Corps requested design proposals from four aircraft firms: Boeing, Lockhead, Douglas, and Consolidated. On September 6, 1940, the Boeing Company received a $3.6 million contract covering the construction of a wooden full-size mock-up and two prototypes. The new bomber received the designation XB-29.

STRETCHING AERODYNAMIC LIMITS

To meet the Air Corps' performance requirements for the new bomber, Boeing engineers stretched existing aircraft technology to the limit. To reduce drag (air resistance) and provide great lift at high speed, designers selected a long, narrow wing incorporating a newly designed, aerodynamically efficient airfoil. Flaps as large as the wings of some fighters would reduce the high landing speed inherent in such a heavy bomber. Flush riveting of most of the aircraft's skin produced a smooth, strong surface. Tight-fitting low-drag cowlings enclosed the B-29's four massive 2,200 hp Wright Cyclone R-3350 engines. Even the aircraft's rounded nose contributed to drag reduction by eliminating a vertical windscreen.

Boeing's design efforts resulted in a combination of flight and landing characteristics that compromised neither. As a result, although the B-29 carried a larger bombload over greater distances at higher altitude and speed than any other bomber of World War II, it proved surprisingly easy to fly.

A TECHNOLOGICAL GAMBLE

For the first time on a combat aircraft, heated pressurized compartments allowed crewmen to fly at high altitudes without bulky clothing and oxygen masks. A 10-m (33-ft) tunnel, 86 cm (34 in) in diameter, ran through the aircraft's two bomb bays and connected two of the compartments. Bunks in the rear compartment allowed crewmen to sleep on long duration flights. The tail gunner's pressurized position remained isolated from the rest of the aircraft.

The complexity of the B-29 represented not only a major technological achievement, but also a significant gamble for Boeing and the Army Air Corps. If unforeseen problems turned up in the B-29's engines or internal systems during flight testing, the entire program could be endangered.

A TROUBLESOME GESTATION

As Boeing proceeded toward the construction of the first prototype B-29, the program began to suffer from numerous delays. Over 900 changes were made to the basic design between 1940 and 1942. One of the most important was inclusion of a new type of defensive armament system incorporating four remotely-controlled machine gun turrets connected to a computer-assisted fire-control system. To provide electrical power for the fire control system, the pressurization system, and the aircraft's massive propellers, designers used over 125 electric motors, necessitating weight reduction for the rest of the aircraft.

To eliminate further delays and speed production of the first prototypes, the B-29 Liaison Committee was established in April 1942 and empowered to make binding decisions for the program. As the year progressed, various subcommittees helped coordinate the assembly of the B-29 prototype, which made its first test flight on September 21, 1942.

THE ENGINE CRISIS

Although the B-29 exhibited excellent flying characteristics, its engines caused problems from the beginning of flight testing. After several near-accidents, an engine fire caused the second prototype to crash on February 18, 1943, killing Boeing's chief test pilot and ten others on board. A Senate investigating committee determined that engine quality control had been deficient, precipitating a crisis for the B-29 program. In response, General Arnold set up the "B-29 Special Project" under General Kenneth B. Wolfe. Arnold expected Wolfe, one of the Army Air Forces' most experienced engineering officers, to ensure that the first B-29 would be ready for combat by the end of 1943.

Improved quality control, a redesigned engine cowling, improved lubrication and better cooling helped to reduce the R-3350's tendency to catch fire. The problem, however, persisted well into the B-29's service life.

SUPERFACTORIES FOR A SUPERBOMBER

Following the Japanese attack on Pearl Harbor, the U.S. Army Air Forces ordered over 1,600 B-29's, even though the aircraft had never been flown. Although Boeing had already begun construction of a massive new factory for B-29s at Wichita, Kansas, the Army recognized that the order far exceeded Boeing's plant capacity.

Chrysler Corporation would produce the new bomber's engine, at a massive plant to be built in Chicago. General Motors' Fisher Division would be responsible for forgings, castings, stampings and various B-29 subassemblies. Bell Aircraft Company would build center sections and fuselages and, after some delays, entire aircraft in Marietta, Georgia. Additional B-29 factories were eventually established by Boeing at Renton, Washington, and the Martin Company in Omaha, Nebraska.

The first production B-29s began to roll off the assembly lines during July 1943. By war's end, the four B-29 assembly facilities and engine factories had produced over 2,000 aircraft and 18,000 engines, a signal achievement.

The B-29 and the Bombing of Japan

CREATING A NEW AIR FORCE

By October 1943, President Franklin Roosevelt had begun to

lose patience with the B-29 program. General Arnold had promised that at least 150 B-29s would be available to begin bombing Japan from China by January 1, 1944. Aware of the President's dissatisfaction, Arnold activated the first B-29 combat unit, the XXth Bomber Command, in late November, and its parent organization the Twentieth Air Force, in April 1944. Arnold selected General Kenneth Wolfe, already deeply involved in the B-29 program, to command the XXth Bomber Command from an airfield near Salina, Kansas. Unlike all of the other Army Air Forces, the Twentieth Air Force would be directly under the command of the Joint Chiefs of Staff.

The mission of the Twentieth Air Force would be the destruction of Japanese war industries as outlined under the "Air Plan for the Defeat of Japan," drafted by Wolfe and formalized by President Roosevelt, British Prime Minister Churchill, and the Combined Chiefs of Staff at the Cairo Conference in November 1943.

CREW TRAINING

Following activation of XXth Bomber Command, General Wolfe prepared plans to train 452 combat crews. As personnel trickled into their bases in late 1943, they found B-29s in such short supply that many were forced to train in older heavy bombers. By the end of the year, the average crew had less than 30 hours of flight time in the airplane they would be taking into combat. Although more B-29s became available for training during early 1944, the crews left for their first combat deployment with much still to learn about their complex, temperamental bombers.

THE BATTLE OF KANSAS

The first B-29s off the assembly lines required extensive modification to make them ready for combat. Under pressure from President Roosevelt to deploy the 150 B-29s of the XXth Bomber Command to India by April 15, 1944, Army Air Forces Commanding General Arnold visited the modification center at

Salina, Kansas, in early March, expecting to find the first contingent of new B-29s ready to begin the long flight to Asia. Arnold was shocked to find that none of the new bombers were ready and no one could say exactly when the modifications would be completed.

To speed up the process, Arnold imposed greater Air Force control over program management, assigned the B-29 priority over all other aircraft programs, and diverted workers from Boeing's assembly lines to the Salina, Kansas, modification center.

Laboring on B-29's parked outdoors in freezing temperatures, Boeing workers modified just enough bombers by the end of March 1944 to equip the first units going overseas. The last of the 150 bombers left by April 15. The episode quickly became known as "The Battle of Kansas."

EARLY B-29 OPERATIONS IN ASIA

The first B-29s arrived in India during May 1944. Early bombing raids against targets in Japanese-held China and Southeast Asia were conducted from air bases in China. The first attack on Japan since the Doolittle Raid, a strike against coke furnaces and steel plants in the city of Yawata, was staged from Chengtu, China, on June 15, 1944.

The B-29 crews operating from China faced enormous obstacles, however. Because Japanese forces blocked overland routes to Chengtu, all food, fuel, bombs, ammunition, and other supplies had to be flown to the base over the Himalaya Mountains from India. In some cases, it was estimated that supply aircraft burned 12 gallons of fuel for every gallon delivered to a Chinese airstrip within striking distance of Japan. Moreover, B-29 crews taking off from Chinese bases had to fly a 5,000 km (3,200 mi) round trip to reach those few cities in western Japan that were within their range. Operations were hampered by mechanical failures, the strain of very long flights at high altitude, and poor bombing results.

BASES IN THE CENTRAL PACIFIC

The "Air Plan for the Defeat of Japan" called for the largest share of the strategic bombing campaign to be conducted from bases in the central Pacific. After the seizure of the Marianas Islands, five great airfields would be constructed there, allowing a new B-29 organization, the XXIst Bomber Command, to begin large-scale bombing of the Japanese home islands. On August 27, 1944, the Twentieth Air Force's Chief of Staff, Major General Haywood S. Hansell, took command of the XXIst Bomber Command and began to formulate plans for the campaign from the Marianas.

BULLDOZERS BEFORE BOMBERS

Although the XXIst Bomber Command faced fewer logistical difficulties than had the XXth, the construction of airfields and support facilities in the Marianas represented a substantial accomplishment. After the capture of the island of Saipan in June 1944 and the islands of Tinian and Guam in early August, Army airfield engineers and Navy Seabees constructed the five largest air bases ever built to that time, each capable of handling several hundred B-29s. With the completion of two airfields on both Tinian and Guam during the spring of 1945, the islands had been totally transformed, setting the stage for the last great air campaign of World War II.

EARLY B-29 OPERATIONS IN THE MARIANAS

Operations from Saipan began on November 24, 1944, reducing the length of a round-trip flight to Tokyo to 4,800 km (3,000 mi). Most significant Japanese targets were now within the range. Additional airfields on Guam and Tinian allowed more B-29 groups to join the offensive.

Still, problems remained. Major General Haywood Hansell, commander of XXIst Bomber Command, wanted to continue the high-altitude precision-bombing techniques first tried in Europe. Crews attacking targets in Japan from 9,000 m (30,000 ft), however, experienced a powerful and unknown phenomenon—jet-stream winds of over 320 km/h (200 mph). These high winds either pushed bombers along at ground speeds approaching 800 km/h (500 mph) or slowed them nearly to a standstill. Bombing accuracy was very difficult to achieve. Hansell ordered his bombers to attack at lower altitudes, but unpredictable weather often obscured targets anyway. By the end of 1944, B-29s had dropped 1,550 tons of bombs during seven raids on Japanese aircraft factories and steel plants. It was estimated that only one bomb in 50 had fallen within 1000 feet of its target.

"Oh, I get that lonesome feeling
When I hear those engines whine,
Those 29's are breaking up
That old gang of mine.
There goes Jack, there goes Bill
Down over Tokyo.
We all hope it's home we go
How soon we do not know.
A goddamned Zeke rammed old Pete,
We wept to see him go,
Heavy flak riddled Jack,
He couldn't make Iwo.
Oh they say it's thirty missions
But it's more like twenty-nine,
Those 29s are breaking up
That old gang of mine."

Song by an anonymous B-29 crewman, sung to the tune of "Those Wedding Bells Are Breaking Up That Old Gang of Mine"

CITIZEN AIRMEN

As the U.S. Army Air Forces expanded dramatically during World War II, it drew in men from every geographical region and background in America. Although the Air Force provided practically no flying opportunities for anyone other than white males, the B-29 units nevertheless contained a remarkably diverse mix of airmen. Almost all were volunteers, motivated by patriotism and sense of wartime duty. Flight pay, the prospect of rapid promotion, and the glamour of aviation attracted others. As one of the Army Air Forces' highest priority units, the Twentieth Air Force attracted the best flyers among those still training in the United States.

Although many senior officers came from combat units, most B-29 crewman had not yet been overseas when they arrived at the great airfields in the Marianas. These citizen airmen faced an enormous responsibility—to take a complex, often dangerously temperamental aircraft into combat halfway around the world and deliver what their superiors hoped would be the final knockout blow against Japan.

A HAZARDOUS BUSINESS

Although loss rates for American bomber crews bombing Japan rarely approached those suffered by those over Germany, combat aircrews in the Pacific nonetheless faced a host of dangers, particularly during the early stages of the Marianas campaign. Operating B-29s at the limit of their performance was often disastrous for crews attempting to take off with a full load of fuel and bombs. Japanese anti-aircraft fire and fighters sometimes posed a significant threat over the target. Nor was abandoning a wounded B-29 over Japan a good idea—capture by the Japanese often meant execution.

The 2,400 km (1,500 mi) return flight over open ocean proved too much for many weary aircrews in damaged bombers. Others ditched at sea after running out of fuel on the long return flight. Although patrol aircraft and submarines rescued many downed crews, others disappeared into the Pacific without a trace. By war's end 417 B-29s had been lost in combat and through operational accidents with 3,015 crewmen listed as killed, wounded, or missing in action.

HAVENS FOR DAMAGED BOMBERS

By the spring of 1945, B-29 losses had dropped to very low levels on most missions. Although some bombers continued to be lost to battle damage or lack of fuel during the long return flights, emergency airfields constructed in Iwo Jima, roughly halfway between Marianas and Japan, provided a much need haven for aircraft unable to limp home. Establishment of bases capable of handling B-29s on Okinawa, after its final capture in June 1945, provided another escape option for crippled aircraft. Finally, Japanese air defenses proved rather less than formidable against B-29s bombing from low-altitude at night. These defenses became even less effective as a result of bombing, naval blockade, and the general deterioration of Japanese society during the spring of 1945. By war's end, Japanese air defenses had claimed only one of every five B-29s lost during the war.

A SHIFT IN TACTICS

Dismayed with the poor results achieved by XXIst Bomber Command under General Haywood Hansell, General Arnold fired Hansell and appointed Major General Curtis E. LeMay, a veteran of the European air campaign, on January 20, 1945.

Under pressure to attack Japanese cities with incendiary bombs, LeMay instituted radical changes in the tactics employed by the B-29s. Instead of high altitude daylight precision attacks, his bombers would conduct area raids at night, flying very low altitudes. Under those circumstances, enemy air opposition and antiaircraft defenses were expected to cause fewer problems. LeMay stripped the aircraft of their guns, ammunition and three crewmen, raising the operational bomb load for a single airplane from three to six tons. Most of the bombs would be incendiaries. Reasoning that dispersed factories could be destroyed and civilian morale shattered by burning residential areas, LeMay ordered his crews to bomb by radar, with an entire city, or a major section of it, as the target.

MODEL M-50 INCENDIARY BOMB

Along with the Model M-69 and M-47 incendiary bombs, the M-50 provided XXIst Bomber Command with the ideal weapon for burning Japanese cities. B-29s released bundles of individual

M-50s, which burst to scatter the individual bomblets at a preset altitude. Although not as effective as the jellied gasoline-filled M-69, the magnesium-filled M-50 was virtually impossible to extinguish.

BURNING JAPAN

The fire bombing campaign, which began in earnest with the great raid against Tokyo on the night of March 9–10, proved destructive beyond LeMay's wildest expectations. During the next five months, LeMay's bombers destroyed one half of the total area of 66 cities—burning 178 square miles to the ground. By the beginning of the summer of 1945, the destruction wrought by the B-29s was so complete that LeMay warned his superiors that by September he would run out of targets.

The cities of Hiroshima, Kokura, Niigata, and Nagasaki, however, had been largely spared from the aerial onslaught. The task of destroying them would be given to a unit recently arrived in Tinian's North Field—one trained to drop atomic bombs.

The World's First Atomic Strike Force

"...start training crews to drop the bomb, if and when we make it and drop it."
Henry H. "Hap" Arnold, Commanding General, Army Air Forces, to his deputy Lt. Gen. Barney Giles, 1944

By the summer of 1944, Manhattan Project scientists had made significant progress on the atomic bomb. Slowly but surely, the Army Air Forces had worked most of the glitches out of the B-29. It was time to create and train a combat unit to deliver the new weapons.

The Army Air Forces quickly realized that a standard bomber group would not be able to carry out the mission. To ensure secrecy, a uniquely organized, self-contained group was needed. For eight months, this "composite group" trained in isolation for a mission, the details of which were kept secret even from them.

Only on August 6, 1945, when the "Enola Gay" returned safely from its atomic attack on Hiroshima, would the 509th Composite Group understand their own role in history.

SELECTING AN ATOMIC COMMANDER

"You have to put together an outfit and deliver this weapon. We don't know what it can do...you've got to mate it to the training, the ballistics—everything. These are all parts of your problem."

General Uzal Ent to Lt. Colonel Paul Tibbets, September 1944

Almost a full year of planning went into selecting a commander for the new 509th Composite Group. Three days before a decision was reached, Paul Warfield Tibbets' name was added to the list of nominees. After an unorthodox interview designed to test his fundamental honesty, Tibbets was told he would command a unit that would be responsible for dropping an atomic bomb.

In 1944, "atomic power" did not have much meaning. Only after Tibbets learned that the atom bomb would have "an explosive power equal to that of several thousand tons of TNT," would he begin to understand the colossal potential of his mission.

PAUL W. TIBBETS: "AN INDEPENDENT OPERATOR"

Paul Warfield Tibbets was an obvious choice to command the 509th. Born in 1915, Tibbets' love of aviation led him to abandon his medical education to pursue a far less promising career in aviation at age 22. Joining the U.S. Army Air Corps cadet program in 1937 earned his father's wrath but also secured him a place in history.

By fall 1944, he had extensive combat experience, including the first daylight raid by an American bombing squadron on German-occupied Europe. As a 97th Bombardment Group officer in the North African and European Theaters he had gained leadership experience. A veteran of the B-29 testing program, he was one of the most experienced Superfortress pilots.

Tibbets offered more than his stellar service record. According to his memoirs, he "gained a reputation as an independent type of operator. In the European theater, [he] was called on to do things for which no formula or standards had been established." An innovator, he took on a project with an underdeveloped airplane and an undeveloped bomb and successfully executed it.

CREATING THE 509TH COMPOSITE GROUP

"Never before and never again would such a group exist."
Paul Tibbets, 1993

Standard bomb groups were comprised of four bomber squadrons, plus maintenance and ordnance squadrons. The 509th Composite Group was not a standard unit. Instead, it was comprised of one bomb squadron with its own, dedicated support squadrons. Grouping bomber and support squadrons together under one central command was an unorthodox but necessary strategy for keeping the 509th's mission secret.

The U.S. Army Air Forces selected various squadrons for the Group, while Tibbets hand-picked pilots and crewmen with whom he had experience flying. In addition to reviewing each candidate's performance record, the Air Forces made extensive security checks on each potential member. In late summer 1944, qualified squadrons and individuals were detached from their parent organizations and reassigned to what would become the 509th Composite Group.

THE 393RD BOMBER SQUADRON

Before Tibbets' took command of what would become the 509th, the Army Air Forces had already selected a bomber squadron to form the core of Tibbets' atomic strike force. One of Tibbets' first tasks was to approve the choice of the 393rd.

The members of the 393rd had already completed two-thirds of their training in Nebraska and were eagerly anticipating the day they would be ordered to move to the Pacific. To the surprise and disappointment of the combat-ready 393rd, they received a transfer to an air base in Utah.

Although pleased with the bomber squadron's superior training record, Tibbets asked the Army Air Forces to assign a few others, with whom he had previously served, to the 509th. Integrating this elite group with the bomber squadron added one more dimension to Tibbets' complex assignment.

THE 393RD'S UNIFORM PATCH

The members of the 393rd continued to wear their flight jackets with the 393rd insignia even after they had been transferred into the 509th Composite Group. After the war, the 393rd's insignia was changed to incorporate the mushroom cloud into its imagery.

TOM CLASSEN AND THE 393RD

Lt. Col. Tom Classen, a distinguished combat veteran and experienced pilot took command of the 393rd in the early months of 1944. All but a few of its members were inexperienced. Classen quickly turned them into a combat-ready squadron.

After the 393rd bomber squadron became a part of the 509th Composite Group, Classen's role changed. Classen continued to train bomber pilots, but Tibbets also assigned him broader responsibilities. As Tibbets' Deputy Commanding Officer, Classen oversaw the Group's everyday affairs.

SOMETHING NEW: A MILITARY POLICE COMPANY

Attaching a military police squadron to a bomber squadron was "something entirely new," according to the 509th yearbook. Guarding the 509th's atomic secrets, however, was a full-time job. While Tibbets prepared his air crews to deliver the bomb, the 395th Military Police Company completed a rigorous training program that prepared them to meet any enemy ground forces as well as curious fellow troops or civilians.

1ST ORDNANCE SQUADRON

The members of the 1st Ordnance Squadron were responsible for assembling the atomic bombs. In a unit unique to all standard Army organization, they worked closely with the

Manhattan Project scientists.

The technical and military security requirements for the squadron were exacting. The Army Air Forces accepted only one-fifth of those who met the basic qualifications. They warned those chosen that their jobs would be hazardous due to the experimental stage of the work.

THE 1ST ORDNANCE SQUADRON
YOU'RE GOING TO BE A HERO

"Colonel, if you get any trouble from anybody, you can call on me."

General Henry "Hap" Arnold to Paul Tibbets

"...if this is successful, you'll be a hero. But, if it fails, you'll be the biggest scapegoat ever."

General Uzal Ent, Commanding General of 2nd Air Force, to Paul Tibbets

Tibbets was given "broad authority" for someone of his rank. Bypassing the usual chain of command, Tibbets answered directly to "Hap" Arnold, or to Leslie Groves, the head of the Manhattan Project. While this autonomy would greatly aid Tibbets in carrying out his mission, it would sometimes cause ridicule and envy among other B-29 groups.

TIBBETS' PRIVATE AIRFORCE

In wartime, personnel transfers were not uncommon. Faced with training an entirely new group of men, commanding officers often requested the transfer of men with whom they had flown in combat. With luck, the Army Air Forces met their requests.

With the help of "Silverplate," the code name for the Army Air Forces' involvement in the atomic project, Tibbets successfully transferred anyone he chose to the 509th. He selected men who had been part of his regular bomber crews in Europe and North Africa. Others he had worked with on the B-29 testing and training program.

Tibbets was not altogether successful at integrating crewmen he hand-picked with the bomber squadrons of the 393rd. Within themselves, however, each 393rd bomber crew was a tightknit group, loyal to each other, and entirely dependent on each other in the air.

OLD FRIENDS

Tom Ferebee, who had been the bombardier in Tibbets' regular crew in Europe, was Tibbets' first choice for his 509th crew. Ferebee would take the bombardier's position on the first atomic mission—to Hiroshima—and acted as Tibbets' unofficial adviser. Ferebee recommended "Dutch" van Kirk, the regular navigator, and Wyatt Duzenbury, the regular first engineer, from their European bomber crew.

Tibbets also selected a number of airmen he had met in the B-29 training program, including pilots Robert Lewis, Charles Sweeney and Don Albury, and gunnery instructor, George Robert Caron.

RADAR COUNTERMEASURES

Although 509th navigators would learn to navigate without radar, Jacob Beser was assigned to the 509th group as a radar countermeasures officer. Beser, an engineering student, would help develop a system that would detect and block enemy radar. Because of the nature of his job, Beser was one of the few members of the 509th besides Tibbets who was told the mission's atomic secrets.

WENDOVER AIR FORCE BASE: "LEFTOVER, USA"

In the fall of 1944, the various squadrons of the newly formed 509th Composite Group met at Wendover Air Force Base in Utah. Described as "Leftover Field" by Bob Hope, Wendover was "the end of the world, perfect" according to Tibbets. The base was close to a bombing range, reserved for the 509th's use, and close to Los Alamos, where Manhattan Project scientists were designing the atomic bombs. Tibbets knew that his men would detest the base's primitive conditions and isolation. Because the base offered so few distractions, however, Tibbets was sure that he would command their full attention to the mission.

ARRIVAL AT WENDOVER

"Don't ask what the job is. That is a surefire way to be transferred out."
Paul Tibbets to the 393rd, September 1944

Rats, heat, desert, primitive accommodations, rancid drinking water, and termites welcomed the 393rd flight and ground crews to Wendover Air Force Base. Barbed wire and military police were everywhere. Nothing within sight gave them a clue to why they had been transferred to Wendover instead of the Pacific.

The first meeting with their new commanding officer intrigued them but hardly satisfied their curiosity. Tibbets told them that they had been "brought here to work on a very special mission." He divulged little more, but did add, "You are going to take part in an effort that could end the war."

"The place sounded so...awful that there just had to be a good reason for my being there."
Jacob Beser, 1975

"WELCOME TO ALCATRAZ"

"Don't ask any questions. Don't answer any questions from anybody not directly involved in what we will be doing."
Paul Tibbets, September 1944

Members of the 509th quickly learned that Tibbets intended to enforce the strictest security precautions. The Manhattan Project sent 50 special agents to help the military police unit monitor the 509th. They tapped phone calls, censored mail, and used subtle means to remind the unit that they were always under surveillance.

Tibbets counted on working the 393rd so hard that they would not have time to complain about Wendover, the often-irritating security measures, and their apparently lost chance to go overseas. While at Wendover, the 393rd crews learned a new way of flying and gained more experience flying B-29s.

WILLIAM "DEAK" PARSONS AND THE BOMB

Months before the various squadrons of the 509th assembled at Wendover, Manhattan Project scientist and Navy Captain William "Deak" Parsons was developing a fusing device that would trigger the atomic bombs to explode at a specified altitude above their targets. He was also designing the casings for the two atomic bombs. In the fall of 1944, Parsons flew with Ferebee to test drop the various experimental bomb casings and determine the best design.

"PUMPKIN" MISSIONS

On each training flight, 509th bomber crews dropped bombs filled with high explosives. Manhattan Project scientists stationed at a safe distance from the aiming point, analyzed the bomb's flight pattern, watched to see if the bomb's fusing mechanism worked, and investigated the bomb's impact.

Shaped like the "Fat Man" type bomb and painted bright orange, these bombs earned the nickname "pumpkins." The pumpkin missions were a vital element in the test phase of Manhattan Project bomb development.

OUT OF THE BOMB'S WAY

Manhattan Project scientists calculated that the bomb's explosion would cause a shock wave powerful enough to destroy an airplane flying too close. To prepare their crews to safely escape the predicted shock wave's effect, Tibbets and Classen taught the 393rd crews to roll their planes in a steep, diving turn after they dropped their bomb load. Executing this maneuver ensured that they would be miles from the blast site by the time the bomb exploded.

Tibbets expected his pilots to learn how to execute the highly unorthodox escape turn. He did not, however, explain to them why their lives and the lives of their crews depended on mastering this maneuver. Caught by surprise the first time he experienced the turn, Tibbets' tail-gunner said it felt "like a roller coaster."

LOTS OF FUN

Tibbets, a perfectionist, had great expectations for the 509th. Tension levels rose as his officers and enlisted men followed a high-paced training schedule, performed unorthodox flying maneuvers, and worked under seemingly excessive security precautions. Activities from hiking in the canyon country surrounding the base to gambling at the State Line Casino relieved the tension.

SPECIAL TRAINING: BATISTA FIELD, CUBA

In January 1945, Tibbets sent ten of his fifteen crews to Cuba for special training. Under Tom Classen's charge, the crews carried out long-distance navigational training over water at night. They also continued practicing high-altitude bomb runs.

THE UNTOUCHABLES

No matter what stunts the members of the 509th pulled, invoking the code name *Silverplate* rescued them from the consequences of their high jinks. They soon earned the reputation of being "untouchable." To some extent, Tibbets encouraged his crews' spirited off-duty antics. He believed that they helped build *esprit de corps*.

OVERSEAS: THE 509TH GOES TO TINIAN

In June 1945, the 509th Composite Group travelled to its overseas base on the small Pacific island of Tinian. By the time the 509th arrived on Tinian, in June 1945, the 313th Bombardment Wing was well-established, having participated in dozens of missions over Japan. The 313th Bombardment Wing, composed of 192 B-29 crews, arrived on Tinian in December 1944 and occupied the island's North Field. With his Silverplate clearance, Tibbets, however, was able to displace 313th combat veterans from some of the island's best accommodations on North Field.

One step closer to the war, the 509th practiced dropping conventional bombs, grew increasingly impatient with security measures, and tried to entertain themselves. They anxiously awaited the day when they would finally carry out their mysterious mission.

BOMBING ISLANDS: ROTA, TRUK, MARCUS ISLAND

Training missions in the Pacific began on June 30, 1945. Each mission focused on a different aspect of combat flying, including navigational techniques, instrument calibration, and visual and radar-aided bomb drops. The nearby islands of Rota and Truk provided targets for the crews in training.

A "flurry of excitement" accompanied the announcement of the Group's first combat mission. On July 6, five crews bombed the runways of the Japanese airfield on Marcus Island. During the Marcus Island raids, the 509th dropped various sizes of bombs on the island with varying degrees of success and with little enemy resistance.

BOMBING "THE EMPIRE": JAPAN, 1945

On July 20, 1945 the 509th made its first airstrike on Japan. Ten crews loaded their planes with Fat-Man shaped high-explosive bombs, called Pumpkins, and took off at 0200 hours. More than twelve hours later, all ten crews returned safely to Tinian. Because of poor weather conditions, however, only five crews had been able to bomb their primary targets visually. Four had used radar to drop their bombs on secondary targets. The tenth had jettisoned its bomb load in the ocean because of engine failure.

Before dropping the atomic bomb, the 509th flew three more "Pumpkin" missions to Japan. Largely due to variable weather conditions, the results of these missions ranged from "fair to unobserved" to "effective and successful." From these missions to the Nagasaki raid, cloud cover posed a constant threat to the 509th's success.

TENSION IN PARADISE

From the moment Tibbets' crews arrived, the other B-29 squadrons stationed on Tinian questioned them. Why had the 509th supplied its own mechanics instead of using the already existing support squadrons on the island? Why did the 509th fly ten-plane bombing runs instead of standard hundred-plane-strong raids? Why was the 509th fed luxuriously in a separate mess while other bomber squadrons based on Tinian ate regular military rations? Why did the 509th members refuse to divulge information about their mission?

Envy and curiosity sparked one Tinian inhabitant to write a poem dedicated to razzing the inactive and seemingly unimportant 509th.

SURVIVAL GEAR

The commander of the 313th Bombardment Wing already stationed on Tinian quickly learned that Tibbets' crews "knew more about airplanes and navigation" than his combat veterans. But the 509th had not yet learned about air sea rescue, ditching and bail-outs, dinghy drill, and survival, even though extensive training at Wendover and Batista Field had prepared them to operate their B-29s with great precision. Each crew member was fitted with a survival vest equipped with items that would help him if he had to abandon his airplane.

GETTING AROUND

By the time the 509th arrived on Tinian, the island looked like "a huge airport." Seabees had erected quonset huts, constructed runways, and built an extensive network of roads. Tinian had reminded one New York City-born Seabee of the island of Manhattan and had laid out the streets according to its plan.

Based at Tinian's North Field, the 509th bartered with the Seabees to obtain vehicles to get around the island. William "Locke" Easton, pilot, and other 509th members, traded liquor for Seabee-built scooters.

WAITING TO "WIN THE WAR"

As at Wendover, the 509th followed a rigorous training schedule. After completing their training in the Pacific, however, they found they had a surprising amount of leisure time. Swimming, horseshoes, baseball, and racing scooters helped them bide their time until Tibbets finally called them to carry out their mission that "was going to win the war."

The B-29 Superfortress "Enola Gay"

On August 6, 1945, the "Enola Gay" dropped an atomic bomb on Hiroshima, Japan, and changed the face of warfare. This aircraft, Army Air Forces serial number 44-86292, only received its name on the night before the mission, when Col. Paul Tibbets named the aircraft after his mother.

Manufactured under license by Martin Aircraft in Omaha, Nebraska, the "Enola Gay" was delivered to the 393rd Bombardment Squadron, 509th Composite Group, on June 14, 1945. Like the other "Silverplate" aircraft, it was specially modified for its atomic mission. All gun turrets were removed except for the tail guns and the aircraft incorporated the latest technology: the newest version of the huge R-3350 engines, Curtiss Electric reversible propellers and pneumatic bomb-bay doors.

The "Enola Gay" arrived at Tinian on July 2, 1945, and flew its first combat mission with conventional bombs four day later. After returning to the United States in November 1945, the aircraft was modified for the Bikini atomic tests of 1946. It flew back to the Pacific in April 1946, but was not used in those tests.

THE MARKINGS OF THE "ENOLA GAY"

The stencils of crew names on both sides of the nose were added after the Hiroshima raid and do not include all those who were on the mission. Omitted from the twelve who flew on August 6 were crew members who were from the Manhattan Project or were closely related to the bomb: Capt. (USN) William

S. Parsons, "Little Boy" project leader and bomb commander, Lt. (USAAF) Morris R. Jeppson, Parson's assistant in arming the atomic bomb, and Lt. (USAAF) Jacob W. Beser, the radar countermeasures officer. Not all ground crew who worked on the "Enola Gay" were included in the stencils either.

The "Enola Gay" flew on August 6 with the "circle R" tail markings of another B-29 squadron to confuse Japanese intelligence. The 509th's regular tail insignia was a horizontal arrow in a circle. The four small "Fat Men" markings on the port side of the nose were added after the war and indicate the number of times the aircraft carried an atomic bomb.

THE RESTORATION OF THE "ENOLA GAY"

In July 1946, the Air Force stored this historic aircraft at Davis Montana AFB, Arizona. Col. Tibbets flew it to Park Ridge, Illinois, on July 3, 1949, where it was accepted by representatives of the Smithsonian. The "Enola Gay" was moved to Pyote AFB, Texas, in February 1952 and it remained there until December 2, 1953, when it made its last flight to Andrews AFB, Maryland, just outside Washington, D.C. In 1960–61, Smithsonian technicians disassembled the "Enola Gay" and stored its components indoors at what is now the Paul E. Garber Preservation, Restoration and Storage Facility in Silver Hill, Maryland.

Restoration began at the Garber Facility in December 1984 and was completed in (month) 1995. It was by far the largest aircraft restoration project ever undertaken by the National Air and Space Museum, consuming over 50,000(?) person-hours. Except for some historic post-Hiroshima markings, the aircraft has been returned as far as possible to its configuration of August 6, 1945. This extremely thorough restoration will allow the preservation of the "Enola Gay" for decades and even centuries into the future.

WHEN WILL THE "ENOLA GAY" BE ASSEMBLED?

The huge size of this four-engine bomber has made it infeasible to reassemble the whole aircraft anywhere inside the National Air and Space Museum building, or even at the Museum's Garber Facility outside Washington. Therefore, except for a propeller and a few other smaller components, this exhibit contains only the forward fuselage section, which is slightly less than two-thirds of the airplane's original length.

The "Enola Gay" will be reassembled and put on permanent display at the Museum's new Extension building at Washington Dulles Airport, once that facility is completed sometime in the next decade.

THE "LITTLE BOY" ATOMIC BOMB

A bomb of this type was dropped by the "Enola Gay" on Hiroshima, Japan, on August 6, 1945. Unlike the "Fat Man" plutonium bomb dropped on Nagasaki, the "Little Boy" used uranium 235 as the critical material. Inside the bomb, a shortened smooth-bore 76.2 mm (3 in) naval gun fired a uranium bullet at target rings also made of uranium 235. At the moment of impact, a critical mass was formed, initiating a nuclear explosion. Due to the gun barrel and the heavy casing, the "Little Boy" weighed over four metric tons (8,900 lb), almost as much as the much larger "Fat Man."

The bomb casing shown here was a "War Reserve" training version of the "Little Boy" and was built after the war. Except for the absence of electronic firing circuitry and nuclear material, this bomb casing is virtually identical to the Hiroshima weapon.

THE MISSIONS

Little more than four weeks after their arrival on Tinian, the 509th Composite Group dropped two atomic bombs on Japan. On August 6, pilot Paul Tibbets and his crew of the *Enola Gay* conducted the first atomic strike in history, dropping a gun-type "Little Boy" bomb on the city of Hiroshima. Three days later, Charles Sweeney, piloted the *Bockscar* and its crew on the second and last atomic attack of the war. Because of bad weather over the primary target—the industrial city of Kokura—Sweeney's crew dropped their implosion-type "Fat Man" bomb on Nagasaki instead.

MISSION NO. 13: THE FIRST ATOMIC STRIKE

In early August 1945, tension rose among the 509th crew members as they anticipated Tibbets' order to "deliver the bomb." Even though their commanding officer still withheld many details from them, the 509th sensed their mission's momentous nature.

A few days before August 6, the projected mission date, Tibbets selected seven crews to attend briefings for Mission No. 13, the first atomic strike. Tibbets and other officials listed targets and described the immediate effect of the bomb, but did not reveal its atomic nature to the excited crews.

AUGUST 4: THE FIRST BRIEFING

Tibbets ordered seven crews to attend the first briefing, on August 4. Although many of them arrived at the briefing hut in high spirits, their mood quickly changed. Military police, armed with carbines, surrounded the building and inside, curtains were drawn. In the darkened hut, they quietly awaited their commanding officer's arrival.

Tibbets was to the point. He told them the bomb was ready to be dropped, announced crew assignments and then unshrouded bulletin boards to reveal aerial photographs of the potential target cities.

SUBSTITUTIONS

Tibbets announced that No. 82's regular crew, with a few substitutions, would deliver the bomb. He assigned himself to the pilot's position, van Kirk as the navigator, and Ferebee as the bombardier. For the most part, Tibbets' crew selections did not surprise the 509th. Bob Lewis, No. 82's regular pilot, however, was greatly disappointed with his assignment as co-pilot.

As Commanding Officer, Tibbets reserved the right to make

changes. He had experiences flying in combat with Ferebee and van Kirk and had the utmost faith in them. The final strike crew, regardless of its overall high skill level, however, had never flown a combat mission together. This situation made some of the crew members uneasy.

"SOME WEIRD DREAM"

"It was like some weird dream, conceived by one with too vivid an imagination."

Radio operator Abe Spitzer's unsanctioned diary, Tinian 1945

After Tibbets announced crew assignments and described primary and secondary targets, Manhattan Project scientist and Navy Captain Deak Parsons briefed the crews about the bomb. He was not able to show them the film footage of the Trinity explosion, because the projector failed. Even without visual evidence to dramatize the bomb's potential effect, however, Parsons's personal descriptions of the bomb test still astounded the 509th.

Even if Parsons had divulged the mission's atomic secrets to the crews, this information might not have made a significant impression on them. Aside from the few engineering students among them, the majority of the 509th members had gained their information about atomic power from the pages of science fiction novels.

PROTECTIVE GOGGLES

Deak Parsons explained that the bomb's blast would create such a bright flash that crews near the explosion would need to wear goggles, similar to those worn by welders, to protect their eyes. Turning the knob on the nose bridge would change the goggle's darkness. Parsons warned that they must adjust the knob to the darkest setting during the bombing.

LITTLE BOY GOES TO TINIAN

On July 26, the U.S.S. *Indianapolis* arrived at Tinian. Aboard the veteran naval cruiser were the gun and bullet elements of the Little Boy bomb. That same day, two air transports departed for Tinian, each carrying a uranium target.

Once all parts were delivered to Tinian, Manhattan Project scientists and 509th Ordnance specialists began to assemble the bomb, but did not arm it. Deak Parsons, the 509th's atomic bomb specialist, had seen a significant number of B-29s crash on the North Field tarmac. Having considered the possible gruesome results if the *Enola Gay*, loaded with a live atomic bomb, crashed on take-off, Parsons decided to finish arming the bomb once the *Enola Gay* had reached cruising altitude.

On August 1, Manhattan Project commander Groves received a telex informing him that pre-flight assembly of the bomb had been completed and that the mission could be flown any time the weather permitted.

"A TICKLISH PROCEDURE": LOADING THE BOMB

Silverplate B-29 bomb bays had been specially modified to carry their unusually large and heavy bombs. Because there was little clearance with the bomb bay catwalks and only a single shackle and adjustable sway braces held the bomb, loading it was "a rather ticklish procedure," according to one engineer.

0000–0235 HOURS: AUGUST 6

In the early hours of August 6, seven of the 509th's fifteen crews crawled from their cots or tore themselves from their card games to attend one last pre-flight briefing. After eating a quick meal and attending a religious service, they headed off to the flight line where their planes waited.

When they arrived, they were surprised to find camera lights illuminating the field and more than 100 people on the tarmac. Feeling like moviestars, they granted interviews, nervously milled around, and made final checks on their airplanes. Around 2:20 a.m., Tibbets "called a halt" so that they could complete preparations for takeoff.

Tibbets distributed Operations Order #35 to 509th officers.

The order specified that the bomb type to be used was "special" but did not mention that it was atomic.

Tibbets and his crew did not wear flak vests and parachutes during most of the flight. They put on protective gear only after they reached enemy territory.

Each crew member was issued an ashtray before going on board. Tibbets, an ardent pipe smoker, made sure to bring his "smoking equipment" with him on the *Enola Gay*.

A PERFECT PERFORMANCE

Every step of the mission—takeoff, arming the bomb, finding the target, dropping the bomb—posed a potential problem. With the help of favorable weather conditions, however, Tibbets and his crew successfully and safely carried out their mission.

Tibbets recognized that the *Enola Gay,* loaded with bomb and fuel, was 15,000 pounds over its designed takeoff weight limit. Using almost the entire runway, he expertly lifted the plane into the air. At 0300, fifteen minutes after takeoff, Deak Parsons and Morris Jeppson, carefully began the final bomb assembly. Three hours later, the *Enola Gay* and its two escort planes met at the designated rendezvous point above Iwo Jima.

For the remaining hours of the flight, the crew took turns napping and "George," the automatic pilot, steered the bomb toward Japan. Approximately two hours before "bombs away, " Jeppson activated the bomb. They arrived at their target 17 seconds late and Ferebee came very close to the designated aiming point. Groves described the mission as a "perfect performance."

ARMING THE BOMB

"The bomb was now independent of the plane. I had a feeling the bomb had a life of its own now that it had nothing to do with us."

Bob Lewis, Enola Gay's *co-pilot comments on the activation of the bomb*

At 7:15 a.m. (6:15 a.m. in Hiroshima) the weather scout plane over the city of Hiroshima reported to Tibbets that the cloud cover was favorable for a visual bombing of the city. Tibbets announced to his crew, "it's Hiroshima."

At 7:30 a.m., one hour and forty-five minutes before "bombs away," assistant weaponeer Morris Jeppson once again entered the bomb bay. Throughout the flight, three green plugs inserted into the forward part of the bomb had inactivated the electronic firing circuitry. Jeppson's final task was to replace the green plugs with the red plugs that would open the firing circuit.

BOMBS AWAY

Tibbets handed over control of the plane to bombardier Ferebee and navigator van Kirk. Ferebee trained the plane's Norden bombsight on the target. Then, van Kirk fed Ferebee updated calculations on wind speed and altitude, which Ferebee, in turn, entered into the bombsight's computer. Using the target as a base point, it automatically corrected the course of the airplane. At 17 seconds after 9:14 a.m. (8:14 a.m., Hiroshima time), Ferebee flipped a switch which turned over control of the plane and the bomb to the bombsight's computer. One minute later, it automatically dropped the bomb.

The lightened plane lurched upward, Tibbets took back the controls and turned the *Enola Gay* in the practiced violent escape turn. Eleven miles from the blast, a flash of light filled the cockpit and the first of two shock waves hit the plane. Tibbets announced, "Fellows, you have just dropped the first atomic bomb in history."

FIRST ATOMIC BOMB: HIROSHIMA

"The flash after the explosion was deep purple, then reddish and reached to almost 8,000 feet; the cloud, shaped like a mushroom, was up to 20,000 feet in one minute, at which time the top part broke from the 'stem,' and eventually reached 30,000 feet."

"The stem of the mushroom-like column of smoke, looking now like a giant grave marker, stood one minute after the explosion upon the whole area of the city, excepting the southern dock area. This column was a thick white smoke, darker at the base, and interspersed with deep red.

"Though about fifteen miles from the target when the explosion occurred, both escort aircraft, as well as the strike plane, reported feeling two shock waves jar the aircraft. Approximately 390 statute miles away from the target area, the column of smoke still could be seen piercing the morning sky."

509th Composite Group Administrative Report

"I don't believe anyone ever expected to look at a sight quite like that. Where we had seen a clear city two minutes before, we could now no longer see the city."

Co-pilot Bob Lewis, post-war interview
Courtesy of Frank Shelton

"That city was burning for all she was worth. It looked like...well, did you ever go to the beach and stir up the sand in shallow water and see it all billow up?"

Jacob Beser, radar countermeasures officer

As Tibbets tamped down the tobacco in his pipe, he commented to Bob Lewis on the bomb's impact. "I think this is the end of the war."

A HERO'S RETURN

Over 200 officers and enlisted men waited anxiously for the *Enola Gay*'s return. Twelve hours and thirteen minutes after it left Tinian, Tibbets landed the plane on North Field.

General Carl Spaatz, commander Strategic Armed Forces in the Pacific, and "all the ranking military brass that could be mustered in the Marianas at that time," met the crew as they disembarked. To Tibbets' surprise, Spaatz greeted him, shook his hand, and then pinned a Distinguished Service Cross to his rumpled overalls.

Atomic Might

The Japs well knew,—they had been warned
Of the Allied might that was being formed
But they chose to die for the Rising Sun
And proudly stuck to their ill made gun.
But a thunderous blast, a blinding light,
Brought the 509th atomic might.

It was the 6th of August, that much we knew
When the boys took off in the morning dew,
Feeling nervous, jumpy, sick and ill at ease
They flew at the heart of the Japanese,
With a thunderous blast, a blinding light,
And the 509th's atomic might.

Below like a miniature checker board
Lay a Japanese town in one accord,
Unknowing the might that lay in store
It went to the shelters, the rich and poor,
That's when the thunderous blast, and blinding light
Came from the 509th's atomic might.

From out of the air the secret fell
And created below a scene of hell.
(?)
Has there been displayed such a sight,
As the thunderous blast, the blinding light,
Of the 509th's atomic might.

From ear to tongue, from tongue to press
The story spead (?),—stupendous—nothing less!
From pole to pole, around the earth,
Folks knew now of our powerful worth,
With thunderous blast, the blinding light,
Of the 509th's atomic might.

Oh, God!—that when this War doth cease
And again we turn our thoughts to peace
That you will help us build,—not devastate,
A life of love and truth,—not hate,
Without the thunderous blast, the blinding light
Of the 509th's atomic might.

Sgt. Harry Barnard

In response to the poem, "The 509th Is Winning the War," which had questioned the 509th presence on Tinian, a 509th member wrote "Atomic Might."

"THE GREATEST THING IN HISTORY"

"This is the greatest thing in history."
President Harry S. Truman, August 6, 1945

Sixteen hours after the 509th dropped the "Little Boy" bomb on Hiroshima, President Truman made a radio broadcast in which he announced the atomic bomb to the American public.

While President Truman informed the United States, Hap Arnold sent a cable to Gen. Carl Spaatz, ordering him to enlist B-29 squadrons in an extensive propaganda campaign in the Pacific. In less than 24 hours of receiving the order, Spaatz had arranged for pamphlets, which described the destructive power of an atomic attack, to be printed and dropped over the Japanese islands.

Text of Truman's August 6 Statement on the Bomb

Sixteen hours ago an American airplane dropped one bomb on Hiroshima, an important Japanese Army base. That bomb had more power than 20,000 tons of T.N.T. It had more than two thousand times the blast power of the British "Grand Slam" which is the largest bomb ever yet used in the history of warfare.

The Japanese began the war from the air at Pearl Harbor. They have been repaid many fold. And the end is not yet. With this bomb, we have now added a new and revolutionary increase in destruction to supplement the growing power of our armed forces. In their present form these bombs are now in production and even more powerful forms are in development.

It is an atomic bomb. It is a harnessing of the basic power of the universe. The force which the sun draws its power has been loosed against those who brought war to the Far East.

Before 1939, it was the accepted belief of scientists that it was theoretically possible to release atomic energy. But no on knew any practical method of doing it. By 1942, however, we knew that the Germans were working feverishly to find a way to add atomic energy to the other engines of war with which they hoped to enslave the world. But they failed. We may be grateful to Providence that the Germans got the V-1's and V-2's late and in limited quantities and even more grateful that they did not get the atomic bomb at all.

The battle of the laboratories held fateful risks for us as well as the battles of the air, land and sea, and we have now won the battle of the laboratories as we have won other battles.

Beginning in 1940, before Pearly Harbor, scientific knowledge useful in war was pooled between the United States and Great Britain, and many priceless helps to our victories have come from that arrangement. Under that general policy the research on the atomic bomb was begun. With American and British scientists working together we entered the race of discovery against the Germans.

The United States had available the large number of scientists of distinction in the many needed areas of knowledge. It had the tremendous industrial and financial resources necessary for the project and they could be devoted to it without undue impairment of other vital war work. In the United States the laboratory work and the production plants, on which a substantial start had already been made, would be out of reach of enemy bombing, while at that time Britain was exposed to constant air attack and was still threatened with the possiblilty of invasion. For these reasons Prime Minister Churchill and President Roosevelt agreed that it was wise to carry on the project here. We now have two great plants and many lesser works devoted to the production of atomic power. Employment during peak construction numbered 125,000 and over 65,000 individuals are even now engaged in operating the plants. Many have worked there for two and a half years. Few know what they have been producing. They see great quantities of material going in and they see nothing coming out of these plants, for the physical size of the explosive charge is exceedingly small. We have spent two billion dollars on the greatest scientific gamble in history—and won.

But the greatest marvel is not the size of the enterprise, its secrecy, nor its cost, but the achievement of scientific brains in putting together infinitely complex pieces of knowledge held by many men in different fields of science into a workable plan. And hardly less marvelous has been the capacity of industry to design, and of labor to operate, the machines and methods to do things never done before so that the brain child of many minds came forth in physical shape and performed as it was supposed to do. Both science and industry worked under the direction of the United States Army, which achieved a unique success in managing so diverse a problem in the advancement of knowledge in an amazingly short time. It is doubtfull if such another combination could be got together in the world. What has been done is the greatest achievement of organized science in history. It was done under high pressure and without failure.

We are now prepared to obliterate more rapidly and completely every productive enterprise the Japanese have above ground in any city. We shall destroy their docks, their factories, and their communications. Let there be no mistake; we shall completely destroy Japan's power to make war.

It was to spare the Japanese people from utter destruction that the ultimatum of July 26 was issued at Potsdam. Their leaders promptly rejected that ultimatum. If they do not now accept our terms they may expect a rain of ruin from the air, the like of which has never been seen on this earth. Behind this air attack will follow sea and land forces in such numbers and power as they have not yet seen and with the fighting skill of which they are already well aware.

The Secretary of War, who has kept in personal touch

with all phases of the project, will immediately make public a statement giving further details.

His statement will give facts concerning the sites at Oak Ridge near Knoxville, Tennessee, and at Richland near Pasco, Washington, and an installation near Santa Fe, New Mexico. Although the workers at the sites have been making materials to be used in producing the greatest destructive force in history they have not themselves been in danger beyond that of many other occupations, for the utmost care has been taken of their safety.

The fact that we can release atomic energy ushers in a new era in man's understanding of nature's forces. Atomic energy may in the future supplement the power that now comes from coal, oil, and falling water, but at present it cannot be produced on a basis to compete with them commercially. Before that comes there must be a long period of intensive research.

It has never been the habit of the scientists of this country or the policy of this government to withhold from the world scientific knowledge. Normally, therefore, everything about the work with atomic energy would be made public.

But under present circumstances it is not intended to divulge the technical processes of production or all the military applications, pending further examination of possible methods of protecting us and the rest of the world from the danger of sudden destruction.

I shall recommend that the Congress of the United States consider promptly the establishment of an appropriate commission to control the production and use of atomic power within the United States. I shall give further consideration and make further recommendations to the Congress as to how atomic power can become a powerful and forceful influence towards the maintenance of world peace.

MISSION NO. 16

While perfect timing characterized the Hiroshima raid, urgency and haste affected the second. Mission planners felt it was necessary to conduct another atomic raid before the Japanese had time to "recover their balance." When they received the news that deteriorating weather conditions threatened to postpone the mission by a week, they quickly changed the projected mission date from August 11 to August 9.

Accelerated preparations introduced a high level of risk into every step of the mission. Although problems occurred from bomb assembly to bomb delivery, Charles Sweeney and his crew successfully dropped their bomb on Japan and returned safely.

"With the success of the Hiroshima weapon, the pressure to be ready with the much more complex implosion device became excruciating... Everyone felt that the sooner we could get off another mission, the more likely it was that the Japanese would feel that we had large quantities of the devices and would surrender sooner."

Post-war interview with member of the "Fat Man" assembly team Bernard O'Keefe

ADDITIONAL BOMBS

"Additional bombs will be delivered on the above targets as soon as made ready by the project staff..."

Gen. Handy, Acting Army Chief of Staff, to Gen. Spaatz, Commander, Strategic Air Forces in the Pacific, July 25, 1945

There was no separate order to drop the second bomb. Acting on the July 25 directive, the 509th Ordnance Squadron and Manhattan Project scientists began to prepare the implosion-type Fat Man bomb for the second mission. The primary target for that raid would be the Japanese arsenal at Kokura.

ONWARD TO KOKURA

At pre-flight briefings similar to those before the Hiroshima flight, Tibbets assigned six crews and described the two potential targets, Kokura and Nagasaki. The mission's weaponeer then briefed them on the atomic bomb. In the early hours of August 9, crews headed for the airfield.

Heated discussions between Tibbets and crew members took precedence over interviews that morning. A preflight check of the strike plane, *Bockscar*, piloted by Charles Sweeney, uncovered a malfunctioning fuel pump. With no time to fix the defective pump, Sweeney suggested changes in the flight plan. To save fuel, he would rendezvous with the escort planes over the coast of Japan instead of Iwo Jima and would make a refueling stop in Okinawa on the return trip to Tinian.

To add to the mechanical problems, weather conditions were unfavorable. Forecasters predicted that the crews would fly through tropical rain squalls all the way to Japan. At 0347, Sweeney lifted the *Bockscar* off the tarmac. In the sky, "flashes of lightening [sic] stabbed into the darkness with disconcerting regularity."

MONITORING THE BOMB

On the Hiroshima flight, the assistant weaponeer made the final arming of the Little Boy gun-type bomb about two hours before the bomb drop. Because the *Bockscar* flew according to a different flight plan, weaponeer Richard Ashworth armed the Fat Man implosion-type bomb minutes after *Bockscar* left Tinian.

A MISSED RENDEZVOUS

The *Bockscar* crew reached the rendezvous point one minute ahead of schedule at 9:09 a.m. (8:09 a.m., Japan time) Bock's instrument plane arrived three minutes later. Bock made a visual sighting of Hopkins' camera plane, but lost contact with it. Because they had been ordered to maintain radio silence at that point, they could not inquire about its location. Without Hopkins, Sweeney and Bock circled the rendezvous point, waiting for the arrival of the third plane. After forty-five minutes, it had not appeared. Unsure about their escort's status, but concerned about diminishing fuel reserves, they proceeded to the target.

KOKURA: THE BOMBING THAT NEVER HAPPENED

Although weather scouts had reported that both primary and secondary targets were clear for visual bombing, by the time the *Bockscar* crew arrived over Kokura, at 9:44 a.m. (Japanese time), a thick haze obscured the city. Ironically, smoke from a regular B-29 incendiary attack on a neighboring city had shrouded Kokura. Sweeney made three passes over the city, but each time bombardier Kermit Beahan announced "No drop."

Tense moments passed as Sweeney waited for his flight engineer's report on the plane's fuel reserves. Kuharek's calculations revealed that just enough fuel remained to drop the bomb on the secondary target and return to a "friendly air field." Sweeney alerted special air-sea rescue forces that ditching the aircraft was a possibility. He then turned the *Bockscar* toward the secondary target of Nagasaki.

THE SECOND ATOMIC BOMB: NAGASAKI

To their dismay, the *Bockscar* crew found Nagasaki obscured by thick cloud cover. Faced with jettisoning the bomb, weaponeer Ashworth opted to use radar, even though they had been ordered to bomb visually.

While on the Hiroshima flight, bombardier Ferebee had steered the plane to the target with the Norden bombsight, *Bockscar* bombardier Kermit Beahan temporarily gave up control. Although accounts vary, the most popular remembrance of the bomb drop is that, at the last minute, Beahan exclaimed "I have the target, taking control." A hole broke in the clouds and Beahan dropped the bomb. At 11:02 a.m., Japanese time, the "Fat Man" tumbled from the *Bockscar*'s bomb bay and seconds later, exploded, 2,600 m (8,500 ft) from the intended target.

The return trip was equally tense. By the time the *Bockscar* reached Okinawa, fuel reserves had dipped dangerously low.

Sweeney's "Mayday" calls did little to clear the crowded Yontan Airfield runway. Firing signal flares finally roused a response. After refueling and reporting to Tibbets, they took off for Tinian, where they received a subdued welcome.

UNIT 4: GROUND ZERO

Before the Bomb: Two Cities At War

HIROSHIMA, JAPAN: A MILITARY CITY

On the morning of August 6, 1945, Hiroshima was the seventh largest city in Japan, with a population of some 350,000. Located on the southwestern shore of the main island of Honshu, where the delta of the Ota River enters the Seto Inland Sea, the city took its name from the Hiro-shima-Jo ("Broad-island-castle"), a fortress established by a local lord in 1594.

Hiroshima was a prefectural capital, and a key economic center for western Japan. In April, 1945, the Second General Headquarters, which would plan and lead the attack against the expected American invasion, was also established in Hiroshima. Supplies for Imperial forces in China, Southeast Asia and the Pacific had passed through the city's Ujina port throughout World War II.

HIROSHIMA AT WAR

Hiroshima had escaped the incendiary bombing campaign that was destroying many smaller towns. Puzzled, some residents of the city speculated that the U.S. Army Air Forces had spared the city because of its beautiful location on the Inland Sea. Others believed that the city was protected because so many Japanese American families had emigrated to America from the region. One wild rumor even suggested that Hiroshima was the birthplace of President Truman's mother.

Convinced that the B-29s passing over the city each night would eventually strike Hiroshima, city officials prepared for an attack. Concerned that flooding would result from the destruction of a dam above the town, they issued bamboo floats to the leaders of neighborhood associations, and ordered that similar floats be constructed for everyone in the city. Students were released from class and put to work clearing firebreaks in the center of the town. Sand

and water buckets were kept filled. When the attack came, the people of Hiroshima were determined to be prepared.

HIROSHIMA, 8:15 A.M., AUGUST 6, 1945

The morning of Monday, August 6, was sunny and hot in Hiroshima. By 7:00 a.m. people were pouring into the city center to begin the work day. In addition to the usual officers and factory workers, merchants and shop keepers, some 8,300 junior and senior high school students were laboring to demolish 2,500 buildings that had been evacuated to create firebreaks in six districts of the city.

The first air raid warning of the day sounded at 7:09, as "Straight Flush," a B-29 weather aircraft piloted by Capt. Claude Eatherly, appeared over the city. "Enola Gay," accompanied by two other B-29s, "The Great Artiste" and "Number 91," approached Hiroshima from the northeast one hour later. At precisely 8:15:17 the Little Boy bomb was released from the *Enola Gay*. Forty-three seconds later it detonated 580 m (1,870 ft) over the Shima Hospital.

NAGASAKI, JAPAN: WINDOW ON THE WEST

Founded in the 12th century, Nagasaki is located on the southwestern island of Kyushu, where the Nakashima and Urakami rivers enter the East China Sea. On August 15, 1549, the Jesuit father Francis Xavier landed on Kyushu and founded the first Christian missions in Japan. Intrigued by the new religion, and by Western firearms, Japanese leaders at first tolerated the Spanish and Portuguese presence at Nagasaki. After 1587, however, they banned Christianity and severely persecuted its adherents.

For two-and-a-half centuries, from about 1600 to 1850, all foreign contacts with Japan were made through Nagasaki, where a small group of Dutch East India company traders were tolerated on the tiny island of Dejima in the harbor. Nagasaki retained its importance as a center of Western economic and cultural influence following the opening of Japan in 1854.

Christians re-emerged who had remained secretly faithful during the centuries of persecution. Nagasaki was once more the center of the Catholic Church in Japan.

NAGASAKI AT WAR

In August 1945, Nagasaki had a population of about 270,000 people and was a major industrial center. One of the most important shipyards in the nation was located in the harbor. The great naval base of Sasebo was nearby. The giant battleship *Musashi* was based here during the closing months of WWII. In addition, the city was home to a variety of factories critical to the war effort, including the Mitsubishi Steel Works.

NAGASAKI, 11:02 A.M., AUGUST 9, 1945

The morning of Thursday, August 9, was mild and humid in Nagasaki. The skies were fairly clear at 8:30 a.m., when a B-29 weather aircraft flew over the city. By mid-morning, however, a weather front moving in from the East China Sea had spread a thick layer of cloud over Nagasaki.

Having been forced to abandon their primary target, Kokura, because of haze and smoke, the B-29s *Bockscar* and *The Great Artiste* were running low on fuel as they approached Nagasaki. The bombardier of *Bockscar* made a radar approach, but released the "Fat Man" bomb through a momentary break in the clouds at 11:02 a.m. The weapon exploded 503 m (1,540 ft) above the Urakami River Valley, 2.5 km (1.5 mi) from the intended target in the center of the city.

NAGASAKI, AUGUST 10, 1945

Mr. Yosuke Yamabata, a resident of Nagasaki, set out with his camera early on the morning of August 10, 1945. He spent the day walking through the shattered Urakami Valley, capturing scenes of the incredible destruction—and the faces of those who, for the moment, at least, had survived. Mr. Yamabata himself died only a few years after the war, probably from his exposure to residual radiation.

"The Incredible Avalanche of Light"

"There was a blinding white flash of light, and the next moment—Bang! Crack! A huge impact like a gigantic blow smote down upon our bodies, our heads and our hospital."

Dr. Tatsuichiro Akizuki, Franciscan Tuberculosis Hospital, Nagasaki

"Flash! The incredible avalanche of light seemed to last for several seconds...momentarily the bright August sun was completely absorbed and negated by it."

Ms. Kimie Akabae, Nagasaki

THE FIRST UNSPEAKABLE SECOND

The two bombs dropped on Hiroshima and Nagasaki were quite different, but the sequence of events after the detonation of each weapon was about the same.

0.0 second: The temperature at the epicenter (burst point) reaches several million degrees within one-millionth of a second following detonation. All of the material composing the bomb become ionized gas and gamma rays—electromagnetic radiation of very short wavelength (0.01 to 10 nanometers).

0.1 second: A fireball with a diameter of 15 meters (50 ft) and a temperature of some 30,000 C (540,000 F) has formed. Radiation in the form of alpha and beta particles, gamma rays and neutrons (3% of the total energy of the bomb) streams out in every direction. Alpha and beta particles do not reach the ground. Neutrons and gamma rays reach the ground almost instantly and are responsible for the initial radiation damage to living organisms as well as the irradiation of soil and structures in the area of the blast.

0.15 second: The fireball is expanding, but a shock wave expands even more rapidly, heating the air until it becomes luminous. As the air begins to cool, the hot inner core of the fireball becomes visible for the first time. It will remain visible for some ten seconds.

0.2 second: The temperature at the core of the expanding

fireball is now about 7,700 C (13,900 F). Thermal energy released by the explosion (35% of the total energy) ranges from near ultraviolet to infrared wavelengths. The vast amounts of infrared energy generated during the 0.2–0.3 seconds following the explosion cause most of the initial thermal burns to human beings.

1 second: The fireball reaches its maximum diameter of 200-300 m. The blast (50% of the total energy) is now complete. The overpressure at the *hypocenter* (the spot directly under the explosion) at Hiroshima is estimated to have reached 4.5 to 6.7 tons per square meter, 45-67% of normal atmospheric pressure. Maximum pressure at the Nagasaki hypocenter may have been as high as 10 tons per square meter. The blast wave generated by the explosions moved through the air and across the surface of the ground at approximately the speed of sound until it dissipated.

PIKA!

"Someone shouted, 'Look, a parachute!' We looked up and saw something falling slowly... Suddenly, 'Pika!' There was a tremendous flash, and everything turned completely dark."

Taeko Teramae, third year student, Shintoku Girls' High School, Hiroshima

Few survivors who were close to the center of the Hiroshima or Nagasaki explosions would remember hearing the sound of the blast. What none of them would ever forget was the *Pika*— the flash of incredibly brilliant light and heat that occurred as a nuclear explosion heated the sky to luminescence. The burst of light was quickly followed by a tremendous air pressure wave that bent steel bridges, toppled buildings and reduced wooden houses to kindling.

"Then a tremendous flash of light cut across the sky...It seemed like a sheet of sun."

Rev. Kiyoshi Tainimoto, from "Hiroshima" by John Hersey (1946)

"The moment there was a flash, it felt as though thickly mixed paint was thrown at me, and I thought that heaven had fallen. At that instant, I was burned from face to shoulder to navel."

Tada Makiko, housewife, Nagasaki

"Suddenly there was a brilliant flash, like a photographer's magnesium flash...Then came the blast with a deafening bang and I felt as though I had been kicked in the guts...The world was black."

F.J. Johnston, Australian prisoner-of-war in Nagasaki, 1945

A MOMENT FROZEN IN TIME

The flash of light generated at the moment of detonation cast shadows on walls, steps, buildings and even stands of bamboo in Hiroshima and Nagasaki. The unbelievable heat, which reached 3,000 to 4,000 C (5,400 to 7,200 F) at ground level under the explosions, altered the color of the surrounding material, etching the shadows in place. Human flesh was horribly burned and, near the hypocenters, people were vaporized altogether.

People caught in the open within one kilometer of the blast experienced temperatures so high that the dark, heat-absorbing pattern of their clothing was burned into their flesh.

HIBAKUSHA

Hibakusha ("explosion affected person") is a term that has been applied to atomic bomb survivors for the past half century. Some hibakusha still bear the mark of their experience in the form of keloid scars. They have suffered the psychological pain of surviving an experience that took the lives of friends and loved ones. Many have suffered the post-war prejudices of their countrymen, who believe that survivors were tainted by exposure to radiation. All of them are aware of the fact that they have a higher than average chance of developing leukemia or some other cancer. Only they can tell you what it is like to survive an atomic explosion.

Two Cities in Chaos

HIROSHIMA: THE FIRST HALF HOUR

Hiroshima stands on a flat river delta, with few hills to protect sections of the city. Moreover, the bomb was dropped on the city center, an area crowded with wooden residential structures and places of business. Beneath the column of smoke that rose over the city following the explosion, tens of thousands were already dead or dying.

Even before the fires began to race out of control, the physical destruction of buildings and other structures within 2 km (1.2 mi) of the blast was virtually complete. The sheer force of the explosion had shifted the position of a large steel bridge close to the hypocenter; flattened all wooden buildings and steel frame structures; and collapsed the floors and roofs of reinforced concrete buildings designed to withstand earthquakes.

NAGASAKI: THE FIRST HALF HOUR

The pattern of destruction in Nagasaki was shaped by the geography of the city. The bomb was dropped over the Urakami Valley, a residential and industrial area. The center of Nagasaki, the harbor, and the historic district were shielded from the blast by the hills flanking the Urakami River. In the affected area, however, an estimated 12,000 buildings were destroyed by blast or burned in the fires resulting from the bomb.

As a result of a more powerful bomb and the focusing effect of the surrounding hills, physical destruction in the Urakami Valley was even greater than in Hiroshima. Virtually nothing was left standing. Worshippers in neighborhood shrines and temples and in the great Urakami Cathedral, died at their prayers. Children died in their classrooms, prisoners in their cells, workers at their machines.

"Houses and trees were leveled as far as the eye could see, and fires were beginning to break out in the ruins. At the side of the road I saw the corpse of a man who had been guiding a horse cart, still on his feet with his hair standing on end like wire...The river was filled with dead and half-dead; burned children were screaming, 'Mommy! Mommy!'; and mothers searched for their children, calling out names in faltering voices."

Ms. Hide Kurokawa, Nagasaki

FIRESTORMS

In both cities, the intense heat generated by the explosions created fires near the hypocenter. Fed by broken gas and electrical lines, the initial fires spread out of control. Fire stations and equipment had been destroyed, fire fighters were dead or injured, water pipes were ruptured.

High winds created fire storms within one half hour of the blast. In Hiroshima, where conditions for such a conflagration were perfect, winds within the firestorm reached a maximum velocity of 65 km/h (40 mph) 2-3 hours after the blast. In the center of the firestorm, temperatures reached 1,899 C (3,450 F). Wood and fabric burst into spontaneous flame. The steel structures of bridges and buildings twisted out of shape. Objects of metal, glass and stone were shattered, melted and fused.

A SEA OF FLAMES

The gigantic firestorm in Hiroshima ultimately destroyed 13 square kilometers (5 square miles) of the city. Almost 63% of the buildings in Hiroshima were completely destroyed and nearly 92% of the structures in the city had been either destroyed or damaged by blast and fire.

Because of the hilly geography of Nagasaki and the location of the hypocenter away from the city center, the conflagration there was limited to the Urakami Valley and part of downtown. It was nonetheless devastating—some 22.7% of Nagasaki's buildings were consumed by the flames.

THE FIRST HIROSHIMA MUNICIPAL GIRLS' HIGH SCHOOL

On the morning of August 6, 1945, 544 first and second year students and eight teachers of the First Hiroshima Municipal Girls' High School were clearing rubble to create a fire break near the south side of the Seifukuin Temple in the district of Zaimoku-cho, some 300-500 m (1000-1650 ft) from the hypocenter. They took the full force of the blast and heat. Most died instantly. A few apparently survived the initial explosion only to die in the flames that followed. It is estimated that perhaps 16 of the 544 girls survived.

"...on the following morning I bandaged my head—I too was burned and injured—and went to the work site. Many of the students'...eyeballs had popped out, all the way out. And their mouths were ripped open by the blast, their faces were burned, their hair gone, their clothes were burned off all over their bodies, and they were blown helter-skelter by the blast... the girl's school uniforms were burned off completely; they were completely stripped...naked. It was just like, well, a scene from hell."

Zoroku Miyagawa, Principal, Hiroshima First Girls' High School, December 3, 1945

SHATTERED LIVES

Many individuals who were close to ground zero in the two cities were never found. Their bodies were consumed by the heat and blast of the explosion, or burned beyond recognition in the firestorms that followed. Scattered here and there among the ashes, a handful of objects survived to remind family members of cherished loved ones who had simply vanished.

SCENES OF DESTRUCTION: HIROSHIMA AND NAGASAKI, AUGUST 7–10, 1945

"They all had skin blackened by burns...They had no hair because their hair was burned, and...you could not tell whether you were looking at them in front or in back... They held their arms bent [forward]...and their skin—not only on their hands, but on their faces and bodies too—hung down... I can picture them in my mind, like walking ghosts..."

A grocer, Hiroshima

"And one thing that has never disappeared from my mind was...a girl in the rain of about eighteen or nineteen years old, and she had no clothing on her body but half of her panties, which did not cover her. She took a few steps toward me, but, as she was ashamed of her situation, she...crouched on the ground...and asked me for help...and when I looked at her hands, I saw the skin was burned off, as if she were wearing gloves. Her hair was disheveled and her breast was red from burns...I was at a loss."

A Hiroshima factory worker

"Many corpses were found at places where there was water— rivers, old wells, cisterns, ponds and the like. People who did not die instantly had, it appears, exerted themselves to the limit in their search for water."

A member of the Marine Transport Rescue Team, Hiroshima, 1945

"At the side of the road I noticed a young boy standing beside a...pine tree, and the vision made me stop in my tracks. His legs were spread open in a running posture and his hands were thrust forward as though he were about to grasp something. It was the corpse of a boy, frozen like a statue...I noticed a dead kitten clamped to the...pine tree in front of the boy...obviously having jumped onto the tree to avoid his grasp, and its body was covered in the scorched and frizzled remains of fur. Without disintegrating or falling from the tree, it glared with eternally locked eyes in the direction of the boy."

Ms. Chise Setuguchi, Nagasaki

COPING WITH CHAOS

In Hiroshima, and in the Urakami section of Nagasaki, the devastation was staggering. Hiroshima had suffered the loss of city and prefectural officials, military leaders, hospitals and medical professionals who might have organized the relief effort. A steady stream of half-naked, bleeding and burned survivors staggered away from the center of destruction. Surviving doctors and nurses established make-shift relief stations, but beds, essential medical supplies, and trained personnel were in desperately short supply.

Relief parties moving into the devastated areas discovered

that there were few people left to rescue. Their biggest task was the recovery and disposal of tens of thousands of corpses. Those who had died immediately were buried beneath the rubble of the city. Those who had lived for a few minutes or hours longer were piled deep on bridges and along the river banks, or floating in the rivers, where they had sought to escape the firestorm.

"Some time after dark, a whistle and a horn blew; the Relief Train and an Army truck had arrived. The train was packed...But the truck was even worse; bodies were piled so high [that] surely another could not have been added. Neither dead nor living, nor male and female, could be distinguished among the overlapping bodies...their hair was burned crisp and wrinkled; their clothes were in tatters; exposed skin was badly burned and blood soaked...their faces, backs, arms and legs had been pierced by countless glass, wood and metal splinters...and some kind of pitch-black substance, like coal tar, stuck to their heads and bodies."

An intern on duty at the Omura Naval Hospital, Nagasaki, August 9, 1945

"I threw myself into the search for my family and cast about the still hot rubble. Before long the tips of my shoes burned and my toes stuck out, and my hands became swollen with blisters...looking on the road, I found a charred corpse that seemed to be my wife in front of our neighbor Mr. Baba's house. I intuited that the dead baby on her back was our one year old daughter Takako. However, I was never able to find our eight year old son Tateki and our eldest daughter Mariko."

Tsuneo Tomimatsu, Nagasaki

"On the fifth day of duty we were assigned to disposal of the countless corpses floating in the rivers, bobbing up and down with the waves caused by the ebb and flow of the tide. The corpses were retrieved by boat and transported to shore. Several dozen bloated, naked bodies was a sight too gruesome to look upon. When we reached out and grabbed the hand of a decayed corpse, the skin just slipped off; it was very difficult to haul them into the boat."

A member of the Marine Transport Rescue Team, Hiroshima, 1945

A STORY OF SURVIVAL

"I thought she was dead, but finally found her alive. I hoped that she could at least die at home, so I borrowed a cart from a neighbor and went to Kuba to take her home. I had brought her up since she was two years old after her father died...I took her to the Red Cross Hospital every day. I remember someone taking our picture on the way back from the hospital... She was so pitiful, burned on the left side of her body, face and arm. I still cry when I think of it."

Mrs. Kohide Matsuda, 1973

"We gathered scraps of lumber and made a neat pile...We carried the children's bodies over and placed them on the pile with Umito in the middle. I dressed Umito in a nightshirt of Michiko's I found in the ruins of our house and on top of that put his uniform trousers that had a tag saying 'Matsuo 1-6' sewn on the lining. I covered little Hiroto and Yukiko with blankets—the last gesture of love I could make for my children. We stacked another heap of wood over their bodies. I said a small prayer, lit the fire below their heads, and then passed the match to the four corners of the pile."

Atsyuki Matsuo, Nagasaki

COUNTING THE DEAD

The chaotic conditions in both cities following the disaster made it difficult to prepare an accurate account of the human dimension of the tragedy. This was complicated by the fact that death from radiation poisoning incurred at the time of the bombing might not claim its victim for days, weeks, months or years after the event.

Several studies based solely on the disposal of bodies set the initial toll for Hiroshima at between 42,000 and 93,000 individuals. Those counts are, however, undoubtedly low and incomplete. A more accurate survey combining body counts, unresolved missing person reports and interviews conducted by neighborhood associations during the year following the bombing suggests that as many as 130,000 individuals lost their lives as a direct result of the bomb up to the beginning of November 1945. A similar survey by the Nagasaki officials set the final death toll for that city at 60,000 to 70,000.

A Deadly New Threat: Radioactivity

RADIOACTIVE FALLOUT: THE "BLACK RAIN"

Following the atomic explosions, nuclear fission products of uranium and plutonium, radioactive isotopes that had escaped fission, and other material irradiated by neutrons from the bombs, were carried high into the atmosphere. The enormous amount of material thrown into the air, combined with the heat and thermal currents generated by the growing firestorms, led to rain in both cities within 30-40 minutes of the bombing.

The "black rain," as it came to be known, carried the radioactive materials back to earth in the form of fallout. The sticky, dark, dangerously radioactive water stained skin, clothing and buildings. Contact with the skin, ingestion through breathing, or the consumption of contaminated food or water resulted in radiation poisoning.

"I went to report to the dean of the college that the patients had been evacuated, but I found him covered by a raincoat and lying asleep on a hill-side vegetable patch with terrible wounds all over his body. Large drops of black-colored rain were falling and spattering on the raincoat. I thought to myself for the first time that Japan had lost the war."

Dr. Takashi Nagai, Nagasaki

THE INITIAL RADIATION FROM THE BOMB

The nuclear weapons dropped on Hiroshima and Nagasaki expended about 3% of their total energy in the generation of ionizing radiation—high-energy particles and rays with sufficient energy to "ionize" neutral atoms, that is, to strip electrons away from them. While some of this ionizing radiation is absorbed by the air, neutrons (electrically neutral sub-atomic particles) and gamma and X-rays (extremely high energy forms of light), did reach the ground and damage living tissues exposed to them. Close to the hypocenters of the explosion, dosages were high enough to be immediately lethal, provided the exposed person was not already killed by flash, blast or fire.

INDUCED RADIOACTIVITY

The Hiroshima and Nagasaki bombs also created induced or residual radioactivity. The initial burst of radiation from the bombs irradiated the soil and all other materials in the area of the blasts. The absorption by all kinds of substances of slow neutrons from the explosions was particularly important. New forms (isotopes) of chemical elements were created that themselves emitted ionizing radiation.

On August 13–14, 1945, Japanese physicists investigating the area near the hypocenter at Hiroshima found unusual levels of radioactivity in the soil, in the bones of a horse, and in the sulphur of electrical insulators on utility poles. Ultimately, scientists would identify a variety of unusual radioactive elements in the soil, roofing tiles, asphalt, and concrete near ground zero in the two cities.

RADIOACTIVITY AND LIVING TISSUE

Living tissue may be exposed to ionizing radiation either directly, as in exposure to an atomic explosion, or through exposure to or ingestion of materials emitting residual radiation. In either case, the danger is the same.

Ionizing radiation transforms a neutral atom into a charged ion that may bond to another atom, altering the structure of the original molecule, the way it reacts chemically, and the function it performs when part of a living organism. These altered molecules may act as poisons, hindering the normal functions of the cell of which they are a part.

MANHATTAN PROJECT SCIENTISTS AND THE RADIATION EFFECTS OF THE BOMB

The American, British and refugee scientists who designed the Hiroshima and Nagasaki bombs were aware of the dangers of radioactivity. Since the beginning of the twentieth century, experimenters with radioactive materials had suffered ill-effects, as had workers who had painted radium watch-dials and instruments.

At the time of the first atomic bomb test in New Mexico in July 1945, Manhattan Project scientists had expressed concern over the possibility of radioactive fallout on people downwind of the test site. The very high level of radioactivity produced by the "Trinity" test explosion nonetheless came as something of a surprise.

Most scientists, however, continued to believe that radiation poisoning would not claim many victims when the atomic bomb wᴄs dropped on Japanese cities. Those individuals most in danger of such poisoning, they reasoned, would already have died as a result of blast and heat.

THE MYSTERIOUS "A-BOMB DISEASE"

At first, the medical professionals who treated bomb victims in Hiroshima and Nagasaki were overwhelmed with the traumatic effects of the bombs. Individuals had been crushed, struck by flying objects and burned. The severe nature of the burns suffered by survivors exposed to the initial flash were [sic] particularly shocking and surprising. In some cases, the fabric pattern of clothing had actually been burned into the skin.

The real puzzle, however, came from individuals who suffered from unexplained loss of appetite, nausea and vomiting, abnormal thirst, diarrhea, and a general malaise. In up to 30% of the survivors, the symptoms occurred alone or in combination within a half-hour to three hours after the explosion. By August 17 in Hiroshima(?), 181 unexplained fatalities had resulted from these types of symptoms.

"The bodies of the dead students from the school where I taught had been collected for the most part, but now an increasing number of students who had no visible injuries were dying. They developed a fever several days after the explosion; their hair fell out completely; and thick blackish-red blood began to flow from their gums. Finally, they sputtered hysterically in the throes of fever and then died one after another. There were others who went insane, and apparently seized by some unknown fear, refused to come out of the toilets and closets. The school dormitory had to be closed temporarily, and I began to receive word that many of the young girls who had gone home to recuperate were also becoming sick and showing the above symptoms."

Ms. Chie Setoguchi, Nagasaki

"My sister soon developed diarrhea, and unsightly purple blotches appeared on her skin. This was the final signpost. She began to mumble deliriously. I had heard that water was not good for an injured person, but I gave her as much as she wanted because I knew the end was near."

Ms. Hisae Aoki, Nagasaki

THE MYSTERY IS SOLVED

New symptoms appeared during the days and weeks following the bombing. Skin hemorrhages and lesions appeared on the face, chest, neck and upper arms, often complicated by infections. There was widespread hair loss, internal hemorrhaging, and reddening and pain in the larynx, gums and palate. The symptoms appeared in some 61% of all Hiroshima survivors who had been within one kilometer of the hypocenter, and only 7% of those who were exposed over five kilometers from ground zero.

By the end of the first week of September 1945, it was becoming clear to physicians in the two cities, and to American authorities, that the A-bomb survivors were suffering from radiation poisoning. This was confirmed by analyses of blood and bone-marrow samples from victims. It had also become apparent that individuals exposed to fallout, and those who had been exposed to induced radiation during the hours and days following the explosion had also contracted radiation poisoning.

"An old woman...died within a few days of the bomb, showing many spots on her body...I know it is terrible to say this, but those spots were beautiful. They were just like stars—red, green-yellow and black—all over her body, and I was fascinated by them."

Physician, Hiroshima

"We heard the new phrase, 'A-bomb disease.' The fear in us became strong, especially when we could see certain things with our eyes: a man looked perfectly well when he rode by on a bicycle one morning, suddenly vomiting blood then dying...Soon we were all worried about our health, about our own bodies—whether we would live or die. And we heard that if someone did get sick, there was no treatment that could help. We had nothing to rely on, there was nothing to hold us up."

A Buddhist Priest, Hiroshima

SHORT-TERM MORTALITY AT HIROSHIMA AND NAGASAKI

Over 90% of individuals within 500 m (1600 ft) of the hypocenters at Hiroshima and Nagasaki died. At a distance of 1.5 kilometers (roughly one mile) over 2/3 of all people were casualties, and 1/3 died. Half of the individuals exposed at a distance of 2 km (1.2 mi) were casualties, 10% of whom died. Casualties dropped to 10% at distances over 4 km (2.4 mi). Most of those who received high dosages of radiation close to the hypocenter died immediately or during the first day. One third of the total number of fatalities had occurred by the fourth day; 2/3 by day 10; and 90% by the end of three weeks.

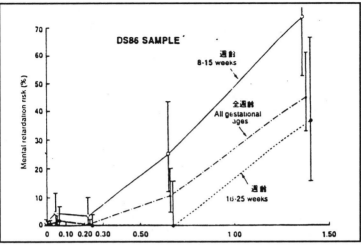

Particularly distressing is the incidence of mental retardation among those exposed during their first 8 to 25 weeks in their mothers womb. Those who received a dost of 1 Gray, in the womb, had approximately a 20% risk of mental retardation. These children had both unusually small head size and later were found to have low IQ and school performance. IQ scores showed a linear decline with increasing radiation dose.

LONG-TERM RADIATION EFFECTS IN HIROSHIMA AND NAGASAKI

The immediate crisis in Hiroshima and Nagasaki had passed by the end of December 1945. Individuals who had suffered from radiation poisoning had either died or, apparently, recovered. It soon became obvious, however, that exposure to radiation created longer-term health problems.

Thermal burns were covered with disfiguring scars known as keloids. Severe anemia and other blood disorders, cataracts, sterility in both sexes, and menstrual irregularities appeared. Children exposed to radiation while in the womb faced a 20% risk of being mentally retarded. Some exposed children were born with unusually small heads or other deformities.

"In April 1952, Yoshimasa entered T. Elementary School.

When the name Yoshimasa Yoshida was called, he responded, but, unable to understand the teacher's order to rise, he remained seated blankly...The result of the [intelligence] test we requested was, after all, really quite low... We left the school gate just when the cherry blossoms were in full bloom. Hearing the healthy children's voices singing behind us, I burst into tears. Yoshimasa, who was skipping ahead of me, looked back and smiled..."

Mrs. Jirokichi Yoshida, mother of a retarded child exposed to radiation in utero

CANCER AMONG SURVIVORS

Fifty years after the atomic bombing of Japan, it is apparent that the incidence of some cancers is significantly higher among bomb survivors than in a normal population. The first cases of leukemia (a cancer of the blood) appeared in Nagasaki in 1945 and Hiroshima a year later. The disease climbed to a peak among survivors during the years 1950-1953. A survivor who received 1 gray (100 rads of ionizing energy absorbed per kilogram of body tissue) in August 1945 is almost five times more likely to contract leukemia than a normal individual.

The incidence of cataracts of the eye and cancers of the urinary tract, breast, lungs, colon, esophagus and stomach are also higher among atomic bomb survivors. Genetic damage is apparent in the non-reproductive cells of atomic bomb survivors. The impact of this damage on the offspring and descendants of survivors has been studied carefully, but there is no significant evidence that genetic problems have been passed to future generations.

"How would people look at me. The more I thought about it the more apprehensive I became...The burns on my back did not heal for fifteen years, and I had to receive treatment for them continuously. After a skin transplant operation in 1960 the wounds finally covered over, but ulcers soon formed in the [keloid] scars. The ulcers got worse and five years ago I entered another hospital and received another operation to remove them. Subsequently, I have been in and out of the hospital repeatedly...

According to my doctor, modern medical science still knows of no efficient method to treat these lesions."

Sumiteru Taniguchi, Nagasaki

THE ATOMIC BOMB CASUALTY COMMISSION

Anxious to obtain a better understanding of the effects of radiation on large populations, the U.S. government established an Atomic Bomb Casualty Commission (ABCC) under the auspices of the National Academy of Sciences in 1947. The ABCC would eventually identify 120,000 bomb survivors, establish their precise location and radiation dosage, and monitor their health over an extended period.

The ABCC was bitterly criticized in Japan for its refusal to provide health services to victims. The decision was based on a reluctance to draw patients away from Japanese physicians and on the American perception that treating the survivors would amount to an admission of guilt for the bombing. From the Japanese perspective, it simply appeared that the U.S. government, through the ABCC, regarded the atomic bombing of Japan as an experiment and the survivors as guinea pigs.

In an attempt to ease the situation, the ABCC was reorganized in (yr.?) as the Radiation Effects Research Foundation (RERF), with joint Japanese–American participation.

The Radiation Effects Research Foundation, still active today, has proven invaluable in advising on the treatment of victims of subsequent nuclear disasters, including the 1986 explosion of the Soviet reactor at Chernobyl.

SADAKO AND THE THOUSAND PAPER CRANES

Sadako Sasaki was two years old when she was exposed to radiation 1600 m (1 mi) from the hypocenter in Hiroshima. In 1955, the healthy twelve-year-old girl, the fastest runner at the Noborimachi Primary School, was diagnosed as suffering from acute leukemia. According to Japanese folk belief, cranes live a thousand years and are a symbol of good health. Sadako spent the last months of her life attempting to fold one thousand paper cranes. When she died in October 1955, she had completed only 964. Her classmates finished the rest.

Determined to raise funds for a monument to Sadako and the other child victims of the atomic bomb, the young people of Hiroshima began a letter writing campaign to schools across Japan. The effort captured the public imagination, raised seven million yen ($20,000) and established Sadako as a symbol of the cost of war in the nuclear age. Today her statue stands in the Hiroshima Peace Memorial Park, adorned with thousands of the paper cranes that arrive each year from school children around the world.

UNIT 5: THE LEGACY OF HIROSHIMA AND NAGASAKI

The introduction of nuclear weapons into the world, and their first use at Hiroshima and Nagasaki, left powerful legacies beyond the long-term radiation effects on the survivors. For Japan, the United States and its Allies, a horrific war was brought to an abrupt end, although at a cost debated to this day; for the world, a nuclear arms race unfolded that still threatens unimaginable devastation. The bombings of Hiroshima and Nagasaki cannot be said to have simply caused either the end of the war or the nuclear arms race, but they have exercised a profound influence as military and political acts, as symbols of the arrival of the nuclear age, and as a glimpse of the realities of nuclear war.

Japan Surrenders

The sudden surrender of Japan on August 14, 1945—only eight days after the bombing of Hiroshima and five days after Nagasaki—have led many to believe that the atomic bomb alone forced the Japanese government to accept defeat. Actually, the bombings were one of two major shocks to Japan. The other was the Soviet Union's declaration of war on August 8/9, which destroyed the hopes of the Japanese elite for a compromise peace through Moscow. The Soviet declaration was immediately followed by a massive surprise attack on the Japanese Army in north China.

The bombing of Hiroshima and Nagasaki nevertheless played a crucial role in ending the Pacific War quickly. Some have argued that no atomic bombs were needed to shock the Japanese leadership, because a peace agreement was already possible if Emperor Hirohito's position had been guaranteed. Others have argued that only one bomb was needed and that the destruction inflicted on Nagasaki was unnecessary. These matters remain hotly contested, but the surrender of Japan was doubtlessly a critical legacy of Hiroshima and Nagasaki.

HIROSHIMA AND THE SOVIET DECLARATION OF WAR

For days after the bombing of Hiroshima, the Japanese government had only sketchy information. The destruction was so massive that the city was effectively cut off from the rest of the world. The shock effect of Hiroshima was thus largely derived from President Truman's August 6 announcement of the nuclear attack, repeated on Allied radio stations. That announcement simultaneously revealed to the world the ultra-secret Manhattan Project.

The atomic bombing of Hiroshima also shocked the Soviet dictator, Joseph Stalin. He had promised to enter the Pacific war, but the offensive was not planned until mid-August or later. Afraid that the war would be over before the Soviet Union could gain a share of the spoils, on the evening of August 7, Moscow time, Stalin ordered Soviet forces to attack the Japanese Army in north China twenty-for hours later, at midnight August 8/9, Far Eastern Time. Shortly before that, the Japanese ambassador was handed a surprise declaration of war.

THE EMPEROR INTERVENES

"The time has come when we must bear the unbearable...I swallow my own tears and give my sanction to the proposal to accept the Allied proclamation..."

Emperor Hirohito, August 10, 1945

The Japanese government and military leadership was unable to meet until August 9, after the Soviet declaration of war. Throughout the day, the peace faction, led by Foreign Minister Togo, was stalemated by the military hard-liners, who would not accept surrender. Even the news of the Nagasaki bombing did not change the situation. The key stumbling block was the preservation of the monarchy. Togo argued for accepting the Allies' Potsdam Proclamation, as long as it "would not comprise any demand which would prejudice the prerogatives of His Majesty as a Sovereign Ruler."

The political deadlock provoked an emergency conference with Emperor Hirohito in his air-raid bunker, beginning around midnight, August 9/10. At the end, the Emperor clearly stated his wish that Japan offer surrender on Togo's terms.

TRUMAN AND THE EMPEROR QUESTION

"From the moment of surrender the authority of the Emperor and the Japanese government to rule the state shall be subject to the Supreme Commander of the Allied Powers who will take such steps as he deems proper to effectuate the surrender terms."

U.S. note to Japan, August 10, 1945

The Japanese surrender offer of August 10, which sought to keep Emperor Hirohito on the throne, provoked disagreement among President Truman's advisers. The President's Chief of Staff, Admiral Leahy, argued for immediate acceptance. Secretary of State Byrnes felt, however, that the Japanese condition would lead to "the crucifixion of the President" by an angry public demanding "unconditional surrender." Truman eventually instructed Byrnes to dodge the issue by sending a note that said nothing about the ultimate fate of the Emperor.

NO THIRD ATOMIC BOMB

On August 10, during discussions of the Japanese surrender offer, President Truman ordered that no more atomic bombs be dropped without his consent. He told Commerce Secretary and former Vice President Henry Wallace that he did not like killing "all those kids." Although he had written in his Potsdam diary in July that the target for the first bomb would be "purely military," he clearly understood after Hiroshima that whole cities and their inhabitants were the target.

General Groves, the head of the Manhattan Project, held up the shipment to the Pacific of the plutonium 239 core for another "Fat Man" bomb. Otherwise it would have been available for a mission from Tinian around August 24. The original primary target for the Nagasaki mission, Kokura, would probably have been chosen, although there was some talk of attacking Tokyo. Further plutonium cores could have been shipped to the Pacific approximately every three to four weeks thereafter. But no uranium 235 for a "Little Boy"-type bomb would have been available for some months.

A "LIVING GOD" SPEAKS

The failure of the American note of August 10 to clearly guarantee the Emperor's position provoked another dangerous deadlock in the Japanese ruling elite. The militarist hard-liners felt that there was no choice but to fight the war to the bitter end. After some careful maneuvering by the leaders of the peace faction, Marquis Kido and Foreign Minister Togo, the Emperor called another emergency conference in the Imperial Palace air-raid bunker on August 14. Hirohito once again broke the deadlock by asking that the government accept the American terms.

During the night of August 14/15, ultra-right-wing military officers tried to overthrow the government to prevent the surrender, but the attempt failed because of lack of support in the Army. At noon, Tokyo time, August 15, 1945, the Japanese people for the first time heard the voice of the Emperor on the radio. His recorded message was hard to understand, because it was in archaic, court Japanese, but it conveyed stunning news: Japan had lost the war.

In all Allied countries, that same day was one of riotous celebration: V-J Day. World War II was over.

The Cold War and the Nuclear Arms Race

"A single demand of you, comrades, provide us with atomic weapons in the shortest possible time. You know that Hiroshima has shaken the whole world. The equilibrium has been destroyed. Provide the bomb—it will remove a great danger from us."

Soviet dictator Joseph Stalin, mid-August 1945, to Munitions Minister Vannikov and chief nuclear scientist Kurchatov

Hiroshima and Nagasaki cannot be said to have caused either the Cold War or the nuclear race between East and West, but the first use of these weapons nevertheless had profound effects. The Soviet Union had had a small nuclear project since 1942, but the news of the bombings spurred it into a crash program. Stalin would have wanted to acquire the atomic bomb in any case, but Hiroshima and Nagasaki were frightening demonstrations of the power of these weapons.

Following the Soviet Union's lead, Great Britain, France and China all started their own bomb projects. By the 1960's, two bombs had become tens of thousands of bombs.

THE FAILURE OF INTERNATIONAL CONTROL

Immediately after World War II, American scientists pushed the idea of "international control": all atomic weapons would be put in the hands of the United Nations to prevent a worldwide arms race. The United States government proposed a version of that idea called the "Baruch plan," after the chief American delegate to the U.N. Atomic Energy Commission, Bernard Baruch.

To many in the United States, the Baruch plan looked like an unprecedented offer to give away America's greatest military secret, but to the Soviet Union, the plan appeared to guarantee the continuation of the American nuclear monopoly, at least in the short run. Fear and mutual distrust between the two sides prevented the plan from being enacted. As conflicts over the fate of Eastern Europe and other regions heated up in the late 1940s, the Cold War ended any possibility of even limiting a nuclear arms race to a smaller number of weapons.

MORE BOMBS AND BIGGER BOMBS

On August 23(?), 1949, the Soviet Union exploded its first atomic bomb. The Truman administration responded with a crash program to build a "hydrogen bomb" that would harness the fusion power fueling the Sun and the stars. When the United States exploded the world's first thermonuclear device on November 1, 1952, it was nearly *one thousand times* more powerful than the Hiroshima and Nagasaki bombs. An entire Pacific atoll was vaporized and the fireball was so huge it could have enveloped much of the island of Manhattan. The Russians responded with their first primitive thermonuclear device in 1953 and their first full-scale hydrogen bomb in 1955.

The United States and the Soviet Union also began to build large numbers of smaller "tactical" nuclear weapons for use on the battlefield and in short-range attacks. Great Britain staged its first atomic test in 1953 and exploded a hydrogen bomb in 1958. As a result, the number of nuclear weapons in the world skyrocketed into the thousands in the 1950s.

THE VOYAGE OF THE *LUCKY DRAGON*

After Hiroshima and Nagasaki, fear of the radiation effects of nuclear weapons grew, but it was the hydrogen bomb tests of the mid-1950s that made nuclear "fall-out" into a world-wide issue. Particularly important was the United States' "BRAVO" test of March 1, 1954. The bomb was twice as powerful as planned and radioactive dust fell on the natives of Rongelap Atoll and on the Japanese fishing vessel, the *Lucky Dragon No. 5*. When the boat returned to Japan two weeks later, the crew was suffering from the classic effects of radiation sickness. One crew member died.

The *Lucky Dragon* incident profoundly shocked Japan. A panic broke out about the possible radioactive pollution of tuna fish. In America, many were angered by government denials that radiation had anything to do with the fishermen's illness.

THE RISE OF THE ANTI-NUCLEAR MOVEMENT

The hydrogen bomb tests of the mid-1950s and the *Lucky Dragon* incident energized the anti-nuclear movement around the world. Although there had been movements ever since 1945 to "Ban the Bomb" and advocate "One World or None," nuclear fall-out and the frightening power of the new "H-bombs" made the arms race much more personally threatening to many around the world.

The cities of Hiroshima and Nagasaki became especially

important as international symbols of the dangers of nuclear war. Commemorations had been held every year in the two cities on the anniversaries of the bombings, but it was the tenth anniversary ceremonies in 1955 that first gathered wide international attention.

DIDN'T THEY ALL GO CRAZY?

One of the strangest myths that emerged out of the growing fear of nuclear weapons was the belief that the aircrews on the Hiroshima missions all had gone insane and killed themselves. These stories had their root in the troubles of a former 509th Composite Group pilot, Claude Eatherly. On the Hiroshima mission, Eatherly had commanded one of the B-29s used as weather planes, but had not directly witnessed the bombing. An unstable personality, Eatherly committed burglaries in the mid-1950s and began to claim that guilt had driven him over the brink. Rumors soon spread that he was the commander of the "Enola Gay" and that all the crew members had similar troubles.

Eatherly was also exploited by Soviet-bloc propaganda, which often used peace and anti-nuclear slogans in a hypocritical way to attack the United States. In fact, no other 509th crew members had mental problems or claimed to have felt guilty for having done their duty as servicemen in wartime.

A WORLD GONE "M.A.D."

In the late 1950s and early 1960s, the United States and the Soviet Union both developed intercontinental nuclear missiles that threatened nuclear annihilation of both sides within minutes instead of hours. "M.A.D."—Mutual Assured Destruction—was one acronym coined to describe this terrifying new reality. On the one hand, nuclear "deterrence" seemed to insure for the first time that wars between the great powers were no longer possible. On the other, human civilization itself could be destroyed if deterrence failed. During the Cuban Missile Crisis of 1962, that possibility came frighteningly close to reality.

NUCLEAR WASTE AND HUMAN EXPERIMENTS

Fear and the urgent need to build nuclear weapons produced other problems: widespread nuclear pollution, accidents and experiments on humans to determine the dangers of radioactivity. On all sides, the production of bomb fuel left huge quantities of nuclear waste. These wastes created massive clean-up problems and sometimes have engendered dangerous accidents. In 1959, a chemical explosion at a Soviet nuclear-weapons plant contaminated a huge area in the Ural Mountains with radioactive materials, killing hundreds.

The need to know about the radioactive effects of nuclear war and nuclear-weapons production also led on both sides to human experiments and the exposure of soldiers to above-ground bomb tests. Particularly shocking has [sic] been revelations of the injection of patients in the United States in the 1940s and 1950s with radioactive materials. But the other power undoubtedly also staged such experiments.

ARMS CONTROL?

The Limited Test Ban Treaty of 1963 ended most bomb-testing in the atmosphere, although not by the new nuclear powers, France and China. Arms control agreements were also concluded by the superpowers in the 1970s. Yet none of these stopped a relentless build-up of nuclear weapons. At its apogee in the mid-1980s, there were nearly *70,000* warheads in world stockpiles, 98% of which were held by the United States and the Soviet Union.

On average, each of these warheads were tens of times as powerful as the Hiroshima and Nagasaki bombs. If that explosive power were evenly distributed, every man, woman and child on Earth would be hit by the equivalent of several tons of TNT.

THE COLD WAR ENDS—REAL NUCLEAR DISARMAMENT BEGINS

In 1987, U.S. President Ronald Reagan and Soviet President

Mikhail Gorbachev signed the first arms control agreement that actually resulted in the demolition of deployed nuclear weapons. The Intermediate Nuclear Forces (INF) Treaty eliminated a whole class of weapons—short and medium-range missiles.

It was a harbinger of much more fundamental agreements signed by the two sides after the stunning collapse of the Soviet Union and its empire between 1989 and 1991. At long last, strategic missiles and bombers were actually taken off alert and scrapped, beginning 1992. But the danger of nuclear war has not disappeared. Even today, the United States, Russia, other former Soviet republics, Britain, France and China have many thousands of nuclear weapons aimed at each other. The threat of global nuclear war has apparently vanished, but the possibility of nuclear weapons being used may have actually increased.

A Soviet SS-20 and an American Pershing missile, like those destroyed under the INF Treaty, can be seen in *Milestone of Flight* (Gallery 100).

NUCLEAR PROLIFERATION AND NUCLEAR TERRORISM

Although the Cold War is over, an increasing danger is the acquisition of nuclear weapons by more nations and even by terrorist groups. Already during the 1960s and 1970s, Israel appears to have built a number of nuclear warheads and India actually tested a nuclear device. South Africa built a few warheads similar to the Hiroshima gun-type bomb, although it has apparently become the first nation to dismantle all its nuclear weapons. Other nations who attempted, or who are still attempting to build atomic warheads include Iran, Iraq, Pakistan and North Korea. As the danger of global nuclear war has gone down, the possibility of a local use of nuclear weapons has increased.

It is also possible that terrorist groups could acquire enough plutonium, either through from existing nuclear electric production or from the former Soviet republics, to build a crude device.

FIFTY YEARS OF THE NUCLEAR DILEMMA

A half century after the arrival of nuclear weapons in the world and their employment on Hiroshima and Nagasaki, the nuclear dilemma has not gone away. Some feel that the only solution is to ban all nuclear weapons. Others think that this idea is unrealistic and that nuclear deterrence—at a much lower level—is the only way that major wars can be prevented. One thing is clear, the nuclear "genie" is out of the bottle and, for the foreseeable future, the human race will not be able to eliminate the knowledge of how to build nuclear weapons. The dilemma is not about to disappear.

THE STRUGGLE OVER HISTORY

DEFINING THE
HIROSHIMA NARRATIVE

BY BARTON J. BERNSTEIN

Unbeknown to Americans, in mid-February 1945, when President Franklin D. Roosevelt was only into the fourth week of his fourth term, Harvey H. Bundy, a special assistant to Secretary of War Henry L. Stimson, cast what he called "a draft of a possible Presidential statement to be made when S-1 [code name for the atomic bomb] is used."[1] Little did Bundy or Stimson know that a different man, Harry S. Truman, would be the Chief Executive when the weapon was first used, in August 1945.

When returning in early August by sea from the three-power Potsdam conference, that new president received word, to his delight, that the United States had dropped an atomic bomb on Hiroshima, on August 5th (Washington time). During the Potsdam meetings, Truman had both approved the use of the bomb on Japan and also the release of a presidential statement to announce the event. That public statement, based partly upon Bundy's February draft but recast by others, declared on August 6th:[2]

Sixteen hours ago an American airplane dropped one [atomic] bomb on Hiroshima, an important Japanese Army base. That bomb had more power than 20,000 tons of T.N.T....

The Japanese began the war from the air at Pearl Harbor. They have been repaid many fold. And the end is not yet. With this bomb we have now added a new and revolutionary increase in destruction to supplement the growing power of our armed forces....

We are now prepared to obliterate more rapidly and completely every productive enterprise the Japanese have above ground in any city. We shall destroy their docks, their factories, and their communications. Let there be no mistake; we shall completely destroy Japan's power to make war.

It was to spare the Japanese people from utter destruction that the ultimatum of July 26 [the Potsdam Proclamation] was issued at Potsdam. Their leaders promptly rejected that ultimatum. If they do not now accept our terms they may expect a rain of ruin from the air, the like of which has never been seen on earth. Behind this air attack will follow sea and land forces in such numbers and power as they have not yet seen.

Truman's statement threatened both continued atomic bombings and conventional bombings, as well as the prospects of invasion, unless Japan surrendered. By describing Hiroshima simply as "an important Japanese Army base," this prepared announcement intentionally distorted facts and contrived to omit the salient facts, predictable well in advance, that most of the killed and injured would be non-combatants. The army base was not the aiming point, and Japanese troops probably constituted under a quarter of Hiroshima's large population.[3] In addition, the Potsdam Proclamation, with its demand for unconditional surrender, had not been conceived primarily to avoid the use of the atomic bomb or to prevent the killing of more Japanese, but, rather, to try to achieve Japan's surrender before the A-bomb could be used. That was a subtle but powerful difference. Also, the official statement substantially exaggerated the power of this uranium weapon, which was later estimated as equivalent to only about 13,000 tons of T.N.T.[4]

Three days later, after the Hiroshima bombing, which killed at least 80,000 and possibly over 100,000 (including about 10,000 Koreans), the United States dropped a second nuclear weapon, this time a plutonium bomb, killing at least 35,000 and perhaps closer to 60,000 at Nagasaki. The use of this second bomb had been virtually automatic, because the original order to the Air Force had directed it to drop A-bombs "as made ready."[5] The second bomb was made ready by August 9th because bad weather was forecast for the next few days, and therefore scientists were urged to work on the bomb to get it ready for use before bad weather set in. The original target had been Kokura, but it was clouded over, and therefore the B-29, *Bockscar*, dropped its lethal cargo on the secondary target city.

In Washington, President Truman publicly explained, "We have used it against those who attacked us without warning at Pearl Harbor, against those who have starved and beaten and executed American prisoners of war, against those who have abandoned all pretense of obeying international laws of warfare." That statement, perhaps intentionally, eroded any distinction between non-combatants, who were the major target, and the central government and the Japanese military, which had initiated and brutally conducted the war. In his public statement, Truman went on to say, "We have used it [the A-bomb] in order to shorten the agony of war, in order to save the lives of thousands and thousands of young Americans."[6]

At the White House, Truman had just received a demand from Senator Richard Russell, a powerful Democrat, who probably articulated the thoughts of most members of Congress and of most Americans: "we [should] cease our efforts to cajole Japan into surrendering in accordance with Potsdam Declaration [Proclamation]. Let us carry this war to them until they beg us to accept unconditional surrender." Russell went on to urge that if the United States did not have enough A-bombs to continue such nuclear attacks, then "carry on with the fire bombs" on Japanese cities until more A-bombs could be produced.[7]

Truman responded the day after the Nagasaki bombing, telling Senator Russell, "I know that Japan is a terribly cruel and uncivilized nation in warfare but I can't bring myself to believe that, because they are beasts, we should ourselves act in the same manner." Truman went on to say: "For myself, I certainly regret the necessity of wiping out whole populations because of the 'pigheadedness' of the leaders of a nation and, for your information, I am not going to do it unless it is absolutely necessary." He ended with this one-sentence paragraph: "My object is to save as many American lives as possible but I also have a humane feeling for the women and children in Japan."[8]

In Tokyo on the night of the Nagasaki bombing, Emperor Hirohito intervened in the deliberations of the deeply split Japanese cabinet to persuade the "militarists" to join with the peace forces on behalf of a conditional surrender. Hence, that day, on August 10th, the Japanese government offered to surrender with the single provision that the victors allow the maintenance of the imperial system. In Washington, top presidential advisers divided on this crucial matter, and finally they cast an intentionally ambiguous reply, suggesting but not guaranteeing continuation of the emperor.[9] That same day, President Truman informed his cabinet that he had given orders to stop the atomic bombing. On the 10th, as Truman told his cabinet, in the words of one member, "the thought of wiping out another 100,000 people was too horrible. He didn't like the idea of killing...'all those kids.'"[10] Truman did, however, sanction the continued conventional bombing of Japanese cities, adding to the massive devastation in recent months of over 60 Japanese cities, the killing of many thousands of non-combatants, and the destruction of both housing and industry.

In the United States, most Americans were delighted by the use of the second A-bomb, and many looked forward, as did Senator Russell, to continued nuclear bombings of Japan. But the head of the Federal Council of Churches, a large Protestant organization, sent President Truman a very different message. "Many Christians," the telegram stated, are "deeply disturbed over the use of atomic bombs against Japanese cities because of their necessarily indiscriminate destructive efforts...."[11] Truman speedily replied, "the only language they [the Japanese] seem to understand is the one we have been using to bombard them." He ended with these pungent words: "When you have to deal with a beast you have to treat him as a beast. It is most regrettable but nevertheless true."[12]

At about the same time, within Japan, its divided government was unable to reach a consensus on whether to accept or reject the American ambiguous response until the emperor again intervened in deliberations. Hirohito declared that the American reply was adequate, and that it should be speedily accepted. Despite a small attempted military coup at the palace, where army dissidents sought to overturn this decision, Emperor

Hirohito's voice was heard the next day, on August 14th, informing his subjects that their nation had surrendered.[13]

For Japan, the war had ended after virtually a decade. For the United States, it had ended after nearly four years, but a number of Americans regretted that only two atomic bombs had been used on a hated enemy. In public opinion polls in the late summer and early autumn of 1945, the vast majority (about 85 percent in August)[14] of Americans endorsed the use of the atomic bomb on Japanese cities. In a September poll, only 4 percent thought it should not have been used, while 27 percent would have used it on an area where there were no people, but 43 percent favored using it on one city at a time, and another 24 percent would have "wiped out cities." In a poll with slightly different questions in October 1945, the approval was even greater. In that poll, 23 percent concluded that more than two A-bombs should have been quickly dropped before Japan had a chance to surrender.[15]

For those comparatively few Americans who worried about the use of nuclear bombs to help end the war, Ralph McGill, editor of the *Atlanta Constitution*, phrased the widely shared sentiments: All weapons are equally acceptable. "The atomic bomb is fully as moral as the shotgun, the spear, the ax, the percussion cap rifle,...the tommy gun,...the slingshot of David...," he wrote. Physicist Philip Morrison, after visiting Hiroshima, asserted that the atomic bombing was justifiable because the United States had been in "a war for survival; more than that, a war for the defense of culture itself." Capturing the enthusiasm and the general approval, versifier Edgar Guest expressed the near-consensus in these four lines:[16]

The power to blow all things to dust
Was kept for people God could trust,
And granted unto them alone
That evil might be overthrown.

The "official" version of what might be called the Hiroshima narrative easily carried the day: The bombs had been necessary to end the war quickly and avoid the dread invasions with many American casualties; there were no likely alternatives to using the bomb; and the use of the bomb on enemy cities had been necessary, patriotic, and just.

EARLY CRITICISMS AND OPPOSITION TO THE ATOMIC BOMBING

Not surprisingly, pacifists generally abhorred the use of the weapons on cities, for they opposed killing and especially the slaying of non-combatants. Analyzing Catholic responses, one historian concluded, "No prominent Catholic theologian, periodical, or newspaper endorsed the atomic bombing of Japan."[17] To some Catholic leaders, condemnation of the use of the A-bomb followed from their earlier moral disapproval of obliteration bombing, which violated their ethical-religious precepts by killing non-combatants. In that view, even if the atomic bomb did hasten the ending of the war and save American soldiers' lives, the use of the weapon on civilian populations was indefensible.

John Foster Dulles, at the time a prominent Protestant layman, and some Protestant religious leaders in the Federal Council of Churches lamented the use of the bomb by "a professedly Christian nation...."[18] In early 1946, a Federal Council of Churches special committee condemned the atomic bombings on various linked grounds: there was no advance warning; the targets were mostly civilians; Japan's strategic position was already hopeless; and the bombings were unnecessary to the winning of the war.[19]

The Federal Council's committee sharply phrased its report:

Even though use of the new weapon last August may well have shortened the war, the moral cost was too high. As the power that first used the atomic bomb under these circumstances, we have sinned grievously against the laws of God and against the peoples of Japan. Without seeking to apportion blame among individuals, we are compelled to judge our chosen course inexcusable.

At the same time, we are agreed that these two specific bombing sorties cannot be properly treated in isolation from the whole system of obliteration attacks with explosives and fire-bombs, of which the atomic attacks were the stunning climax. We are mindful of the incendiary raids on Tokyo, and of the saturation bombings of Hamburg, Dresden, and Berlin.

The conservative editor of *U.S. News*, David Lawrence, deplored the mass killing, questioned the need for the use of the A-bombs, and concluded that Japan had already been defeated and was trying to surrender. The right-wing *Chicago Tribune*, perhaps primarily eager to pummel a Democratic president, also objected to the use of the atomic bomb.[20]

In the Pacific, in a largely unnoticed statement, General Douglas MacArthur, the triumphant American commander, also stated that the atomic bombing had been unnecessary. Perhaps inspired by pride, and possibly even annoyed that he had not been able to direct the massive invasion on Kyushu scheduled for November 1st, MacArthur (in words crafted by General Bonner Fellers) declared, "neither the atomic bombing nor the entry of the Soviet Union into the war forced Japan's unconditional surrender." He credited the victory to the conventional warfare conducted by the United States on the land, in the air, and on the sea while virtually dismissing the use of the A-bomb.[21]

In mid-summer 1946, the United States Strategic Bombing Survey, earlier instructed by Stimson and Truman to analyze bombing in the Pacific war, issued what could have been a devastating report undermining much of the official Hiroshima narrative. In words cast by vice-chairman Paul Nitze, a future defense "hawk," the report declared: "Based on a detailed investigation of all the facts and supported by the testimony of the surviving Japanese leaders involved, it is the Survey's opinion that certainly prior to 31 December 1945, and in all probability prior to 1 November 1945, Japan would have surrendered even if the atomic bombs had not been dropped, even if Russia had not entered the war, and even if no invasion had been planned or contemplated."[22]

At the time, Americans had no way of knowing that this report had twisted evidence, suppressed some substantial counter-evidence, and therefore had produced unsubstantiated conclusions, which could be undercut by interviews the Survey had conducted in Japan.[23] Strangely, despite editor David Lawrence's enthusiasm for the report, which nicely dovetailed with his contentions, the Survey's conclusions won little favor and provoked little doubt in America.

Despite some dissents, the official Hiroshima narrative was safely in place. What the Survey's conclusions could not significantly dislodge, some speculative thoughts—briefly stated by Norman Cousins and Thomas K. Finletter, a future Secretary of the Air Force—could not appreciably affect. In mid-1946, in the *Saturday Review of Literature*, these two men suggested that the Truman administration had avoided a noncombat demonstration, and rushed to use the bomb, in order to end the war before the Soviet Union could enter the Pacific war. In that little-noticed but arresting interpretation, the use of the A-bomb was connected with anti-Soviet purposes, and the way that the United States chose to try to end World War II was connected to the American effort to shape the postwar peace.[24]

In August 1946, many literate Americans were jostled the publication by the *New Yorker* of John Hersey's "Hiroshima." It was widely reprinted, read in four special half-hour broadcasts on one of the radio networks, and then issued as a book, quickly becoming a best seller. Hersey's often matter-of-fact treatment, his calm but passionate telling of the stories of six people—five Japanese and a German Catholic priest—conveyed, dramatically, the horror of the atomic bombings as human experience.[25]

Consider, for example, Father Wilhelm Kleinsorge's errand of fetching water in Asano Park, only to encounter about twenty soldiers: "their faces were wholly burned, their eyesockets were hollow, the fluid from their melted eyes had run down their cheeks.... Their mouths were mere swollen, pus-covered wounds." Or when the Reverend Kiyoshi Tanimoto tried to aid an injured woman, "her skin slipped off in huge, glove-like pieces" as he sought to take her by the hands.[26]

"Hiroshima," first as an essay and then as a book, may have briefly reopened the moral question of whether America should have used the bomb. But its very focus on the sufferers as part of a human tragedy, in which resourcefulness and quiet heroism also warrant admiration, undoubtedly also had the effect of turning attention from the decision to use the bomb to the effects of the bomb.

Thus, it may well have been possible for readers to regret the suffering, to admire the resiliency of the survivors, to lament the use of the bomb, and to see it as a necessity. In a war where atrocities were massively committed and many millions died, readers could conclude that the bomb was the most dramatic event in that terrible conflict characterized by mass death. Such thinking would have barred celebration in 1946 of the use of the bomb, but it might still have allowed some to view the bomb as "deliverance," and not as a weapon whose 1945 use on cities merited condemnation.[27]

Whatever the general understanding and regrets produced by Hersey's powerful essay, it prompted Norman Cousins, editor of the *Saturday Review of Literature*, to return, in September 1946, to express at greater length his condemnation of the dropping of the atomic bomb on Japan. Using harsh language, he spoke of "the crime of Hiroshima and Nagasaki." Why, he asked, had American leaders not first given Japan a noncombat demonstration of the bomb together with a surrender ultimatum? This question was crucial, Cousins asserted, because "we have learned...that Japan was ready to quit even before Hiroshima," and therefore there was no merit to the contention that the atomic bombings had been necessary to save American lives.[28]

DEFENDING THE OFFICIAL HISTORY: CONANT, STIMSON, AND THEIR AIDES

Viewed objectively in the summer of 1946, such challenges—by the Federal Council's committee, by some nuclear scientists, by the Bombing Survey, by Hersey and Cousins, and by some others—were like small waves on the usually calm sea of near-consensus on the official Hiroshima narrative. There was no groundswell of opposition, no organized effort to probe and raise more questions, no substantial effort to challenge Truman, Stimson, and their cohorts directly and forcefully.

But in Cambridge, Massachusetts, at Harvard University, its president, James Conant, who had been a major adviser on the wartime A-bomb project and who had even suggested the nuclear targeting of cities, worried as he pored over the emerging literature of dissent. The problem, Conant explained to his wartime associate, Harvey Bundy, the prominent State Street attorney who had served Secretary of War Stimson as a special assistant, was that the criticisms were not coming just from "professional pacifists and...certain religious leaders," but from others including "nonreligious groups and people taking up the same theme." In his letter to Bundy on September 23, 1946, Conant contended that the dangers were considerable:[29]

This type of sentimentalism...is bound to have a great deal of influence on the next generation. The type of person who goes into teaching, particularly school teaching, will be influenced a great deal by this type of argument. We are in danger of repeating the fallacy which occurred after World War I [when] it became accepted doctrine among a group of so-called intellectuals who taught in our schools and colleges that the United States made a great error in entering World War I....A small minority, if it represents the type of person who is both sentimental and verbally minded and in contact with youth, may result in a distortion of history.

To guarantee that the official version of the Hiroshima history would not be challenged successfully, Conant wanted Harvey Bundy to have his former boss, Henry L. Stimson, a respected Republican, publish an authoritative essay defending the use of the atomic bomb on Japan. Probably Conant knew that Harvey Bundy's younger son, McGeorge Bundy, was already at work drafting Stimson's memoir of public service, and thus the Harvard president recognized that the two men would undoubtedly be preparing a chapter or more on the A-bomb decision. Conant's aim was to have a version published separately, in some distinguished magazine, so that Stimson in calm, measured words could skillfully squelch the emerging dissent without ever directly engaging the dissenting arguments. Basically, what was needed, in Conant's judgment, was a carefully framed narrative that implicitly but never argumentatively or defensively presented the decision to use the bomb as reasonable, necessary, and just.[30]

In preparing to help his son, McGeorge, and Stimson with the essay, Harvey Bundy put together a draft. In it, he phrased two sets of themes that, because of Conant's purpose of avoiding unsettling admissions, never made it into the final essay, which was published in *Harper's Magazine* (February 1947),[31] to wide public acclaim. Here are those two unsettling themes: that some policymakers had believed before Hiroshima that "unless the bomb were used it would be impossible to persuade the world that the saving of civilization in the future would depend on a proper international control of atomic energy"; and that some policymakers "saw large advantage to winning the Japanese War without the aid of Russia...."[32]

Stimson worried deeply about the article as it went through drafts, and the former Secretary of War seriously considered not publishing it. As he explained to his longtime friend, Supreme Court Justice Felix Frankfurter, who years before had been one of Stimson's assistants: "I have rarely been connected with a paper about which I have so much doubt at the last moment. I think the full enumeration of the steps in the tragedy [the atomic bombing of Japan] will excite horror among friends who heretofore thought me a kindly minded Christian gentleman but who will, after reading this, feel I am cold blooded and cruel."[33] Bucking up his former chief, Frankfurter fired back an ardently enthusiastic endorsement: The essay was splendid, and Stimson was the right man to make "the facts...known."[34]

Among the "facts" was the matter of American casualties (dead, wounded, and missing) predicted by American officials before Hiroshima if one or both American invasions—one had been scheduled on Kyushu for November 1, 1945, and the second at Honshu, tentatively scheduled for March 1, 1946—had been launched against Japan. Somehow, McGeorge Bundy and Stimson, contrary to the summer 1945 military estimates, produced a remarkably high number of "over a million casualties." In a sentence that was to become a major source for the continuing Hiroshima narrative, the published article asserted, in Stimson's apparent words: "I was informed that [the two invasions] might be expected to cost over a million casualties, to American forces."[35]

Nowhere, in Stimson's diaries and official Secretary of War papers, in the files of the Joint Chiefs and the President, and in related military archives, did any high-ranking, American official in summer 1945 forecast any number like a million American casualties or even a half-million, let alone "over a million." At a fateful meeting of the Joint Chiefs with Truman, as well as with Stimson and others, on June 18, 1945, General George C. Marshall, the army chief of staff, had actually forecast, in the words of the diary of Admiral William Leahy, that the operation on Kyushu "will not cost us in casualties more than 63,000 of the 190,000 combatant troops estimated as necessary...."[36] At that same White House meeting, Admiral Leahy, the chairman of the Joint Chiefs, had suggested that the casualty rate might be about 35 percent. Probably he meant 35 percent of *that 190,000* "combatant troops," though it is not impossible, but only unlikely, that he meant 35 percent of the total American force of about 767,000.[37]

After that mid-June White House meeting, the Japanese

buildup on Kyushu did increase greatly. By late July and early August 1945, informed by decoded Japanese cables, General Marshall worried about the possibility of high casualties in the Kyushu operation.[38] But there is no evidence, even in that period shortly before and after Hiroshima, when the Kyushu invasion still seemed possible, that he thought that American casualties would be astronomical.

In Stimson's *Harper's* article, the "over a million" number skillfully helped to legitimize the use of the bomb and to foreclose debate. Much of the article shrewdly emphasized the themes of saving American lives, of there being no practical alternative to the use of the bomb, and that the decision had been "carefully considered." These themes were linked to the rest of the article's presentation: that American leaders had assumed since 1941 that the bomb was a "legitimate" weapon to be used against the enemy; that no leader dissented from that belief and that the bomb was used to save American and Japanese lives; and that top-level scientist-advisers had endorsed the intention to use the bomb on Japan. He emphasized that speedy victory, not use or avoidance of use of the weapon, had been the controlling factor.

The article's tone was not of celebration or enthusiasm, but rather of necessity and of duty—to select the "least abhorrent choice." Patriotism and humanity, he seemed to be saying, had created the grim necessity of killing "over a hundred thousand Japanese" to end the war. "[The bomb] stopped the fire raids, and the strangling blockade; it ended the ghastly specter of a clash of land armies."[39]

Stimson's article had excluded evidence that might have both enriched understanding and raised unsettling questions: that the wartime A-bomb project had been systematically kept secret from the Soviet Union; that some advisers had expected that the bomb's use on Japan might also intimidate the Soviets and render them tractable in the postwar period; and that the bomb's likely influence on the Soviet Union had often helped to shape policy and been the subject of deliberations.

Deftly, Stimson's article avoided the Bombing Survey's conclusions that the use of the A-bomb had "in all probability" been unnecessary in order to avoid the invasion of Japan, and that the Japanese surrender would probably have occurred before November without the use of the bomb. Citing the Survey, Stimson's article instead stated, "all the evidence that I have seen indicates that the controlling factor in the final Japanese decision to accept our terms of surrender was the atomic bomb."[40] That carefully framed sentence, by suggesting more than it asserted, managed to imply that the bomb had been essential to producing an early surrender—and that the Bombing Survey fully agreed.

The essay's calm use of previously classified documents, and its reliance on the personal authority of Henry Stimson as the author, with no acknowledgment of the role of young Bundy, helped guarantee that the article achieved its hidden purpose: ratifying the official version of the Hiroshima narrative.

Former Under Secretary of State Joseph Grew did privately complain to Stimson that the article had failed to treat adequately a crucial issue: that a pre-Hiroshima guarantee of the emperor's position would, in Grew's judgment, have produced an earlier surrender, obviating both the use of the bomb and the November invasion. Grew reminded Stimson that they had both campaigned during the summer of 1945, within the administration, for such a guarantee. In privately raising this issue, Grew was strongly arguing that the administration's insistence on unconditional surrender had needlessly prolonged the war. Thus, for Grew, the use of the bomb had been unnecessary—and avoidable.[41]

Perhaps Grew's letter propelled Stimson and Bundy, when slightly recasting the *Harper's* article for inclusion in Stimson's 1948 memoir, to make an important revision in the text. His published memoir, when discussing the administration's pre-Hiroshima refusal to guarantee the emperor's position, stated, "only on this question did he [Stimson] later find...that the United States, by its delay in stating its position, had [possibly] prolonged the war."[42] The unstated implication, undermining much of Stimson's A-bomb argument, was that there might well have been a "missed opportunity" and that the bomb then might well have been unnecessary.

No reviewer of the book noticed this significant addition, or commented on this important sentence. For defenders of the use of the bomb, the book version simply confirmed their faith. For the comparatively tiny group of doubters and opponents, in contrast, the book version probably went largely unread—except perhaps in a few cases.

UNKNOWN AND LITTLE-NOTICED CHALLENGES TO THE "OFFICIAL" HISTORY

General Bonner Fellers, who had crafted MacArthur's September 1945 statement implying that the use of the A-bomb had been unnecessary, was outraged by Stimson's article. Fellers believed, incorrectly, both that there was widespread American sentiment, especially in the churches, that "the dropping of the atomic was an atrocity," and that Stimson and Truman were trying to defend themselves in preparation for the 1948 presidential campaign.[43]

Ex-President Herbert Hoover, a recipient of Fellers's expressed suspicions, had himself strongly but privately condemned the 1945 use of the A-bomb. It "revolts my soul," he had said. According to a recent Hoover biographer, the former president, in the biographer's summary words, had stated, "use of the bomb had besmirched America's reputation."[44]

In counseling Fellers, who had crafted an article to rebut some of Stimson's claims, Hoover recommended some revisions, based upon his own interpretation of recent history: "the Japanese were prepared to negotiate all the way from February 1945... up to and before the time the atomic bombs were dropped; ...if such leads had been followed up, there would have been no occasion to drop the bombs.[45]

Hoover, probably sometimes eager to believe the worst about Truman, a Democrat, and about Stimson, an ardent internationalist who had joined the wartime Roosevelt cabinet, was basing his interpretation upon recent claims by an American naval intelligence officer, who had too smoothly flattened out the jagged pieces of recent history and of wartime Japanese government attitudes and efforts. The record of wartime Japanese government intentions and attitudes was less clear—but there was adequate evidence, consistent with Grew's postwar conclusions, to allow reasonable analysts to argue that there *may* have been a missed opportunity.

Though never publicly attacking Truman for the use of the bomb, Hoover had publicly implied a moral rebuke. He had called the bomb "the most terrible and barbaric weapon that has ever come to the hand of man." Its major use, he had stressed, was "not to kill fighting men, but to kill women, children and civilian men of whole cities as a pressure on governments." Despite Truman's characterization of Hiroshima substantially as "an important Japanese Army base," Hoover implied that the target had been primarily non-combatants, and he suggested that he found such use "barbaric."[46] His implications had attracted no public attention, and he was undoubtedly reluctant to attack the administration publicly on this moral and political issue.

Unlike Hoover, who often seemed to crave Truman's approval, physicist Leo Szilard, a Hungarian émigré who had helped inspire establishment of the A-bomb project, publicly deplored the use of the atomic bomb on Japan. In the early postwar years, despite secrecy-classification restrictions, Szilard managed to reveal that he had organized various pre-Hiroshima petitions among scientists in an effort to head off use of the atomic bomb. Acting out of deeply rooted moral concerns, he had wanted both to save Japanese lives and to prevent the Soviet-American nuclear-arms race that he foresaw if the United States used the bomb, especially without prior information to the Soviets.[47]

In the early postwar years, Szilard cast a puckish tale, "My Trial as a War Criminal," which indicted his own earlier efforts to produce the bomb and criticized Truman, Stimson, and former Secretary of State James Byrnes for their decision to drop the bomb on Japan. Despite some strained humor to deflect portions of his moral indictment, Szilard's meaning was clear: The use of the bomb had been unnecessary, its use was an atrocity and thus a war crime, and decision makers could justifiably be prosecuted. He purposely delayed publishing this tale until 1949, and then it appeared in the University of Chicago law review, where it was unlikely to attract widespread attention.[48]

In 1949, in a Chicago roundtable discussion, which was soon published in a small-circulation periodical, Szilard narrated his May 1945 efforts, in a meeting with then Secretary of State–designate Byrnes, to prevent the use of the A-bomb. Szilard's little-noticed version of that meeting, later to become a rich source for "revisionist" scholarship on the A-bomb, warrants quotation:[49]

> Mr. Byrnes did not argue that it was necessary to use the bomb against the cities of Japan to win the war. He knew at that time, as the rest of the Government knew, that Japan was essentially defeated and that we could win the war in another six months. Mr. Byrnes was much concerned about the spreading of Russian influence in Europe; Rumania, Bulgaria, Yugoslavia, Czechoslovokia, and Hungary were all living under a shadow cast by Russia... [H]is view that our possessing and demonstrating the bomb would make Russia more manageable in Europe I was not able to share.

Here were major themes: that Byrnes and others knew that Japan was near defeat, and presumably six months from surrender; that the use of the bomb was militarily unnecessary; and that Byrnes understood that and wanted to use the bomb in order to "make Russia more manageable in Europe." In Szilard's version, based upon his recollection, his implicit indictment of Byrnes was far more severe than it was in Szilard's "War Criminal" tale. In Szilard's roundtable recollection, Byrnes was, in effect, being charged with killing many Japanese in order to conduct the early Cold War against the Soviet Union. There was a suggestive but unstated implication that such motivation might also have shaped the decisions of other high-level American policymakers in 1945 to drop the atomic bomb on Japan.

Two years later, some additional seemingly supportive evidence emerged for this line of interpretation, when large parts of the World War II diaries of former Secretary of the Navy James Forrestal were published. Among the important but little-noticed segments was Forrestal's diary entry for July 28, 1945, involving his conversation with Secretary Byrnes at Potsdam, where American leaders were meeting with their British and Soviet counterparts. For July 28th, Forrestal recorded: "Byrnes said he was most anxious to get the Japanese affair [the Pacific war] over with before the Russians got in, with particular reference to Dairen and Port Arthur. Once in there, he felt it would not be easy to get them out...."[50]

This evidence, along with Szilard's 1949 recollection, seemed nicely to fit the speculative conception, published by Cousins and Finletter in 1946, that the United States had rushed to use the bomb on Japan in order to end the war before the Soviets could grab territory in Asia. Such a conception also emphasized that American leaders, in conducting World War II, were very much aware that wartime military decisions could shape the postwar peace snd territorial patterns.

Forrestal's published diaries also seemed to provide substantial support for the various contentions that American leaders, before Hiroshima, knew that Japan was seeking to end the war, and therefore that the use of the bomb was unnecessary. For example, Forrestal's diary for July 13, 1945, stated:[51]

The first real evidence of a Japanese desire to get out of the war came today through intercepted messages from Togo, Foreign Minister, to Sato, Jap[anese] Ambassador in Moscow, instructing the latter to see [Soviet Foreign Minister] Molotov if possible before his departure for the

Big Three meeting [the Potsdam Conference] and if not then, immediately afterward, to lay before him the Emperor's strong desire to secure a termination of the war.... Togo said further that the unconditional surrender terms of the Allies were about the only thing in the way of termination of the war and he said if this were insisted upon, of course the Japanese would have to fight.

And Forrestal's July 24th diary entry, two days before the Potsdam Proclamation demanding Japan's unconditional surrender, reported on another recently intercepted Japanese cable: "the [Japanese] Cabinet in council had weighed all the considerations [and] their final judgment and decision was that the war must be fought...so long as the only alternative was unconditional surrender."[52]

Read imaginatively, or uncritically, this evidence of Japanese "peace feelers" could easily be interpreted to mean that all that had been needed to achieve surrender in July 1945 was for the United States to abandon its "unconditional surrender" demand. And Forrestal's published diaries, revealing far more than Stimson's publications, provided substantial evidence that Grew, Stimson, Forrestal, and Stimson's Assistant Secretary of War, John J. McCloy, had been struggling, unsuccessfully, in the summer of 1945, to modify the surrender terms and to guarantee the maintenance of the imperial system. But the evidence of Japanese "peace feelers" did not make clear what Herbert Hoover and many other critics of the A-bomb too facilely concluded after the war: that the guarantee of the emperor was the only sticking point blocking Japan's surrender before Hiroshima.

What the intercepted cables could suggest, however, was a more moderate conclusion: Japan might have been near surrender, the Japanese government was deeply split on terms, and the guarantee of the emperor was a condition that all members of the otherwise divided Japanese government insisted was essential for surrender. But some members of that government were also insisting upon *additional* terms, and therefore it was unclear—but not impossible—that a Japanese surrender might have been achieved before the use of the bomb. In later years, as more evidence became available, disputes among historians would erupt over just how possible such a surrender might have been.[53]

HIGH-RANKING U.S. MILITARY AND CIVILIAN CHALLENGES TO THE OFFICIAL HISTORY

In the few years after Stimson's article and Hoover's private counter-interpretation, four of America's highest-ranking wartime military officers, joining with General MacArthur's earlier expressed doubts about the use of the bomb, stated or implied that the August 1945 atomic bombing of Japan had been unnecessary. In memoirs between 1948 and 1952, General Dwight D. Eisenhower, the victorious World War II commander in Europe, General Henry H. Arnold, commanding general of the Army Air Forces, Admiral William Leahy, chairman of the Joint Chiefs, and Admiral Ernest J. King, wartime chief of naval operations, raised serious questions about the 1945 dropping of the A-bomb.

Admittedly, their memoir-claims, as with many memoirs, were sometimes less than accurate about past beliefs and actions. These memoirs, sometimes exaggerating pre-Hiroshima beliefs and sometimes fighting postwar bureaucratic battles for larger military budgets, could not—and should not—be taken as necessarily accurate about the pre-Hiroshima decision to use the bomb. But these memoirs also should have cast doubt on some crucial parts of the official history, and have certainly made clear that it was neither unreasonable nor unpatriotic, after Hiroshima, to question whether the 1945 dropping of the A-bombs had been necessary or just.

In 1948, in *Crusade in Europe*, Ike's memoir of his victorious effort in Europe, he claimed to recall and describe his reactions at a July 1945 meeting in Germany, when Secretary Stimson told him of the successful July 16th Alamogordo test and of the intention to use the bomb on Japan:[54]

> I expressed the hope [to Stimson] that we would never
> have to use such a thing against any enemy because I dis-
> liked seeing the United States take the lead in introducing
> into war something as horrible and destructive as this new
> weapon was described to be. Moreover, I mistakenly had
> some faint hope that if we never used the weapon in war
> other nations might remain ignorant of the fact....My
> views were merely personal and immediate reactions; they
> were not based upon any analysis of the subject.

Ike's arresting recollection of moral doubt, as expressed in his
alleged conversation with Stimson, took on greater (but suspi-
cious) clarity as the years passed. By 1963, Eisenhower remembered matters far more vividly. In his 1945 conversation with
Stimson, Ike wrote in 1963, he had opposed use of the bomb "on
two counts. First, the Japanese were ready to surrender and it
wasn't necesssry to hit them with that terrible thing. Second,
[along the lines of his 1948 words], I hated to see our country be
the first to use such a weapon." To all this, according to
Eisenhower in 1963, Stimson "got furious."[55]

Two years after Ike's first memoir, Admiral Leahy, in his own
memoir, *I Was There*, harshly condemned America's use of the
A-bomb on Japan: It did not shorten the war, it was unnecessary,
and it was immoral. Here are his 1950 memoir-words:[56]

> It is my opinion that the use of this barbarous weapon at
> Hiroshima and Nagasaki was of no material assistance in
> our war against Japan. The Japanese were already defeated
> and ready to surrender because of the effective sea block-
> ade and the successful bombing with conventional weapons.
> It was my reaction that the scientists and others wanted to
> make this test [dropping the bomb on Japan] because of
> the vast sums that had been spent on the project....
> My own feeling was that in being the first to use it [the

bomb] we had adopted an ethical standard common to the barbarians of the Dark Ages. I was not taught to make war in that fashion...by destroying women and children.

In this set of judgments, Leahy implied—but never clearly asserted—that he had held similar beliefs before Hiroshima. Perhaps he did—though strangely his diary provides no confirmation. Most likely, he never offered such moral judgments to Truman, Stimson, or anyone else in the highest ranks of the administration before Hiroshima.

In more muted, and somewhat ambivalent terms, General Henry ("Hap") Arnold, air force chief of staff, also raised questions about whether the A-bomb had been necessary. In his 1949 memoir, he revealed that, before Hiroshima, he had outlined a bombing and blockade campaign that "might cause a capitulation of the enemy [Japan]," presumably before the scheduled November 1st invasion. "It always appeared to us [himself and top air force officers]," he stated in this memoir, "that, atomic bomb or no atomic bomb, the Japanese were already on the verge of collapse" in early August, when Hiroshima was bombed.[57]

He did not focus on the possibly crucial difference between a nation being "on the verge of collapse" and its government actually surrendering. He did suggest that the air force, by its conventional bombing, had played the major role in producing Japan's surrender. But he also indicated that the "abrupt surrender of Japan came more or less as a surprise," because he and others had expected that four atomic bombings or greatly increased B-29 conventional attacks might be necessary.[58]

Probably Arnold, as a proud air force officer dedicated in the postwar period to the largest share of the military budget going to his service, was eager, by his memoir, to justify such spending on the air force. In similar bureaucratic-politics fashion, Admiral Ernest King, in his 1952 memoir written with Walter Whitehill, also cast World War II history partly in terms of emphasizing, and even exaggerating, the navy's contributions and capacities. But even allowing for such purposes, King's memoir also raised serious questions about whether, as Stimson had implied, the realistic choice had been between using the bomb or conducting the invasion. King contended that "the dilemma was an unnecessary one, for had we been willing to wait, the effective naval blockade would, in the course of time, have starved the Japanese into submission...."[59]

Shrewd critics might have asked, after reading King's account, how long before victory through blockade? And even what about the likely small, but terribly painful, losses of American forces in the air and on the sea? And such critics, had they been informed, might well have challenged King's false claim that he had argued for the blockade strategy in summer 1945 and lost to Marshall and the army. In truth, King had much earlier wanted the blockade-and-bombing strategy (often called the siege strategy), and not the invasion, but by June 1945, even before the mid-June White House meeting with the President, the Joint Chiefs, and others, King had yielded to Marshall and endorsed a combination of the siege strategy and the invasion strategy. That had been the established policy, endorsed by Truman in mid-June 1945, a month before the successful A-bomb test.[60]

To an attentive public, or even to critical historians, the memoirs of these four World War II military leaders could have raised doubts about the official Hiroshima history, if there had been an inclination to doubt, question, and probe. There was no such inclination. And despite some dissenting studies, by P.M.S. Blackett, a British Nobel laureate in physics, and Hanson Baldwin,[61] a naval academy graduate and the respected military analyst of the *New York Times*, the official history did not come under sustained scrutiny by historians, opinion-leaders, or rank-and-file laypeople. Probably Blackett's argument of anti-Soviet motives compelling the use of the bomb on Japan seemed unbelievable, and Baldwin's likening the use of the bomb to the ruthless tactics of Ghengis Khan probably also offended readers. Even more moderately phrased objections gained no serious attention.

Thus it is hardly surprising that virtually no scholar noticed for roughly a decade the challenging brief comments that former Assistant Secretary of War John J. McCloy, Stimson's wartime assistant, made in 1953, in prestigious Harvard University lectures and then in a slender book, that cast some serious doubts upon parts of the official history. McCloy claimed that at the mid-June 1945 White House meeting, amid the emerging agreement on the commitment to an invasion, that one individual had suggested the possibility of an alternative to the invasion—a warning to Japan of the use of the bomb, and a stipulation of conditional-surrender terms. In 1953, McCloy criticized the policymakers of mid-1945 for not adequately focusing on these possible options, and he suggested that clear conditional-surrender terms might have produced peace without the use of the bomb.[62] That suggestion was close to the thought, or lament, that Stimson had inserted in his own 1948 memoir, in revising his 1947 *Harper's* article. But McCloy's criticism went deeper: He suggested that American leaders had been too attracted to military means in 1945, not properly appreciative of political means, and perhaps not looking for a way of avoiding the use of the atomic bomb on Japan.

These various memoirs, despite their possible liabilities, constituted a rich storehouse of corrosive evidence that, in some analyst's hands, might substantially undermine the official history. There were strong implications, if not contentions, that some policymakers had suggested, before Hiroshima, alternatives to both the bomb and the invasion. And there was serious doubt, in the aftermath of Hiroshima, whether the bomb had been necessary, whether the invasion would have occurred even without the use of the bomb, and whether political means, and especially a guarantee of the imperial system, might have ended the war in about August 1945. Added to all this, at least two military leaders—Eisenhower and Leahy—stated or implied that the use of the bomb had been immoral.

151

EXAMINING JAPAN'S DECISION AND CASTING
DOUBT ON THE HIROSHIMA NARRATIVE

Some substantial doubt was cast upon the official Hiroshima narrative in the mid-1950s, when Robert J. C. Butow, a young American scholar of Japanese history, published a carefully researched book, *Japan's Decision to Surrender*. Based heavily on Japanese documentary materials and postwar interrogations of former Japanese officials, Butow's study was a richly textured, carefully wrought analysis. In it, he intentionally focused, albeit briefly, on the issue that Stimson had briefly raised in his 1948 memoir but had not addressed in his 1947 *Harper's* article: Might different American policy before Hiroshima have produced Japan's surrender without the atomic bombing? "In the light of available evidence," wrote Butow, "a final answer in the affirmative seems possible, even probable."[63]

Butow contended that if Prince Fumimaro Konoye, the Emperor's special representative to discuss peace terms with the Soviets, had been allowed by the Soviets to go to Moscow and had been privately presented with the Potsdam Proclamation's terms a week before they were published, "the war might have ended toward the latter part of July or the very beginning of August without the atomic bomb and without Soviet participation in the conflict." Thus, for Butow, there had been a very likely, but not definite, "missed opportunity." That could also have involved an explicit guarantee of the emperor.[64]

As an honest scholar impressed by the complexity of evidence and by the ambiguity of many situations, Butow did not seek to shape a whole chapter, or a larger part of his book, on the theme of this possible missed opportunity. And his own text often seemed sufficiently ambivalent, and his construction of events in Japan so rich in detail, that his own book at times seemed to minimize this theme of a possible missed opportunity for a surrender without the atomic bombing.

For example, in discusing the efforts of Japan's so-called "peace faction" within the government, Butow wrote, "they recognized in the atomic bomb and the Soviet entry into the war not just an imperative need to give in but actually a supreme opportunity to turn the tide against the die-hards [in the leadership] and to shake the government loose from the yoke of military oppression under which it had been laboring so long."[65] He was suggesting, perhaps unintentionally, that the peace forces might well have not been so emboldened without the recent events of the atomic bombing and Soviet intervention in the Pacific war.

In similar tones, elsewhere in his volume, Butow also noted, though not stressing, the important roles of the atomic bombings and Soviet entry into the war: "these events produced a shock great enough to crack the walls of the prison [of impasse and of maintaining expectations]. Even this shock did not result in an escape but it did force everyone...to face the full and glaring light of day—to acknowledge a fact that could no longer be denied. It was not that the military men had suddenly become reasonable," but they had been startled, and their arguments seemed strained and unconvincing. The question, as Butow emphasized, was whether the militarists would "continue to resist or would they give in?"[66] Ultimately they did give in—when Emperor Hirohito intervened to push for a conditional surrender.

Precisely because Butow's book is a mixture of narrative and analysis, and because he often leaves unclear the exact impact of Soviet entry and the A-bomb on key decision makers (the so-called "peace faction," the militarists, and the emperor) and because he does not always clearly state who made the crucial decisions and whether, for example, Hirohito would have pushed successfully for peace on August 9-10 without the A-bomb and Soviet entry, the book can be read to support different positions. To some honest readers, the bomb was quite probably unnecessary; to other equally honest readers, the bomb may have been necessary. And the matter of the bomb's role is rendered even more complicated by Butow's seemingly honest ambivalence, because Soviet entry so closely followed the Hiroshima bombing that the concatenation of these two blows left Japanese decision makers reeling, and therefore Butow seemed unsure about what might have occurred in the absence of one of these two events. Butow's own thoughtful words, cast just a few pages before the end of his volume, do not resolve these issues: "The atomic bombing of Hiroshima and Nagasaki and the Soviet Union's declaration of war did not produce Japan's decision to surrender, for that decision—in embryo—had long been taking shape. What these events did was to create that unusual atmosphere in which the theretofore static factor of the Emperor could be made active in such an extraordinary way as to work what was virtually a political miracle."[67]

AN "ESTABLISHMENT" HISTORIAN: THE BOMB WAS UNNECESSARY BUT JUST

At a different time in American postwar history, Butow's judgment, though often ambivalent, might have spurred some serious reconsideration of whether the atomic bombing had been necessary to produce Japan's surrender well before the planned November 1945 invasion of Kyushu. But in America, in the 1950s, it is not surprising that no such reexamination occurred in any substantial way. That was a period when, to simplify somewhat, there was more enthusiasm for celebrating America than for critically reexamining recent history. Indeed, despite occasional sparks of Cold War revisionist history by William Appleman Williams, the nature of the recent past seemed relatively settled and the use of the bomb was generally understood, by Americans, to have been reasonable, necessary, and just.

Among the "pillars" of Cold War orthodox history was Herbert Feis, who in the 1950s and '60s was involved in a multivolume project to defend American internationalism, to affirm the need for American involvement abroad in World War II and in the postwar period, to establish that the Soviets were primarily responsible for the Cold War, and to demonstrate that American policy was usually both reasonable and ethical. Funded handsomely by mainline foundations, as a former adviser in the State Department and the War Department, with privileged access to otherwise classified government files, Feis would have seemed, predictably, likely to buttress the official Hiroshima narrative. In 1961, in *Japan Subdued: The Atomic Bomb and the End of World War II*, and then in a revised and retitled 1966 edition, *The Atomic Bomb and the End of World War II*, Feis sought to explain the use of the bomb within the context of how American leaders sought to defeat Japan. In casting his framework explicitly in such terms, and in looking at some disputes over the other possible strategies besides the bomb, he emphasized the basic 1945 issue of how to end the war against Japan. For him, implicitly, the quest to end the war—and not the decision to use the bomb—was central in 1945.

Strangely, perhaps in ways that its "establishment" author did not intend, his two editions occasionally intruded themes and pieces of evidence, often tucked away in a few sentences or in brief paragraphs, that could undermine parts of the orthodox Hiroshima history. Feis sometimes mentioned, but never integrated into his general analysis, the wartime concern by top policymakers about the Soviet Union, their sustained efforts to bar the Soviets from any knowledge of the top-secret Manhattan Project, and some policymakers' awareness that the bomb could help the United States shape the postwar peace. In other hands, these themes might have been integrated into confronting directly, and systematically, the wartime relationship between policymakers' thinking about the atomic bomb and their thinking about the Soviet Union.[68]

Though avoiding such a direct confrontation, Feis in his 1961 edition did seek to treat these issues, albeit in a timid paragraph, toward the end of his often rambling book. After more thinking and possibly with the benefit of additional sources, Feis somewhat revised that paragrph for his 1966 edition. Here is his 1966 statement:[69]

> Some of those men who concurred in the decision to use the bomb discerned other advantages and justifications [besides simply ending the war quickly and saving American lives]. It is likely that Churchill, and probably

also Truman, conceived that besides bringing the war to a quick end, it would improve the chances of arranging a satisfactory peace both in Europe and in the Far East. Stimson and Byrnes certainly had that thought in mind. For would not the same dramatic proof of western power that shocked Japan into surrender impress the Russians also? Might it not influence them to be more restrained?...In short, the bomb, it may have been thought or hoped, would not only subdue the Japanese aggressors but also perhaps monitor Russian behavior.

This brief statement of analysis was not intended to argue that these anti-Soviet purposes had been primary, or even essential, in propelling the use of the bomb. He seemed to mean that such thinking had further confirmed, but not made a crucial difference in, the resolution to drop the A-bomb.

Curiously, in view of his "establishment" allegiances, he asserted that the bomb had not been essential. Trustingly, and uncritically, he based that conclusion on the 1946 Strategic Bombing Survey's finding that "in all probability" before November 1, 1945, the date of the Kyushu invasion, and certainly before the end of 1945, "Japan would have surrendered even if the atomic bombs had not been dropped, even if Russia had not entered the war, and even if no invasion had been planned or contemplated."[70]

Sharply separating the questions of necessity and justness, however, Feis argued that the use of the bomb had been just, both legally and morally. His argument stressed that all the major nations in World War II had sought to develop, and often used, horrible weapons, and therefore the bombing was as justifiable as the employment of these other weapons. In the minds of others, however, his argument could have led in exactly the opposite direction: those other weapons were unjust, and so was the bomb. In fact, some analysts, both during and after the war, had contended that the massive, intentional bombing of non-combatants—whether done conventionally or with nuclear weapons—constituted a violation of ethical standards.[71]

While concluding that the use of the A-bomb was not necessary, he still also sought to defend the use of the second bomb,
the one dropped on Nagasaki. He argued, questionably, that the
war might have continued for some weeks without the second
bomb. Presumably, that same logic could have led him to a different judgment about the first bomb: that it was essential.[72]

Along the way, in discussing the use of the bomb, Feis implicitly rejected Stimson's 1947 claims of pre-Hiroshima estimates
of "over a million" American casualties in the invasions and
Truman's memoir claims (escalated in succeeding drafts by
ghostwriters) that the bomb had saved a half-million American
lives. Feis simply spoke of casualties that might have reached
"hundreds of thousands," which suggested numbers considerably lower than Stimson's and Truman's.[73]

Judged by standards of craftmanship, Feis's two editions had
grave defects. Evidence and analysis were sometimes at odds
with one another, and some arguments seemed to conflict with
others, while various statements were simply never integrated
into the final books. Fortunately for Feis, most reviewers of his
1961 edition, themselves wedded to the official Hiroshima narrative, overlooked the book's substantial weaknesses. And his
1966 edition received similarly generous treatment, with one
notable exception—a review by a young scholar, Gar Alperovitz,
who had recently sought to demolish the orthodox view, promul-
gated by Stimson and perpetuated by others.[74]

ACCUMULATING EVIDENCE POTENTIALLY
CHALLENGING THE HIROSHIMA NARRATIVE

Well before the mid-1960s, evidence had been accumulating
that could challenge important parts of the Hiroshima narrative:
Why were the bombs used? Were there likely alternatives, and
why were they not instead pursued? Was the killing of well over
100,000 Japanese with the atomic bombs justifiable?

Stimson's own 1947 article had mentioned that Under
Secretary of the Navy Ralph Bard had urged an advance

warning to Japan, and Stimson had briefly noted that he had tried to arrange a guarantee of the emperor in the Potsdam Proclamation. In 1948, he had suggested that such a guarantee might have produced Japan's surrender and obviated the bomb. In addition, a number of high-ranking American military leaders published memoirs that explicitly or implicitly challenged whether the atomic bombing had been necessary, some implied that they had raised similar doubts before Hiroshima, and at least two—Leahy and Eisenhower—had criticized the bombing on ethical grounds. Some sources, most notably Forrestal's published diaries, revealing various pre-Hiroshima Japanese "peace feelers," seemed to imply that Truman's unconditional-surrender demand was the only sticking point in blocking Japan's surrender in July 1945, and disclosed that Byrnes had been eager to end the war before Soviet entry. Physicist Szilard also reported that Byrnes had said that the bomb was not necesssry to end the war, but that it was necessary to use the weapon in order to make the Soviets (in Szilard's words) "manageable in Europe." And Butow's book, despite some ambivalence, had asserted that a guarantee of the Emperor would quite probably have produced a surrender before August 1945 and without the A-bomb. In addition, the Strategic Bombing Survey had also undermined orthodox contentions about whether the bomb had been necessary to produce a pre-November 1945 Japanese surrender.

Adding to these sources, Byrnes in a 1960 interview stressed that he and Truman had both wanted to drop the bomb and try to end the Pacific war before the Soviets entered it.[75] And former Under Secretary of State Joseph Grew had emphasized in earlier published memoirs his own efforts to gain an early Japanese surrender by the continuation of the emperor on the throne.[76]

Admiral Lewis L. Strauss, a Hoover Republican who had served as Atomic Energy Commission chairman and had ardently supported the quest for the H-bomb, bitterly entitled his own memoir's A-bomb chapter, "A Thousand Years of Regret." Like Grew, he stressed the Japanese "peace feelers," believed that the war could have been ended by guaranteeing the emperor, and deeply regretted the use of the A-bomb. Physicist Edward Teller, the "father" of the H-bomb, criticized the atomic bombing of Japanese cities and regretted that a non-combat demonstration had not first been tried.[77]

In addition, the recent opening of Henry L. Stimson's diaries provided rich materials linking his own pre-Hiroshima thoughts about the Soviet Union to the A-bomb, and thus presumably shedding great light on the decision to use the weapon. For example, a month after Truman's entering the White House, Stimson recorded this diary entry for May 15, 1945:[78]

The trouble is that the President has now promised apparently to meet Stalin and Churchill on the first of July [the Potsdam conference, later delayed until mid-July] and at that time these questions will become burning and it may be necessary to have it out with Russia on her relations to Manchuria and Port Arthur and various other parts of North China, and also the relations of China to us. Over any such tangled wave [weave] of problems the S-1 [atomic bomb] secret would be dominant and yet we will not know until after that time probably, until after that meeting, whether this is a weapon in our hands or not. We think it will be shortly afterwards, but it seems a terrible thing to gamble with such big stakes in diplomacy without having your master card in your hand.

And on May 31, 1945, after a long meeting with the recently appointed Interim Committee, Stimson summarized in his diary what he had told the group about the A-bomb: "we did not regard it as a new weapon merely but as a revolutionary change in the relations of man to the universe and that we wanted to take advantage of this; that the project might even mean the doom of civilization or it might mean the perfection of civilization [a device] by which the peace of the world will be helped in being secure."[79]

On June 6, 1945, after Stimson met with President Truman and summarized the Interim Committee's thinking and his own conclusions about the A-bomb in the context of international relations, Stimson recorded this in his diary on that day's conversation with Truman:[80]

> I then said that the points of agreement [on the Interim Committee] and views arrived at were substantially as follows:
>
> That there should be no revelation to Russia or anyone else of our work on S-1 until the first bomb had been successfully laid on Japan.
>
> That the greatest complication was what might happen at the meeting of the Big Three [Potsdam]. He told me that he had postponed that until the 15th of July on purpose to give us more time. I pointed out that there might still be delay and if there was and if Russia should bring up the subject and ask us to take them in as partners, I thought that our attitude was to do just what the Russians had done to us, namely to make the simple statement that as yet we were not quite ready to do it....
>
> We then discussed further quid pro quos which should be established in consideration for our taking them into partnership. He said he had been thinking of that and mentioned the same things I was thinking of, namely the settlement of the Polish, Rumanian, Yugoslavian, and Manchurian problems.

At the mid-summer Potsdam conference, after the successful test of the A-bomb at Alamogordo, Stimson in his diary recorded that Truman was delighted by the news, that some advisers including Stimson no longer felt that Soviet entry into the war was necessary, and that Churchill thought that Truman's toughness in dealing with Stalin at the conference was partly attributable to the new power—the successful bomb test. For example on July 21st, Stimson noted that Truman "was tremendously pepped up" by the report of the test. And the next day, talking with Churchill, Stimson was informed that the A-bomb had stiffened Truman's resolve in dealing with Stalin. "Churchill said he now understood how this pepping up had taken place [the bomb] and he felt the same way."[81]

Concern about the Soviets, Stimson's diary revealed, even influenced the selection of A-bomb targets. Before his diary was opened to scholars, they could know only that he had repeatedly deleted Kyoto, the ancient former capital city, from the A-bomb target list in order to protect the shrines. But the opened diary revealed more, as is clear in Stimson's entry of July 24th on his conversation with President Truman: "he was particularly emphatic in agreeing with my suggestion that if elimination [of Kyoto from the target list] was not done, the bitterness which might be caused by such a wanton act might make it impossible during the long postwar period to reconcile the Japanese to us in that area rather than to the Russians."[82]

No scholar reading these, as well as similar, segments of Stimson's diary could deny that pre-Hiroshima thinking often connected the bomb to issues of Soviet policy. In assessing these sources, however, analysts would soon come to argue over whether Stimson's diary, and other archival materials, *established* that anti-Soviet motives were primary, or even important, in shaping the American decision to use the bomb on Japan in August 1945.

ALPEROVITZ'S REVISIONISM: THE A-BOMB HAD BEEN UNNECESSARY AND ANTI-SOVIET MOTIVES DICTATED ITS USE

By summer 1965, near the twentieth anniversary of the atomic bombings, American public opinion had only slightly shifted from the enthusiastic endorsements of the atomic bombings, as reported in the summer and autumn of 1945. In June 1965, when Americans were asked whether they were sorry that their country had dropped the atom bomb or whether they thought "we did the right thing," 13 percent said they were sorry, 72 percent believed it was the right thing, and 15 percent were unsure. In the same poll, 9 percent said they often felt badly about the

1945 use of the bomb, 21 percent said "sometimes," 19 percent said "hardly ever," and 47 percent said "never," with only 4 percent "not sure."[83] Clearly, the published doubts by military leaders, by Grew, Teller, and Strauss, and the suggestions of "missed opportunities" had not significantly altered public understanding, or beliefs, in the twenty years since Hiroshima.

It was in that context in summer 1965 that Gar Alperovitz published his revised dissertation, *Atomic Diplomacy: Hiroshima and Potsdam*, in what was a direct challenge to the established orthodoxy. Broadly conceived as a revisionist interpretation of the origins of the Cold War, the book was primarily devoted to arguing that Truman had helped create the Cold War by reversing Roosevelt's policy on Eastern Europe, that the bomb had greatly influenced this shift, that Truman had generally followed a strategy of delaying a showdown with the Soviets until he had the bomb, that the weapon had shaped his decisions at Potsdam, and that Truman and Byrnes had followed a strategy of "atomic diplomacy" in dealing with the Soviets in the few months after Japan's surrender. Most of these arguments were conceptually related to the book's contention that attracted the greatest attention: that the bomb had not been militarily necessary to end the war before November 1945, that American leaders understood this before Hiroshima, and that they used the bomb primarily for the political purpose of intimidating the Soviets.

At times in the book, Alperovitz treated the decision to use the bomb as an assumption that had not been challenged even when counter-evidence in summer 1945 had allegedly accumulated that Japan was near surrender, that Soviet entry into the war might well force a speedy Japanese surrender, and that the invasion was unnecessary. But in most of the book, he shifted his conception from analyzing the *implementation* of an *assumption* to his explaining the *making* of a *decision* because of the anti-Soviet benefits that were anticipated: intimidating the Soviets, and making them tractable in Eastern Europe. Though claiming that "no final conclusion" was possible, the book's tone and structure seemed to make clear that the author was sure that his analysis had uncovered *the* answer as to why the United States dropped the atomic bomb on Japan without instead pursuing other alternatives. To make his point, he ended his analysis by quoting Szilard's 1949 recollection of Byrnes's thinking, and Alperovitz contended that this statement explained the administration's summer 1945 policy: It was not "neccessary to use the bomb against the cities of Japan in order to win the war [but] our possessing and demonstrating the bomb would make Russia more manageable in Europe."[84]

That line of argument was not new. It could be traced back to Cousins and Finletter in 1946, to P.M.S. Blackett in 1948, to an obscure journalist-historian in the early 1950s, and in somewhat ambiguous form to recent work by a major Cold War revisionist, William Appleman Williams. But unlike his predecessors, Alperovitz's book had many more archival sources, numerous quotes that seemed to establish his case, and hundreds of footnotes that added scholarly authority. As important, the book never seemed angry or polemical, usually appeared careful in phrasing, and possibly disarmed some readers with its dedication to Henry L. Stimson, "a great American conservative."

Planned well before the Vietnam war was a painful issue in America, the book, despite some hostile reviews in the mainline press, soon benefited greatly from the suspicion and mistrust of the American government generated by hostility to the worsening war. Interestingly, the most thoughtful critical reviews were usually by Cold War revisionists, not by defenders of the "establishment" and its history of the A-bombing.

Alperovitz was faulted for his conception, his use of evidence, his understanding of Stimson and Truman, and his relentless advocacy. Despite his initial promise in his preface, where he treated the intention to use the A-bomb as an *assumption*, some critics pointed out that he frequently shifted tactics in the body of the book and often arrayed evidence and conceived of the matter as a "decision." Had he better understood that it was an assumption, and had he started his analysis in the Roosevelt administration with the early thinking about the bomb's use, rather than in the Truman administration, some critics contended, he would have understood the power of the deep-rooted, long-held assumption and constructed his book differently. He would not have gone looking for the overriding reasons why the Truman government used the bomb, because Alperovitz would have understood a subtle but important point: The Truman policymakers had no reason to reconsider the inherited assumption, and it *also* fit their inclinations.[85]

In the view of some critics, this inherent dispute about whether the use of the bomb was a decision or basically the enactment of an inherited assumption made a fundamental difference in understanding the use of the bomb, in explaining the Truman administration's motivation, and in analyzing why some possibly missed alternatives to settle the war differently were not pursued. Put simply, if one accepted the "assumption" interpretation, then only *very powerful* contrary evidence of other ways to gain Japan's surrender might have received a serious hearing. General notions and occasional suggestions would not have been likely to dent the powerful, long-run assumption in 1945 that the bomb would be used on the enemy.

Beyond that fundamental set of problems with the book, some critics contended that Alperovitz had failed to understand that Stimson by the summer of 1945 was not central to the administration's bomb policy, and therefore that Stimson's diary, upon which Alperovitz heavily relied, was not a good source for understanding Truman, his thinking, or his behavior.

Critics also contended that Alperovitz failed to understand that the atomic bombing of Hiroshima and Nagasaki was part of a longer-run process of American city-bombing, possibly dating back to the air war in Europe, and certainly dating back to the Tokyo fire-bombing of March 1945, followed by the fire-bombings of about 60 more Japanese cities prior to the use of the A-bomb. Viewed in that important historical context, the critics maintained, the prospective use of the A-bomb on Japanese cities had not raised profoundly new issues of morality for policymakers in 1945. In multiple ways, according to some critics, the use of the

A-bomb was virtually the implementation of an inherited assumption, and the employment of the A-bomb on cities followed rather easily from the conventional bombing of Tokyo, Kobe, Nagoya, and many other Japanese cities, and possibly also from the earlier bombings of Hamburg, Dresden, and some other European cities. In charging Alperovitz with failing to understand the historical context for the use of the A-bomb, these critics were not approving the earlier massive killing of non-combatants, but the critics were asserting that this historical context was essential to understanding, and explaining, the 1945 use of A-bombs on Japanese cities.

In addition, Alperovitz was sometimes faulted for his use of particular evidence. It was incorrect, some contended, for him to argue that policymakers before Hiroshima had viewed the use of the A-bomb and the role of Soviet entry into the war as equivalent ways of producing a speedy Japanese surrender. In Alperovitz's formulation, some American efforts to delay Soviet entry became important evidence of a *political* decision to *want* to use the A-bomb for America's ulterior purpose—intimidating the Soviets. According to some of Alperovitz's critics, however, American policymakers had not foreseen that Soviet entry into the war was very likely to speed Japan's surrender, and therefore American efforts to impede Soviet entry were not viewed by American policymakers at the time as a missed opportunity for ending the war without using the bomb.[86]

Alperovitz was also criticized over the years for asserting that each member of the Joint Chiefs before Hiroshima had specifically stated that Japan was very likely to surrender unconditionally, and therefore (according to him) they stated that neither the bomb nor the invasion would be necessary. His critics argued that he misused sources, misread at least one crucial document, conflated postwar statements with pre-Hiroshima beliefs, failed to assess memoirs properly, and did not understand that there was no pre-Hiroshima evidence that any of the four chiefs ever said that the use of the A-bomb was unnecessary.[87]

Despite such criticisms, Alperovitz's book had a very important influence on the scholarly dialogue, especially in the late 1960s and the early 1970s. He had raised important questions, emphasized often neglected evidence, and proposed unsettling answers about why the bomb was used and how its use was connected to the Cold War.

REINTERPRETING THE USE OF THE BOMB: BETWEEN FEIS AND ALPEROVITZ

Many of the criticisms of Alperovitz came together in the 1970s in studies by Barton J. Bernstein and Martin J. Sherwin. Aided in part by the opening of new archival sources, these two scholars each investigated the origins of the A-bomb project, stressed that there was an early assumption under Roosevelt that the bomb would be used, and that he had also carefully constructed a policy of excluding the Soviets, unlike the British, from any knowledge of the top-secret Manhattan Project. Despite different emphases, these two historians generally interpreted the use of the bomb as the implementation of an assumption that Truman had inherited, along with many advisers, from Roosevelt's administration. Both Bernstein and Sherwin concluded that strong anti-Soviet attitudes were present in the early Truman administration, but they argued that these attitudes confirmed, rather than controlled, the "decision" to use the bomb. Put differently, these two historians stated, or implied, that the bomb was used primarily to end the war and save American lives—but that this "decision" was made in a context where there was no desire generally, and sometimes a disinclination, to seriously consider alternatives to the use of the bomb.[88]

Both Bernstein and Sherwin contended that there may have been missed oportunities to end the war in a reasonable period without the use of the bomb. Though differing in emphasis, and sometimes on exactly why alternatives were not pursued, these two historians variously suggested that guaranteeing the emperor, awaiting the impact of Soviet entry into the war, and pursuing Japanese "peace feelers" might well have ended the war before the Kyushu invasion. Sherwin was generally more optimistic on this matter than Bernstein, who thought that it was not very likely—though still possible—that any one of these alternatives, if taken alone, would have produced a surrender before November 1945.

Focusing briefly on the Nagasaki bombing, both historians concluded that it was quite probably unnecessary. In their analysis, after the first bomb and Soviet entry, the Japanese government would almost certainly have surrendered at about the same time if there had been no second atomic bombing.[89]

Like Alperovitz and many other historians, both Bernstein and Sherwin greatly regretted the atomic bombings of Japanese cities. Both historians lamented that various alternatives had not instead been pursued. Neither historian dwelled on the small but painful American losses that might have occurred if the war had lingered on a few more weeks or even a month or so after mid-August 1945. They usually focused more sharply on the question of whether the war would have been ended before November 1945, the date for the Kyushu invasion.

Their work undoubtedly helped shift the scholarly consensus by the late 1970s to the following position: The use of the atomic bomb may not have been necessary, the weapon was used primarily to end the war quickly and save American lives, there may have been missed opportunities to end it otherwise, anti-Soviet attitudes helped confirm the long-run assumption that the bomb would be used, and the Nagasaki bombing was undoubtedly unnecessary, whatever one concludes about the Hiroshima bombing. In the lexicon or categorization of historical schools, some would term this "revisionism"; while distinguishing it from Alperovitz's revisionism, many would note that the Bernstein-Sherwin analysis operated midway between Feis's and Alperovitz's positions, and some would even informally term the Bernstein-Sherwin position "anti-revisionism" because of its sharp differences on some important matters with Alperovitz's argument.

To some analysts, the crucial measure for judging membership in a "school" of historical analysis on the A-bomb was the historian's conclusion about the role of anti-Soviet motives in the use of the bomb. To others, the judgment was sometimes more loose, and the standard was whether the historian believed that the use of the bomb had been necessary. Those analysts who employed this "necessity" measure usually did not recognize that their category would merge Alperovitz with Feis, and usually such categorizers did not know that Feis had deemed the atomic bombing unnecessary. Occasionally, the standard was even more general: Did the historians being categorized define the use of the bomb as immoral, unjust, or regrettable?

RATIFYING THE A-BOMB DECISION BUT ALSO RAISING DOUBTS ABOUT ITS NECESSITY

In 1975, in *Air Force Magazine*, issued by the Air Force Association, a pro-service organization supported by air force veterans and the aerospace industry, an official air force historian, Herman Wolk, writing near the thirtieth anniversary of Hiroshima and Nagasaki, published a brief article, "The B-29, the A-bomb, and the Japanese Surrender." Much of that essay focused on the exploits of the B-29s in the war, the pressures by General Arnold, the air force chieftain, on Major General Curtis LeMay to produce dramatic results with this new, expensive bomber, and LeMay's decision to abandon the older tactics of daylight precision bombing and to move to night-time area bombing, beginning with the massive Tokyo fire-raid of March 9–10, 1945.[90]

Celebrating this breakthrough in tactics, which probably killed about 80,000 and injured another 40,000, Wolk wrote with admiration: "The big bombers swept in at low altitude. The Japanese were caught unprepared. In this respect, it was like Pearl Harbor."[91]

According to Wolk, these successful bombing tactics, repeated on other Japanese cities, emboldened LeMay in June 1945, shortly before the mid-June White House meeting on the Kyushu invasion, to promise General Arnold "that by October 1, 1945, Japan's industrial centers would be destroyed and Japan would no longer be able to continue the conflict." "To Arnold," partly in Wolk's own words, "the answer was clear: 'If we could win the war by bombing, it would be unnecessary for the ground troops to make a landing on the shores of Japan.'" Acording to Wolk, "Arnold, LeMay, and other airmen were convinced [in June and July 1945, before the Potsdam meeting] an invasion would not be required," because conventional bombing would win the war before November 1945.[92]

In a segment of his article subtitled "A-Bomb Not Needed: Arnold," this official air force historian concluded that Arnold believed before Hiroshima that dropping the A-bomb was unnecessary. Before Hiroshima, in Wolk's own words, "Arnold declared that in his view it was not necessary militarily to drop the atomic bomb." Was Arnold correct? If the bombs had not been used, would Japan have surrendered before November, the date for the Kyushu invasion? While avoiding a direct answer, Wolk said that "Arnold, Leahy, [LeMay,] and King were convinced Japan could be knocked out before invasion." Implying, incorrectly, like Alperovitz that these four military leaders had given such advice to Truman, Wolk added, with seeming approval, the Strategic Bombing Survey's postwar conclusions that Japan would very probably have surrendered before November 1945 and definitely before the end of the year.[93]

Thus, Wolk, an official air force historian, in what might be termed an unofficial air force journal, mustered the evidence, while often minimizing its ambiguity, to suggest that the atomic bombing had been unnecessary and to stress that air force leaders held that view before Hiroshima. Eager however to defend Truman, Wolk also ended on the loyal theme that Truman had used the bomb "to save lives," and that his decision cannot be easily faulted. But nevertheless the implication lingered, from Wolk's essay, that the president had erred and that he may have used the atomic bombs unnecessarily.[94] Such thoughts, in *Air Force Magazine* in 1975, apparently did not provoke any controversy. There were no challenges to Wolk's scholarship, and certainly not to his patriotism.

At the time that Wolk's essay appeared, it was probably somewhat at odds with popular sensibilities on this issue. In a poll just a few years earlier, in which Americans were asked whether it was necessary and proper, or wrong, for the United States to have dropped the atomic bombs on Japan, 63 percent said "necessary and proper" and 21 percent said "wrong."[95] Wolk, in contrast, seemed to be stating that it was "proper" and quite probably unnecessary. He was very close to Feis—and closer to Alperovitz than most would have recognized.

WORLD WAR II "VETERANS" ENTER THE DISPUTE OVER THE BOMB'S USE

In 1980–81, disputes about the use of the A-bomb briefly burst forth into a few liberal journals of opinion. In the prestigious *New York Review of Books* in 1980, after historian David Joravsky, who specialized mostly in Soviet history of science, had condemned physicist J. Robert Oppenheimer's pre-Hiroshima approval of the use of the A-bomb, journalist Joseph Alsop, who had been a prisoner of war in Japanese camps during World War II, responded with a spirited defense of Truman's use of the bomb.

Alsop's argument, based upon two journalistic books on the Japanese government's policies during summer 1945, was rather simple: Japan would not have surrendered without the atomic bombing, that government was even badly split after the bombing, and the bomb made the crucial difference in producing the surrender; without the A-bomb, the war would have gone on, "costing hundreds of thousands of American soldiers dead or disabled by wounds." In his vigorous but not very informed defense of the reasons for Truman's use of the bomb, Alsop largely disregarded the relevant historical studies of Truman's decision but did assert, repeatedly, that the president had not been "wicked," as Joravsky had implied, but both right and moral.[96]

In rejoinder, Joravsky, focusing briefly on the background of Truman's decision, but not delving deeply into the complicated issues, contended that there had been other ways of ending the war. Joravsky stressed that American policymakers "had no wish [in 1945] to avoid using the A-bomb on Japanese cities [and thus] they gave no serious thought to alternatives." Joravsky pointed to the possibly missed opportunities of pursuing Japanese peace feelers, modifying American terms for Japan's surrender, and trying a non-combat demonstration of the bomb. He contended that historians could not treat the use of the A-bomb as a matter of "tragic inevitability" until they had wrestled with important counterfactual issues: What if alternatives had instead been tried? Not to do so, he asserted, was for the historian to glorify what he called "mass murder."[97]

In important ways, the Alsop-Joravsky exchange, published under a somewhat misleading title ("Was the Hiroshima Bomb Necessary?") unintentionally revealed how little the historical scholarship of 1965–80 on the use of the A-bomb had penetrated beyond history journals and monographs into the general intellectual forum by the thiry-fifth anniversary of Hiroshima and Nagasaki. The issue of the role of anti-Soviet motives in the use of the A-bomb went unmentioned. And there was only brief attention, by Joravsky, given to the fact that some eminent Americans after Hiroshima, if not before, had challenged the morality of the use of the A-bombs.

Judged by polls shortly before and after Alsop's essay, he was clearly wrong to contend that it was "universally fashionable" to believe that the use of the A-bomb had been immoral.[98] Indeed, most Americans overwhelmingly believed the contrary: that the A-bomb had been necessary and just. Possibly in some liberal and many left circles, there was more dispute and doubt. But probably the "pro-use" position still dominated when the issue of Hiroshima and Nagasaki arose in the late 1970s and early '80s.

Perhaps feeling, like Alsop, that an "anti-use" position was triumphing, literary historian Paul Fussell, a former World War II soldier in the Pacific, entered the fray about the 1945 atomic bombings. His spirited essay was entitled, "'Thank God for the Atom Bomb'—Hiroshima: A Soldier's View." He applauded

171

Truman's decision to use the bomb, and dismissed various critics on the explicit grounds that their lives had not been at risk in World War II because they had not even fought in that conflict. Fussell declared that the bomb had saved his own life and that of many soldiers who were destined to participate in the bloody invasion of Kyushu. To add pungency, but without historical warrant, he claimed incorrectly—probably based upon journalist William Manchester's unsupported statement—that MacArthur before Hiroshima had forecast a million American casualties in the invasions.[99]

Stripped to its bare bones, Fussell's argument was that the Japanese had fought viciously, many Americans had already been killed or wounded, and that any available weapon should have been used by the United States to seek to avoid the invasion. Fussell stressed that his was a soldier's perspective, and he insisted that the experience of being in the war and fearing death gave his view greater merit than those of his critics. Unkindly, in an admittedly ad hominem argument, he derided them and their views.

In Fussell's argument, the exact numbers of possible American casualties did not really matter. In his view, the bomb should have been dropped even if it hastened the surrender by only a few days, still saving some American lives. Nor was he concerned that the atomic bombs mostly killed civilians. He answered variously that such killing had been going on for some time, and also that about 10,000 Japanese troops were also slain by the two A-bombs.[100]

Political philosopher and ethicist Michael Walzer sharply, but politely, criticized Fussell's argument. It was, he rightly said, an argument that "there are no limits at all [in war]; anything goes, so long as it helps bring the boys home." But Walzer, relying upon "just war" theory, and perhaps unknowingly echoing the 1945–46 criticisms by editors David Lawrence and Norman Cousins, among others, was asserting the principle of the immunity of non-combatants. The atomic bombings, Walzer correctly stressed, constituted terror bombings. Hiroshima, he contended, was worse than the bombings of Dresden and Hamburg, as well as Tokyo, because "it was more terrifying [and] its long-term effects were literally unknowable by the men who decided to impose them."[101]

Like Joravsky the year before, Walzer emphasized that some men in the American government had believed that a settlement with Japan was possible without either the A-bomb or the invasion. "Surely," Walzer wrote, "some attempt should have been made—not only for the sake of our own soldiers, but also for those...civilian inhabitants of Hiroshima (and Nagasaki too)."[102]

Entering this debate a month later, historian Martin Sherwin drew upon much of the research he had published six years earlier, in his prize-winning *A World Destroyed*. In his 1981 essay, he emphasized an argument from that book: that "the decision to use the bomb, which involved a decision to reject another recommended initiative, *delayed* the end of the war." In Sherwin's judgment, modification of the unconditional-surrender demand and a guarantee of the imperial system, as Grew and Stimson had variously argued for before Hiroshima, could have ended the war before the bomb was ready and thus without it use. In his 1981 essay, Sherwin did not qualify his argument with any "probably" or "maybe." He seemed certain, as did Grew after the war.[103]

But the record of the Japanese peace feelers was, unfortunately, more ambiguous. Certainty, in retrospect, as much as for Grew in summer 1945 in prospect, seems unwarranted.[104] In his essay, Sherwin also edged closer to Alperovitz, a former State Department official, in emphasizing the importance of anti-Soviet motives in shaping the policymakers' decision to use the bomb in 1945 and not to pursue alternatives instead. For Sherwin, a former Navy officer, his shift in interpretation undoubtedly arose from his honest, and sometimes agonizing, reconsiderations of the arguments, the evidence, and the implications of the atomic bombings.

THE USES OF TRUMAN'S DISCOVERED POTSDAM DIARY

In the late 1970s, a few historians had found at the Truman Library the diary, written on loose pages, that the President had kept at Potsdam. Acting separately, three different historians independently published the diary in different journals in 1980.[105] The diary was valuable because it constituted the only contemporary source, just prior to the Hiroshima bombing, in which Truman recorded his own thoughts and actions in his own words. Until the discovery of this diary, historians had relied mostly upon the diaries of presidential associates (Stimson, Leahy, Forrestal, Joseph Davies, and a few others) as well as on official minutes of meetings and postwar memoirs and recollections to seek to understand Truman's pre-Hiroshima thinking about the use of the bomb.

As with many interesting historical sources, these Truman diary entries did not always have a clear meaning on which historians would agree. The problem was that many entries were elliptical, the connections between thoughts not always clear, and the actual meaning often required the historian's effort to establish the context for the entry and to construe the diary's words within the framework of other behavior by the President, and sometimes by his associates, too. Put bluntly, historians, using various standards and means, would have to *interpret* these entries; the process was not automatic, and the "answers" were not self-evident.

Especially arresting, and susceptible to various interpretations, were the following entries, which are excerpted from longer comments by Truman on each of these days in July 1945 at Potsdam:[106]

July 17. Most of the big points are settled. He'll [Stalin] be in the Jap War on August 15th. Fini Japs when that comes about.

July 18. Decided to tell Stalin about it [the A-bomb]. Stalin had told P.M. [Prime Minister Churchill] of telegram from Jap Emperor [actually from the Japanese Foreign Secretary] asking for peace. Stalin also read his answer to me. It was satisfactory. Believe Japs will fold before Russia comes in.

I am sure they will when Manhattan [the A-bomb] appears over their homeland.

July 25. The weapon is to be used against Japan between now and August 10th. I have told the Sec. of War Mr Stimson to use it so that military objectives and soldiers and sailors are the target and not women and children. Even if the Japs are savages, ruthless, merciless, and fanatic, we as the leader of the world for the common welfare drop this terrible bomb on the Capitol [Kyoto] or the new [Tokyo].

He & I are in accord. The target will be a purely military one and we will issue a warning statement [the Potsdam Proclamation of July 26th] asking the Japs to surrender and save lives. I'm sure that they will not do that, but we will have given them the chance.

If taken at face value, which would be an interpretive mistake, the diary entries could seem to mean this: that Truman concluded that Stalin's entry into the war would mean the prompt end of the Japanese war effort; that Truman believed that the bomb would produce a very speedy surrender, and that its use before August 10th would thus mean a Japanese surrender before August 15th (the date promised by Stalin for Soviet entry); and that Truman and Stimson agreed that the A-bomb would not be targeted on non-combatants and would only be used to destroy a military target. In what could be called this "face value" interpretation, Truman presumably believed that the Japanese were seeking peace (on terms acceptable to the United States), and that the war could be ended speedily by pursuing these peace feelers, or awaiting Soviet entry into the war, or using the bomb. In this "face value" interpretation, any one of these three means was *guaranteed* to produce a Japanese surrender very promptly, literally within a few days, and thus the other two means could be comfortably disposed with. Most bluntly, there was a choice: negotiate with Japan; or let Soviet entry produce the surrender; or drop the bomb to produce a surrender before Soviet entry.

The problem is that these so-called "face value" versions are not really so straightforward. For example, what exactly does "Fini Japs when that comes about" really mean? Does it mean *immediate* surrender, or a likely Japanese surrender *soon*? And how soon is soon—a few days, weeks, longer? And did Truman really believe that Japan would actually surrender on August 15th, the date that Stalin had promised for Soviet entry?

If Truman had sincerely believed for more than a few minutes that the war would end by mid-August or earlier, *depending upon what he did*, he would undoubtedly have fired off a directive to his demobilization and reconversion planners in Washington: Prepare definite plans to demobilize the wartime economy, provide for immediate reconversion of military-goods factories, and get essential anti-inflation orders ready for issuance, all by August 2nd, at latest. Truman knew in mid-July that the major postwar domestic political problems he would face, right at the end of the war, were demobilizing the economy, reconverting factories, preventing depression and unemployment, and restraining dangerous inflation. Yet, from Potsdam, he never sent such an order—for immediate action. The reason, undoubtedly, was that he did not actually expect a speedy surrender, certainly not in early or mid-August. The very fact that he did not send such an order reveals that he did not sincerely believe, at least not beyond a few minutes, that Japan's surrender was virtually imminent. The diary entries, when construed in *context*, do not have a "face value" meaning.

To Truman, despite these diary entries, Soviet entry into the war was not the functional equivalent of the use of the A-bomb. The A-bomb, he thought, might greatly help produce Japan's surrender, but there was no guarantee that the desired surrender would occur very soon. Soviet entry had been valued by

Truman primarily for its *military* function of dealing with Japanese armies on the Asian mainland; and the powerful *psychological* effect of Soviet entry on Japanese leaders in Tokyo was not foreseen. In retrospect, however, it is possible to contend that Soviet entry, without the A-bomb, but coupled with the heavy conventional bombing of Japanese cities and the strangling blockade might well have produced Japan's surrender before November 1945.

In understanding Truman's diary entry for July 18th, there is great danger, if not naiveté, in taking literally his words about the "Emperor asking for peace" as an assumption by Truman that the Japanese terms were clear and that they were acceptable to Truman. It is far more reasonable to conclude that Truman's diary entry was intentionally elliptical: Japan is *talking* about peace. Truman knew from other sources (decoded Japanese cables) that the terms did not meet his expectations.

Truman's words about his alleged agreement with Stimson on choosing a "military" target for the A-bomb are more puzzling. The high-level Interim Committee had specified a dual target (a military installation surrounded by workers' houses), and the Target Committee, composed of scientists and military officers, had stressed picking urban targets partly to maximize death and destruction in civilian areas. It is unlikely that Truman was actually misinformed about the targeting by Stimson in their conversation of the 25th, and it is strange that Truman, even a year after the atomic bombings, kept insisting privately that the targets were purely, or almost exclusively, "military." Most likely, on July 25th, and perhaps even in the more distant aftermath of Nagasaki and Hiroshima, the President was engaging in self-deception: He could not bring himself to know, and to admit to himself, the painful fact that the A-bombs, as intended, would and did massively kill non-combatants.

Five years after the Potsdam diaries were first published, and after Bernstein had argued in an introduction against the "face value" interpretation and along the lines of the counter-interpretation presented here,[107] historian Robert Messer returned to this evidence to offer, with some additional materials from Truman's previously unavailable letters to his wife, his own effort to reinterpret the Potsdam diaries. Messer pointed out various ambiguities in the record, argued that issues were still unresolved, but seemed to lean rather close to Alperovitz's 1965 arguments about the reasons for the use of the bomb on Japan: gaining advantages over the Soviets.[108]

More energetically, and acknowledging no ambiguity, Alperovitz himself, in the mid-1980s, after not writing on the subject for nearly twenty years, returned to the questions of the impact of the A-bomb on American policy and why the bomb was used on Japan. He seized upon the Potsdam diary, also exploited Messer's recent work on Secretary of State Byrnes, and reissued his 1965 *Atomic Diplomacy* with an extended new introduction reasserting most of his old conclusions. In that new introduction, however, he did back away from his earlier claims that Stimson had been central in Truman's 1945 A-bomb policy, substituted Byrnes for Stimson as an important architect of 1945 policy, but still did not treat the use of the bomb as the implementation of a long-run assumption.[109]

A few years later, in joining with Messer, who was more inclined also to acknowledge bureaucratic reasons for the use of the bomb, Alperovitz collaborated on what constituted a melding of Alperovitz's 1985 introduction and Messer's 1985 essay into a firm statement that the bomb had been unnecessary to produce Japan's speedy surrender, that American leaders had known this before Hiroshima, and that they had primarily used the bomb for ulterior political, not military, purposes.[110]

SOURCES AND DISPUTES ABOUT AMERICAN CASUALTIES IN THE INVASION(S)

In the mid-1980s, two other analysts[111] assaulted part of the standard Hiroshima narrative when they raised serious questions implicitly about Stimson's 1947 claim that the use of the A-bomb had prevented "over a million" American casualties (dead, wounded, and missing) and explicitly about Truman's contention that it had saved a half-million American lives. Stimson's claim had first appeared in his important 1947 essay, and he had contended that this had been a pre-Hiroshima estimate of the human cost if the invasion occurred. Truman's had appeared in his 1955 memoir, and the number there had been ascribed to General George C. Marshall, the army chief of staff, who had allegedly provided the half-million estimate before Hiroshima.[112]

An examinaton of the drafts (prepared by ghostwriters) for Truman's memoirs showed that the numbers had escalated in later drafts. In the first draft, the number had been "half a million [U.S. and Allied] casualties with at least 300,000 dead." By the final version, the number had been raised to "half a million American lives" saved.[113]

Probably most laypeople, as well as many scholars, did not know that, in military language, there was fundamental difference between the meaning of casualties, which included the wounded and missing with the dead, and fatalities. Literary historian Paul Fussell, in his revised "Thank God for the Atomic Bomb," was somewhat unusual in not conflating casualties with fatalities.[114] Nor did many understand that the ratio of fatalities to total casualties in many of the major Pacific battles was about one to four for American forces. To most, unaware of such distinctions, the bomb's significance was simple: It had saved a half-million or perhaps a million American lives.

In the mid-1980s, Bernstein, citing recently opened Joint Chiefs of Staff papers and related archives, questioned these claims. A study by the Joint War Plans War Committee (JWPC), an advisory committee to the Joint Chiefs, showed that on June 15, 1945, they had roughly estimated (they called it an "educated guess") the following human costs in the three invasion-operations then being considered:[115]

 * the most likely, an autumn 1945 attack on southern Kyushu, followed by the Tokyo plain [in early 1946]— about 40,000 American dead, 150,000 wounded, and 2,500

missing;

* the least likely, an autumn 1945 attack on southern Kyushu, followed by northwestern Kyushu—25,000 Americans dead, 105,000 wounded, and 2,500 missing;

* an autumn 1945 attack on southern Kyushu, followed by northwestern Kyushu and then [in early 1946] the Tokyo plain—46,000 American dead, 170,000 wounded, and 4,000 missing in action.

Clearly, all these estimates fell far short—by at least 454,000—of Truman's later claims of a half-million American dead. And the JWPC's highest estimate, of 220,000 casualties, also fell very far short of Stimson's later claim of "over a million."

At the June 18th White House meeting, according to Bernstein, Admiral Leahy, focusing on the casualty rate for American forces at Okinawa, where the bloody campaign was almost finished, suggested a casualty rate of 35 percent in the Kyushu operation. Bernstein assumed that Leahy meant 35 percent of the *total* American force of about 767,000 which would have translated into about 268,000 casualties, or if the actual Okinawa rate was only about 29 percent, then about 230,000 American casualties. Leahy's numbers, if he meant 268,000 or 230,000, were speedily dismissed by another advisory committee, the Joint Planning Staff (JPS) in the next few weeks.[116]

Dismayingly, Bernstein had forgotten about Leahy's own diary for that June 18th White House meeting. It stated: "General Marshall is of the opinion that [the Kyushu operation] will not cost us in casualties more than 63,000 of the 190,000 combatant troops estimated as necessary for the operation."[117] That entry suggested that Leahy's own estimate, based upon the Okinawa casualty rate, also referred *only* to the 190,000 "combatant troops," and thus Leahy was suggesting about 66,500 American casualties, roughly the same number as Marshall's figure. In effect, then, Marshall and Leahy agreed. Since the ratio of casualties to fatalities was usually about four to one, that translated into about 16,000–17,000 American dead.

Unfortunately, Bernstein's article had not closely examined the period from early July to early August 1945, when the A-bombs were used. Had he done so, he would have recognized, as army historian Edward Drea pointed out in a book a few years later, that the Japanese military buildup on Kyushu increased substantially in this period. Indeed, it more than doubled over Marshall's mid-June 1945 estimate, and MacArthur's own intelligence chief was becoming very uneasy by late July. Marshall himself, with new decoded intercepts of Japanese communications on the buildup, decided in early August, on the day after the Hiroshima bombing, to question MacArthur about whether a landing elsewhere should be conducted instead. MacArthur, undoubtedly eager to lead the Kyushu operation, quickly cabled comforting words to Marshall, who decided to stick with the Kyushu plan.[118]

While Drea's research suggested that the mid-June 1945 American estimates were possibly too optimistic, his own study did not provide any evidence of *specific* higher estimates from July or early August. Read sympathetically, his analysis suggested that the Kyushu casualties might have been about 53,000, including about 14,000 Americans killed or missing, in the first 30 days. Assuming between two and three months for the entire operation on southern Kyushu, those numbers would have roughly translated into 100,000–150,000 American casualties,[119] which compared reasonably well with the 132,500 casualty estimate for Kyushu provided by the JWPC in mid-June 1945.

Neither Bernstein nor Drea discussed a relatively unknown American medical corps estimate of late July 1945, assessing the likely need for blood supplies for the Kyushu operation. It estimated *battle* casualties at about 125,000, though total casualties (including non-battle injuries) were placed at about 395,000. Probably the medical planners, fearful of being caught short of needed blood, were somewhat exaggerating the numbers in their estimates. Nevertheless, their figures for *battle* casualties were remarkably close to the JWPC estimate in mid-June and not far from the number suggested by a sypathetic reading of Drea's book.[120]

The JWPC, Marshall and Leahy in mid-June, the JPS, and the medical planners had all been making estimates *before* Hiroshima. None of those numbers approached the postwar numbers issued by Stimson and Truman, which they claimed they had received from advisers. Nor is there any evidence that any trained, high-level adviser provided such numbers before Hiroshima.

After the war ended, high-level military leaders did discuss the issue of what might have happened if the war had continued and if the invasion(s) had been necessary. They concluded that the suggestion of a half-million American lives saved was exorbitant, that even the claim of 200,000 was high, and that the most reliable estimate was to say fewer than 200,000 lives and possibly only "tens of thousands." It was this correspondence in September 1945, between Lt. General John Hull, assistant chief of the Army's operations division, and Lt. General Ira Eaker, deputy commander of the air force, that further led Bernstein in the mid-1980s to conclude that Truman's claim of a half-million American lives (and presumably also Stimson's "over a million" casualties) had no basis in pre-Hiroshima estimates or in responsible post-Hiroshima military estimates.[121]

At the time of writing his analysis in the mid-1980s, Bernstein had decided not to use another military document, written by a Lt. Colonel Ennis in April 1946, that roughly confirmed these estimates. Ennis, assigned to analyze the cost in American casualties if the A-bomb had not been used and if the Kyushu invasion had been launched, concluded that the total cost in American casualties would have been about 75,000–100,000 and that the war would have ended before the Honshu invasion, which had been tentatively scheduled for March 1946. But Ennis's analysis was flawed by some serious errors about Japanese decision making, and therefore seemed an unreliable, though well-intentioned, counterfactual assessment.[122]

On the basis of the June and early July 1945 estimates, as

well as the Hull-Eaker September 1945 assessments, Bernstein suggested in the mid-1980s that Truman may have felt a need after Hiroshima to exaggerate the numbers of lives saved in order to quell his own doubts. In his essay, Bernstein, because he was not focusing on Stimson, did not seek to analyze Stimson's purposes. But Bernstein's essay, "A Postwar Myth: 500,000 Lives Saved," did stress that this belief in very high casualties had "helped deter Americans from asking troubling questions about the use of the atomic bombs," and he contended that "the destruction of this myth should reopen these questions."[123]

That call for reopening the questions did not mean that the answers were obvious, nor that even lower pre-Hiroshima estimates, in the moral calculus of Fussell or some others, could not justify the use of the atomic bombs on Japan. But the call for reopening the questions was predicated upon the assumption that many Americans, more than 40 years after the atomic bombing, tended often to justify the 1945 use of the weapon because they believed that *so many* American lives were saved. Understanding that a much lower number was likely, if the invasion had occurred, might for some alter the assessment of whether the use of the bombs was necessary and just.

The evidence undermining Truman's earlier "lives saved" claims became even stronger in the early 1990s, when a historian, again working through the Truman archives, showed that a famous Truman letter, sometimes cited to bolster the high numbers, had actually been "doctored" by staff aides to suppress more honest numbers. It turned out that Truman, when queried by an official air force historian in late 1952 about the A-bomb decision, had penned his own response: Marshall had told him, before Hiroshima, that the two invasions of Japan, in Truman's words, would cost "1/4 million [U.S.] casualties [at] minimum as well as an equal number of the enemy." But a staff aide had rewritten Truman's letter to bring it in line with the recollections of "over a million" casualties reported by Stimson in both his 1947 *Harper's* article and his 1948 published memoir. Thus, a staff aide explained to the president, in presenting the rewritten letter, "Your recollection sounds more reasonable, but in order to avoid a conflict [with Stimson's contentions] I have changed the wording to read that General Marshall expected a minimum of a quarter of a million casualties and possibly a much greater number—as much as a million."[124]

While the new scholarship in the mid-1980s and early 1990s on pre-Hiroshima casualty numbers undoubtedly altered some thinking among some scholars of the Truman period and the A-bomb decision, it probably had little effect on the general public. Undoubtedly, most Americans, unaware of this new scholarship, still clung to the older beliefs, which had been buttressed by, among others, journalist William Manchester's unsupported claim, in his best-selling biography of MacArthur, that the General had told Stimson that the invasions would "cost over a million casualties to American forces alone." Trusting readers, with faith in best-selling authors, had no way of knowing that neither MacArthur's nor Stimson's files provided any support for this claim, and that Manchester's two footnoted references, which might have seemed to be the relevant sources for this quotation, were in fact irrelevant to the subject.[125]

Another best-selling author, David McCullough, a former *Sports Illustrated* writer who had become host of a television American-history series and a master of producing "good reads," seemed to provide more support for the half-million claim, in his Pulitzer Prize-winning *Truman*. According to McCullough, in a book that would often be cited by laypeople as the authority, a general on Marshall's staff in June 1945 said that the invasions would cost at least 500,000 American lives and possibly as many as a million. In McCullough's words, that evidence showed "that figures of such magnitude were then used at the highest levels."[126] Actually, McCullough had totally misread that army general's memorandum, the related correspondence, and Marshall's own memo to Stimson. The paper that McCullough incorrectly cited had made, at length, just the opposite point—that an outsider's suggestion of a half-million or million American dead was outlandish. Somehow McCullough had both misread the archival evidence and the scholarship on these archival materials—and then announced a new find.[127] Ultimately, in late 1994, after apparently disregarding some earlier efforts to have him publicly acknowledge his error, he did admit that he had made a mistake. It is unlikely that his belated correction, mentioned in a small newsletter,[128] ever caught up with the popular belief, bolstered by Manchester's volume and McCullough's own *Truman*, that the President had been told before Hiroshima, by Marshall or others, that the invasions would cost over a million American casualties or 500,000–1,000,000 American lives.

No enterprising historian, working through the relevant archives, has ever found any such evidence. All the specific numbers, available in the pre-Hiroshima period, from various experts, are much lower.[129] In view of the fact that the Kyushu operation would have involved fewer than 800,000 American troops, and that the Honshu operation, if it had occurred, would have involved about 1.1 million American troops, it is highly unlikely, even in the worst plausible circumstances, that a million American casualties could have resulted. Had the Kyushu operation proved very costly in American lives and casualties, and had the number of casualties approached even a third (about 260,000 casualties), it is highly unlikely that Truman would have authorized an invasion the next March. Most likely, he would have continued the strangling blockade and the deadly fire-bombing of Japan's cities, which even in summer 1945 was already killing many Japanese non-combatants.[130]

A RACIST WAR, THEMES OF REVENGE, AND OF CITY-BOMBING

In the 1980s, three important books by historians, though not designed to concentrate on the use of the A-bomb, provided a deeper cultural and political context in which to understand the 1945 dropping of the bomb on Japan. In a richly researched and thoughtful analysis, John Dower, a specialist in modern Japanese history, examined the racism in both the United States and in Japan in the fighting of the war. With a powerful under-standing of both cultures, he emphasized the deep racism in each nation. It was a "war without mercy," he argued, in choosing that title for his prize-winning book. On both sides there were powerful themes of cultural and racial superiority, of revenge, and of protecting an embattled nation, believed to be just and righteous. The Japanese, he reminded his readers, explained that the West was pursuing a "selfish desire for world conquest," and therefore that Japan's purposes were moral. In contrast, racism, as well as the "sneak" attack on Pearl Harbor, helped persuade Americans of Japan's, and the Japanese people's, apparently evil ways.[131]

In America, in Dower's generally accepted judgment, the war with Japan was viewed very differently from the way the war with Germany was interpreted. To most Americans, and in official American-government pronouncements, there were usu-ally distinctions between the Nazis, who were defined as evil, and the other Germans, who were often defined as basically decent but as duped or coerced. In short, there were evil German (Nazis) and good Germans. In the American understanding of Japan and the Japanese, however, all Japanese (called "Japs" even in respected American newspapers) were evil. It was not unusual for school children, as well as other Americans, to con-clude, in effect, "The only good Jap is a dead Jap." The Japanese were often protrayed as stealthy, cunning, vicious, and subhuman, as rats or simians. In comics, on posters, and else-where, they had bulging eyes, huge teeth, vicious grins; they deserved to be killed.[132]

Such racist, demeaning images on both sides in the Pacific made that war more vicious than the conflict in Europe. Each had its atrocities, but there were undoubtedly many more in the Pacific war. It was, often, a war of hatred and revenge.

Despite different emphases, two other historians—Michael Sherry and Ronald Schaffer—looked closely at the process whereby the United States had moved to "conventional" city bombing and, ultimately, to the use of the atomic bomb on cities.

Developing arguments that had appeared earlier in studies of the atomic bombings, these two authors, more fully than predecessors, stressed how much the city-bombing had prepared the way morally and politically for the use of the A-bombs. In many ways, these two authors helped focus part of the A-bomb analysis on that context—and on the implications of the mass killing of enemy non-combatants.[133]

Some of the evocative force of Schaffer's and Sherry's analyses can be suggested by reading parts of Schaffer's brief paragraph on the deadly 1945 American bombing: "Corpses scattered or in heaps....Many were huddled together....Elsewhere, remains of the dead looked like irregular pieces of charcoal, or consisted only of skeletons with here and there some charred pieces of soft tissue and clothing....Some people had turned into ashes that scattered like sand in a light wind."[134]

For those who are familiar with the painful descriptions of Hiroshima and Nagasaki, after the August atomic bombings, Schaffer's words may seem hauntingly familiar. But, in that paragraph, he was not describing the results of the atomic bombings. He was, instead, describing the results of the March 1945 fire-bombing of Tokyo, the beginning of General LeMay's new tactics for his B-29s. That successful incineration of the living, followed by similar efforts in other Japanese cities, paved the way for the atomic bombings of Hiroshima and Nagasaki.

NEWLY ANALYZED EVIDENCE ON THINKING ABOUT THE A-BOMBS' IMPACT

Because Japan had surrendered shortly after the bombing of Hiroshima and Nagasaki, many analysts had long assumed that this political impact of the bomb was both foreseen and easily foreseeable in the pre-Hiroshima period. But some unsettling information, often long available to scholars, has raised some doubts about this line of analysis.

On August 2, 1945, for example, Under Secretary of War Robert Patterson, who knew about the imminent use of the A-bomb, queried George Harrison, Stimson's special assistant who often dealt with atomic-energy matters, on whether the War Department should anticipate a speedy Japanese surrender and therefore begin promptly cutting back military-procurement contracts. Apparently Harrison counseled against any changes, presumably because such action could be dangerously premature. In summarizing their conversation that day, Patterson wrote, "It is my understanding that for the time being developments have not reached the stage that would warrant changes in our general munitions program." Should Harrison's analysis soon change, Patterson made clear that he expected Harrison to inform him promptly of the need to revise procurement.[135]

On the same day as the Nagasaki bombing, and after Soviet entry into the war, Harrison responded, again with a somewhat cautious message. He was not prepared to predict a speedy surrender and the need for a cutback in munitions procurement. Rather, he phrased matters far more timidly: "Events of the past few days are now producing evidence which, I believe, will when complete warrant, at least, a resurvey of your program. Whether the evidence when complete will justify any change in strategy or production, I, of course, do not know."[136]

That same day, Secretary of the Navy Forrestal apparently still believed that the invasion of Japan, at least the one in November, might still be necessary. Accordingly, he wrote to the President to try to have Truman appoint a navy man to direct the final campaigns against Japan. Even though Forrestal knew about the use of the A-bomb and Soviet entry, and he had earlier recorded various Japanese peace feelers in his diary, he seemed to think that the war was likely to drag on.[137] Had he expected otherwise, it is unlikely that he would have risked expending some bureaucratic-political capital in obliquely pleading against MacArthur and for Admiral Chester Nimitz, the navy's Pacific commander, to direct the final military operations against Japan.[138]

The day after both Forrestal's request and the Nagasaki bombing, Secretary of War Stimson recorded how uncertain he was about the future course of events in the Pacific war. In his diary that day, he wrote: "The bomb and the entrance of the Russians into the war will certainly have an effect on hastening the victory. But just how much that effect is on how long and on how many men we will have to keep to accomplish that victory, it is impossible to determine." He hoped a peace might be arranged in the next few weeks, in which time, he thought, a third atomic bomb would be ready for use on Japan.

On August 10th in Washington, when Japan's offer of conditional surrender arrived, Stimson was both pleased and surprised by the sudden capitulation. He had been on his way to the airport for a much-needed vacation, and instead rushed to the White House to discuss Japan's offer. At the meeting, other presidential advisers also seemed unprepared for Japan's abrupt surrender. Undoubtedly, some had hoped for this result, but they also were not ready for the sudden good news.[139]

Even after Japan's offer of conditional surrender, and while the Japanese government was pondering America's ambiguous reply on the crucial matter of retaining the emperor, General George C. Marshall was going ahead with tentative plans for the Kyushu operation, including the possible use of about seven to nine atomic bombs accompanying that November 1945 invasion. Such preparations should not be cavalierly relegated to the category of "mere contingency planning." Marshall's concern is strong evidence that, after the Nagasaki bombing but shortly before Japan's formal acceptance of America's terms, he still had serious fears that the war would continue into November.[140]

His tentative plan was to use the A-bombs as tactical weapons (on and near the Kyushu battlefield), and not as weapons against Japanese cities. Little known to historians, Marshall had argued in May 1945, but unsuccessfully, against the use of the A-bomb on cities. Clinging then to the prewar ethical distinction between targeting military installations and soldiers, and not non-combatants, he had briefly pleaded for using the atomic bomb in what he defined as an ethical way.[141] He had quickly lost on this matter, but after Nagasaki he apparently seriously revived the idea in his planning for Kyushu. He believed, on the basis of General Groves's advice, that American troops could safely enter the atomic-bombed area within thirty minutes of the detonation.[142]

Adding to the uncertainty shortly after Nagasaki about the likelihood of the war speedily ending, Major General Clayton Bissell, assistant chief of staff for army intelligence, sent Marshall a report on August 12th about the likely next 30 days in the war. Fearful that Japan might drag out negotiations or refuse to accept America's terms, Bissell warned that even additional atomic bombings "will not have a decisive effect in the next 30 days."[143]

For Marshall and Bissell, as well as for Harrison, Patterson, and Forrestal, and sometimes for Stimson too, even after the use of the atomic bomb, its likely results in producing a Japanese surrender seemed uncertain. But after the war ended in mid-August, it was often common for analysts to assume that it had been clear, before Hiroshima, that one or two atomic bombs would make the crucial difference, producing a speedy Japanese surrender. In Washington, in early August, both before Hiroshima and even after Nagasaki, there was often less optimism. At that time, in the view of some top-level policymakers and their advisers, Japan was probably near defeat. The question lingered whether Japan's leadership would rationally accept that objective situation and move to surrender—and whether the terms would be acceptable to the Truman government.

It was that very uncertainty that had led the President, without any careful thought, to agree at Potsdam to the order that the air force, even after Hiroshima, could automatically continue to use bombs on Japan "as made ready." No one in Washington before the Nagasaki bombing foresaw that one bomb, especially when coupled with Soviet entry into the war, was almost certainly sufficient to propel Japan to surrender.

What seems relatively clear in retrospect did not seem at all clear in prospect. Not to have used the second bomb—quite probably the "unnecessary bomb"—would have seemed unduly dangerous to American leaders. It would have required them to take a risk—to take a chance that the November invasion might occur—in order to save Japanese non-combatant lives. No one in Washington consciously mulled over that alternative. All comfortably accepted the use of that second bomb, and many apparently thought that additional atomic bombs—on Kokura, Niigata, and possibly Tokyo, as well as at Kyushu—might be dropped before the terrible war, beginning for the United States at Pearl Harbor, was brought to a successful end.

MCGEORGE BUNDY (STIMSON'S "SCRIBE") REEXAMINES THE DECISION

Forty-one years after the publication of Henry Stimson's famous 1947 *Harper's* article on the A-bomb, McGeorge Bundy, almost 70 years old, returned to a reassessment and analysis of the 1945 use of nuclear weapons on Japan. Writing no longer as Stimson's hidden ghostwriter, but by 1988, after years of serving as a government adviser, Bundy in *Danger and Survival* openly cast his own interpretation. In it, while reaffirming the rectitude of the use of the bomb in 1945, he also challenged important parts of the Hiroshima narrative.

He lamented that the decision did not receive adequate consideration, and he suggested that there might have been missed possibilities of ending the war without the use of the A-bomb. He disliked the slide toward virtually total war, and focused on the shift from "precision" bombing to area bombing. He also regretted that there had not been a greater pause before moving toward the use of a second A-bomb, implying that the Nagasaki bomb was unnecessary.

Unlike Feis, Bundy did not argue that the August 1945 use of the bomb had been unnecessary, but he did imply that it *might* have been. More than many previous analysts, he dwelled upon the defects of the 1945 decision making process leading to the use of the bomb. Unlike Alperovitz, however, Bundy strongly rejected any contention that anti-Soviet beliefs before Hiroshima had been important, or that they had played any role, in the use of the bomb against Japan.

Unlike Stimson's 1947 article, Bundy's 1988 book chapter ("The Decision to Drop Bombs on Japan") dwelled on the slide away from precision bombing and the wartime acceptance of area bombing as both just and desirable. In an analysis similar to Schaffer's and Sherry's, Bundy lamented, "Both military and political leaders came to think of urban destruction not as wicked, not even as a necessary evil, but as a result with its own military value. Distinctions that had seemed clear when the Germans bombed Rotterdam were gradually rubbed out in the growing ferocity of the war. Commanders continued to speak of great military results, but they were increasingly proud of urban devastation for its own sake."[144]

Bundy correctly noted that Roosevelt, who had earlier opposed the targeting of non-combatants, came to accept this new form of warfare. The newer "morality" led rather easily to General LeMay's strategy of fire-bombing Japanese cities. But unlike Stimson's 1947 article, Bundy in his chapter, drawing upon Stimson's diary, stressed as had other historians, how much the Secretary of War was troubled by the mass bombing of cities. Significantly, however, Bundy, perhaps still protective of Stimson, chose not to quote from painful segments of Stimson's diary in which the aged Secretary had deplored such bombing and then, in what had to be an uncomfortable lurch, in the same meeting discussed dropping the atomic bombs on Japanese cities.[145]

Bundy correctly understood that the intercepted Japanese cables of summer 1945 on possible peace negotiations were too unspecific, and often too confused and possibly contradictory, to meet the needs of Amercian leaders. Quoting in part from the telegram that Japan's ambassador to Moscow (Sato) sent to his Foreign Minister (Togo) on July 15th, Bundy reminded readers that American leaders would have agreed roughly with Sato's blunt words: "...your successive telegrams had not clarified the situation. The intentions of the [Japanese] government and the military were not clear either regarding the termination of the war."[146]

Like a number of other historians, Bundy suggested that

there might have been some missed possibilities to end the war without the bomb. Taken singly, or more likely together, perhaps a warning about the bomb, a warning about Soviet entry, and a guarantee of the emperor would have produced the desired Japanese surrender. But unlike Alperovitz or Sherwin, among others, Bundy stressed, "All these possible means of ending the war without using the bomb are open to question; they remain possibilities, not certainties."[147]

Unlike Alperovitz, who had emphasized anti-Soviet motives in the A-bomb decision, and unlike both Feis and Bernstein, who saw such motives as confirming (as a potential "bonus") such a decision, Bundy speedily dismissed the matter. He purposely narrowed the issues in order to rebut Alperovitz's contention. His "assertion is false," Bundy wrote, "and the evidence to support it rests on inferences so stretched as to be a discredit both to the judgment of those who have argued in this fashion and the credulity of those who have accepted such arguments."[148]

Purposely, Bundy chose not to get into a related subject: Stimson's motives, as stated in the Secretary's own diary, for removing Kyoto from the A-bomb target list. Stimson's concern that the destruction of Kyoto might push the Japanese into the Soviet camp in the postwar period in no way established anti-Soviet motives for the use of the bomb. But Stimson's reasoning did make clear, more strongly than Bundy's chapter, the relationship between pre-Hiroshima thinking about the A-bomb and the actual use of the A-bomb. The bomb was used in a context in which anti-Soviet purposes might also be fulfilled, though such anti-Soviet thinking did not shape, but only confirm, the use of the atomic bomb on Japan.[149]

In quiet but powerful criticism, Bundy implied that Stimson's 1947 article had gravely misled readers, because, contrary to that article, there had not been careful consideration, or systematic deliberation, before the use of the bomb on Japan. The process was not "as long or wide or deep as the subject deserved," Bundy concluded.[150]

Having lamented the fact of urban bombing against Japan,

and having questioned whether the A-bomb was necessary, Bundy was driven, in some agonizing reflection, to try to confront the moral problem of whether such urban bombing and the atomic bombing should have been conducted. As a GI in the Pacific who might well have been in the invasion if the war had not ended, and believing that the urban bombing played an important role in helping to end the war, Bundy avoided giving any direct answer to his own set of questions. Whereas Fussell as an ex-serviceman had been sure about the morality of urban bombing and the A-bomb, and Walzer as a moral analyst affirming the immunity of non-combatants had been equally decisive but on the other side, Bundy ended up somewhat evasively: "If as a company commander I had ventured to take Walzer's view, with officers or men, I think I would have been alone and even to reach the question of taking such a lonely view I would have had to have more understanding than I did [in 1945]."[151]

But for Bundy in 1988, as he undoubtedly understood, the real question was not what he had thought in 1945 as a soldier but what he thought, almost 45 years later, after far more reflection. It was a question he could not answer directly—and indeed the nature of his likely answer remains uncertain to readers, and possibly also to McGeorge Bundy himself. Perhaps he intended, in his closing paragraphs, to suggest his answer, when he said that such moral questions are important and then wrote, "I do not myself find Hiroshima more *immoral* than Tokyo or Dresden"[152] (emphasis in original).

By his phrasing, by his agony, and by his uncertainty, McGeorge Bundy, the former World War II officer, the former ghostwriter (he said he was a "scribe") for Stimson, and the former national security adviser to President John F. Kennedy and Lyndon B. Johnson, made clear that reasonable people, in the aftermath of Hiroshima and Nagasaki, were right to have doubts about the atomic bombings of Japan. His was not a celebration but more often a lament—for the Japanese who died and for the fact of the world that emerged, with great nuclear danger, after the use of atomic weapons in 1945 on Japan. "Whether broader and more extended deliberation would have yielded a less destructive result we shall never know," he wrote. "Yet one must regret that no such effort was made [in 1945.]."[153]

Neither Bundy's 1988 chapter nor Stimson's 1947 article had cast the use of the A-bombs as actions warranting commemoration. Stimson, in calling the bombing our "least abhorrent choice," had treated the decision as a grim, and often unpleasant, necessity. In 1988, Bundy had portrayed the decision makers of 1945 as usually unpained by the prospect of dropping the A-bomb, but Bundy, himself, in looking back, was obviously pained by the decision. Nothing Bundy wrote suggested that America's bombing of Hiroshima and Nagasaki, with well over 100,000 dead Japanese non-combatants, merited a commemoration. For both Stimson and Bundy, in the aftermath, there was nothing to celebrate—though each was grateful that the war had been ended in August 1945. Where they differed, among other matters, was that Stimson in 1947 had sought to foreclose critical examination of the A-bomb decision, and Bundy in 1988 had actually promoted criticism of that 1945 action. In so doing, Bundy had self-consciously but obliquely repudiated his earlier role, when at the behest of Harvard president James Conant, he had sought to help Stimson block scrutiny of the decision to drop atomic bombs on Japan.

THE STATE OF A-BOMB SCHOLARSHIP AND ATTITUDES BY THE EARLY 1990s

By the early 1990s, despite continuing but slipping support in the American populace for the 1945 use of atomic bombs on wartime Japan, the scholarship on this subject had shifted substantially since the early 1960s. By the early 1990s, most historians of the atomic bombing had come to conclude that the bomb was at least probably unnecessary, that the November 1945 invasion would probably (or definitely) have been unlikely even if the bomb had not been used, and that various alternative means, especially if pursued in some combination, would probably (or definitely) have ended the war without either the invasion or the bomb. Feis, Alperovitz, Sherwin, and Messer, among others, were in the "definite" camp. Wolk was unclear, perhaps intentionally, about which camp he occupied, but he seemed to be in the "probably" group. Bernstein and apparently Bundy were in the "probably" camp, though Bundy's counterfactual speculations seemed more hedged than Bernstein's speculations.[154]

For those who argued that the A-bomb had been definitely unnecessary, and that the war would have ended very soon without it, there was little incentive to ask what the cost in American casualties might have been if the surrender had not occurred in mid-August 1945, as it did, but if the war instead had continued for a few more weeks or even over two months, though ending before November. For those, however, who thought that the atomic bombing was probably but not definitely unnecessary, there was also the added question: What if the invasion had actually occurred?

Pro-use analysts might well have sketched an elaborate scenario as a challenge to the "probably" group: a November 1945 invasion, death to somewhat over 15,000–20,000 American soldiers, many more deaths and injuries to Japanese soldiers, and also many deaths to Japanese civilians in the ground battles and in the conventional bombings. In this scenario, in what might be called an unlikely but "plausible worst-case" scenario, pro-use analysts could ask whether the atomic bombings had not actually saved lives—of Americans, of Japanese soldiers, and of Japanese civilians.

Members of the "probably" camp would have to answer, honestly, "perhaps so." If the A-bombs had killed "only" about 120,000, the answer might well be, "yes." If the A-bombs had killed as many as 340,000,[155] then, "undoubtedly not." But for members of the "probably" camp, the issue was often not the number of lives saved or lost, but, rather, the *status* (noncombatant or combatant) of those killed. In the scenario involving an invasion, in which presumably many of the killed Japanese civilians would have been people who had taken up arms, they would have died as combatants, not as non-combatants. Possibly more troubling was the question of whether the atomic bombs or conventional bombs, had such conventional bombing continued into November or December, would have killed more Japanese non-combatants. At that point, the answers again depend in part on how many the two atomic bombs did kill.

In the hypothetical answers to such a "plausible worst-case" scenario, there is, of course, the related problem: Would not more Americans have died in the invasion and successive operations than if the atomic bomb had been dropped when it was? Perhaps it was this lurking question that had made Bundy so uneasy when he sought to face basic ethical issues about maintaining non-combatant immunity. No member of the "probably" camp can comfortably assert, in the absence of the use of the A-bomb, that some additional American lives could not have been lost. What members of the "probably" camp can argue is that the "plausible worst-case" scenario is quite unlikely and that there is a *fundamental ethical* difference between killing soldiers and non-combatants.

That ethical difference rejects the utilitarian arguments about the numbers killed in various scenarios, and stresses the principle of non-combatant immunity. That ethical argument does regard the earlier fire-bombings, as well as the August 1945 fire-bombings and any later similar attacks (including the atomic bombing of cities), as equally immoral. Such a position, to repeat, does not rest on numbers.

In the early 1990s, as in most of the 1980s, this kind of uneasy dialogue did not generally occur among analysts. Instead, the major dispute, perhaps unduly influenced by Alperovitz's work, was over anti-Soviet motives in shaping the A-bomb decision. To Alperovitz, that was the primary reason for Truman's use of the bomb. To Sherwin and Messer, among others, it was not primary but it was very important and probably essential in shaping that decision. To Feis and Bernstein, in contrast, anti-Soviet purposes had undoubtedly confirmed, but not made the critical difference in, the use of the

A-bomb on Japan. In their formulation, the anti-Soviet purposes constituted a kind of "bonus." To Bundy, Alperovitz's analysis was anathema, and Bundy also chose not to address the "bonus" argument. To Wolk, the whole matter probably seemed irrelevant, and he never participated explicitly in this dialogue.

Historians were sometimes unclear on whether they treated the use of the A-bomb as the product of a "decision," defined in the robust sense, or as virtually the implementation of an assumption. Alperovitz's own confusion on this matter, as reflected both in his 1965 book and in his new 1985 introduction, had counterparts often, though in less clear form, in others' works. Yet, most historians did accept that Truman had inherited a strong legacy of assumed use from the Roosevelt administration, and that the new President found no reason to reassess it and challenge it. In that sense, most analysts—stretching from Alperovitz to Bundy—acknowledged that the President had not been seeking to avoid the use of the atomic bomb on Japan.

In some treatments, the theme of the inherited assumption was sometimes linked, often subtly, with notions of bureaucratic momentum. That line of analysis could further blend with a different but related argument: that the administration might also have been wary of not using the bomb, because of the great cost in dollars and diverted resources to produce the weapon. After all, how could the President, with the expenditure of $2 billion, have ever justified not dropping the bomb on the enemy?

The various historians disagreed, sometimes implicitly and sometimes explicitly, on whether key advisers, before Hiroshima, had actually made recommendations in order to avoid the use of the bomb on Japan. In particular, Alperovitz, like Wolk, had claimed to find strong evidence that a number of the military chiefs believed, before Hiroshima, that the atomic bombing was unnecessary. Bernstein, in contrast, challenged that evidence. He further contended that no presidential adviser, including the chiefs, had ever recommended before Hiroshima not using the bomb. He thought, in considerable modification of both Alperovitz and Wolk, that some of the chiefs (especially Leahy and Arnold) quite probably had come to believe that there were other likely ways to end the war before November 1945, but he insisted that they had never given such explicit advice.

This dispute among historians about the pre-Hiroshima thinking and advice of the military chiefs and other advisers was a product of the different historian's standards for evidence. At one extreme, Bernstein greatly mistrusted memoirs and other post-Hiroshima recollections, frequently fearing that they were self-serving. In his judgment, the postwar claims by the chiefs were often arguments that they were developing not to reveal their actual past but to rewrite their past in order to secure larger postwar military budgets for their particular service. At the other extreme, some analysts including Alperovitz and Wolk felt that Bernstein was being unduly demanding. What to him seemed rigorous, they viewed as unsupple and possibly unimaginative.

A number of historians of the atomic bombing, sometimes implicitly drawing in part on the work of Schaffer and Sherry, and possibly on Wolk, stressed that the mass bombing of Japanese cities helped prepare the way for the dropping of the atomic bombs on Hiroshima and Nagasaki. Bundy especially elaborated on this theme, and Bernstein and Sherwin, among others, also briefly developed it in their studies. Alperovitz, perhaps because of his general interpretive framework, never stressed that the conventional bombing had defined the context for the use of the atomic bomb on Japanese cities.

Bundy and Bernstein, in particular, implied that post-Hiroshima attitudes about the 1945 use of the atomic bomb might be quite different if the weapon had not been used on *cities*, with the predictable result of massively killing noncombatants. Bundy, though not critical of Stimson, had lamented the slide toward total war. Like Bernstein and Messer, Bundy sharply challenged Truman's Potsdam diary claim that the bomb was going to be dropped on a "military" target, and not on noncombatants. Both Bundy and Bernstein suggested that Truman was engaging in self-deception.

Less clear, often, in the various studies, was the analyst's own ethical attitude toward the atomic bombing and Truman's use of that very lethal weapon, Sherwin clearly found it immoral, and Alperovitz's analysis, despite his dedicating his book to Stimson, powerfully led in that direction. Messer, too, seemed to fall into that camp. Wolk was loyal to Truman, and unwilling to criticize him. Feis, too, reached a similar conclusion, while arguing explicitly that virtually any weapon was moral. Bundy uneasily shied away from the questions, and Bernstein strongly implied that the use of the bomb on cities, like the fire-bombing of cities, was immoral because of the intended killing of many non-combatants. His work, like Walzer's analysis, assumed the principle of "just war" theory with its emphasis on the immunity of non-combatants.

In none of the major studies did the issue of pre-Hiroshima casualty estimates for American forces dominate the analysis or conclusions on this subject. A number of historians, roughly accepting Bernstein's mid-1980s conclusions on this subject, simply found additional reason to regret the use of the A-bomb and to deplore Truman's decision.

Thus, by the early 1990s, the earlier spirited contentions by Fussell and Alsop had very little effect on the scholarship and dialogue among historians. If anything, Fussell's and Alsop's arguments may have helped inspire a spurt of additional publications, and probably provoked a few scholars to sharpen their analyses, but none seemed to accept any of Fussell's or Alsop's major points. Bundy and Bernstein, however, in a more subdued argument than Alsop's, did emphasize that Japan's leadership up to Hiroshima was deeply divided on whether and how to seek peace. But neither Bundy nor Bernstein used that evidence, as did Alsop, to justify the use of the atomic bomb on Japan.

Some of the analysts—but not Wolk, Bundy or Feis—connected the use of the bomb on Japan to the early Cold War. To Alperovitz, the use of the bomb and postwar "atomic diplomacy" were central to the origins of the Cold War. To Sherwin, Bernstein and Messer, among others, this set of themes was important. Unlike Alperovitz, both Sherwin and Bernstein had even traced an "atomic-diplomacy" theme back to the early Manhattan Project, with Roosevelt's decision to keep it secret from the Soviets and to husband the options for future diplomatic uses of the bomb. Neither Sherwin nor Bernstein argued, unequivocally, that the Grand Alliance would have endured without the intrusion, and use, of the A-bomb. But they implied or asserted that the use of the bomb, partly because of prior secrecy in dealing with the Soviets, did greatly help to sour the peace. That was a line of argument that Feis's own work could suggest, but he steadfastly had denied that there was any postwar "atomic diplomacy" or any connection between America's use of the bomb on Japan and the origins of the Cold War.

Despite differences over the connection of the bomb's use to the Cold War, and some differences over the morality of the atomic bombings, the traditional Hiroshima narrative had been considerably undercut by historical scholarship since the early 1960s. Feis, himself, despite his "establishment" relationships, had been partly instrumental in this process. Sherwin, Bernstein, and Messer, and Alperovitz, who was sometimes treated as a marginal figure, were significant in the reconfiguring of scholarly understanding of why the bomb had been used. In the process of redefining "answers," Bundy's own agonizing work, though not essential to the process of transforming historical understanding, was eloquent testimony to the loose consensus by the early 1990s on the use of the A-bomb in 1945. He, as well as others, had helped assure that Stimson's 1947 article, as well as Truman's memoir-claims, did not dominate, or even significantly define, historical thinking by the early 1990s.

In many ways, the newer conceptions by historians had come to accept parts of the dissident thought, dating back to *U.S. News* editor David Lawrence, Federal Council spokespeople, and other critics like physicist Leo Szilard shortly after Hiroshima. The loose consensus of the early 1990s, despite differences among analysts, often drew upon the postwar doubts about Hiroshima asserted or implied by former Under Secretary of State Joseph Grew, former Assistant Secretary of War John J.

McCloy, Admiral Leahy, Admiral King, General Eisenhower, General MacArthur, and General Arnold, among others. The newer conceptions also sometimes reflected some of the postwar criticisms by John Foster Dulles, well before he was Secretary of State, Thomas K. Finletter, from a few years before he became Truman's Secretary of the Air Force, and former President Herbert Hoover, among others.

Despite the criticisms by many of these notables in the years after Hiroshima, and despite the shift in historical writing by the 1965–90 period, support for the orthodox interpretation of the use of the bomb was still comparatively strong in America. But it had weakened, considerably, since August 1945. Then, about 85 of the population had endorsed the use of the bomb, and only about 10 percent had opposed it. By 1986, slightly over two-thirds (67 percent) believed that the use of the bomb had been "necessary and proper," while about a quarter (24 percent) thought it had been "wrong to drop bombs."[156]

PUBLIC ATTITUDES AND THE 1992–93 PROSPECTS FOR AN A-BOMB EXHIBIT

By the early '90s, perhaps partly reflecting the impact of the newer scholarship, support for the 1945 use of the bomb, though still a majority, had slipped further. The poll results were 55 percent approval and 39 percent disapproval, with a large gender split (72 percent "pro" and 25 percent "anti" among men, and 40 percent "pro" and 53 percent "anti" among women). There was also a substantial racial division, with a slim majority of blacks (45 percent "anti" and 44 percent "pro") opposing the use of the bomb, while whites by a two-to-one ratio (58 percent "pro" and 28 percent "anti") endorsed the 1945 atomic bombing of Japan. In addition, there was also a substantial gap between age groups, with younger people (ages 18–44) about evenly split between approval and disapproval (about 48 percent "pro" and about 46 percent "anti"). while older people (age 45 and above) were more than 2 to 1 in favor of the use of the bombs (64 perent "pro" and 31 percent "anti"). When measured by income, poorer people slightly opposed (48 percent "anti" and 43 percent "pro") the use of the bomb, while the wealthier endorsed its use by over a two-to-one margin (68 percent "pro" and 27 percent "anti").[157]

Suprisingly strong evidence of substantial American doubts about the use of the atomic bombs appeared in another early '90s poll, in which Americans were asked whether, "if the decision had been yours to make," the individual would have ordered the 1945 dropping of the A-bombs or have "tried some other way to force the Japanese to surrender." The results were, 49 to 44 percent, in favor of "some other way." Whites evenly divided, but most blacks (66 percent to 28 percent) preferred some other way. The gender split was very pronounced with men heavily favoring dropping the bomb (61 percent "for," and 33 percent for some other way), while women overwhelmingly supported some other way (64 percent for some other way, and 30 percent for dropping the bomb). The age split was also very sharp, with younger people (age 18–29) preferring some other way by roughly a 2 to 1 ratio (63 percent to 32 percent), and people over 45 generally preferring (about 53 percent to 40 percent) dropping the bomb over some other way. The 30 to 44 age group, in contrast, preferred some other way (53 percent), with many fewer (41 percent) endorsing use of the bomb. Measured by income, poorer Americans (under $15,000) heavily preferred some other way (60 percent for it, and 35 percent for dropping the bombs), while wealthier people (incomes over $50,000) substantially endorsed use of the bomb (55 percent) and a minority preferred another way (40 percent).[158]

On a rather different question, Americans split, 55 percent to 38 percent, about whether the 1945 dropping of the A-bombs had been moral or immoral, with the majority finding that use moral. Blacks and whites did not appreciably differ on these issues, but the deep gender split, revealed in the other polls, was also reflected in this one. Unlike the other polls, however, this poll found the difference of opinion between poorer and wealthier Americans to be comparatively insignificant.[159]

Interpreted collectively, these polls indicated wide differences within the American public, with most Americans endorsing the use of the bomb, most believing its use had been moral, and most preferring that another way had instead been tried to produce Japan's surrender. On some of these issues, the percentage split had been almost 6 to 4 for the bomb's use, but on one important matter—seeking an alternative way—the majority had been slightly against the use of the bomb. On many issues, of course, there had been substantial differences by gender, by age, and sometimes by income.

Depending upon how deeply Americans cared about the A-bomb issues, and whether deep *concerns* were equally spread across various groups, defined by race, gender, age, and income, a public discussion—or a museum eshibit about the 1945 use of the bomb—might find it difficult to please most groups, unless the exhibit was reasonably balanced and unless particular groups did not seek to impose their own views on the exhibit. Put differently, an exhibit that reflected the current historical scholarship could be somewhat at odds with popular sensibilities and opinions, but not necessarily *greatly* at odds with them.

Obviously, any exhibit, to be widely accepted, would have to use a great deal of "on the other hand" and "on the other hand" analysis. It would have to avoid sharp conclusions, not find the A-bombings immoral but note that some analysts thought otherwise, suggest that there might have been other ways of ending the war, and reflect some of the divisions among scholars on crucial issues.

If, however, particular groups or organizations mobilized against an exhibit, even if that exhibit roughly reflected the scholarship, the exhibit could be very vulnerable, unless other equally weighty groups and organizations entered the fray to constitute a strong countervailing pressure. Such vigorous political dispute would not have been welcomed by any museum contemplating such an exhibit, but the poll data did suggest that there could be very substantial support for an exhibit that probed questions about the bomb's use, avoided implications that the bomb had been used for racist reasons,[160] and recognized the importance, after nearly a half-century, of looking at the A-bomb decision, its background, and its legacy. With the end of the Cold War, amid beliefs that the bomb had also helped prevent a Soviet-American war, an examination of the 1945 bomb decision and a brief look at the broader history could be enlightening.

From the perspective of the early 1990s, if the poll data had helped guide a museum's anticipation of likely political difficulities in putting together an A-bomb exhibit, the project should have seemed politically possible[161] and educationally useful. With such aims, after the Smithsonian had withstood political assaults involving its recent exhibit on the American west, curators embarking on a A-bomb exhibit should have felt both cautious and reasonably comfortable. Up to 1992-93, recent evidence suggested that even controversial exhibits would not seriously injure the Smithsonian Institution, the particular branch museum, or its director and staff. Some limited controversy, even if unsettling, might be interpreted by curators and others as evidence of education—the challenge, on the basis of scholarship, of traditional beliefs and unconsidered conventional assumptions.

With a generally liberal American press, and its normal willingness to tolerate and even support such educational enterprises, such an exhibit, if viewed from the perspective of 1992 or early 1993, should have seemed intellectually attractive. It would be a challenge to put together, but it would probably receive a generally fair reception. Such guarded optimism, of course, assumed that no powerful group or organization, which might be offended by the exhibit, could turn the tide—and persuade the press, the Congress, and various pundits that there were no justifiable questions about why the A-bombs had been used in 1945 on Japanese cities.

Ideally, such an exhibit would not want to raise questions about the courage and purpose of American servicemen in World War II, but instead should provide sufficient evidence of heroism and sacrifice to allay the anxieties of veterans. Yet, such an exhibit might still run into some difficulty with the 180,000-member Air Force Association, which resented that the National

Air and Space Musum was no longer doing "gee-whiz, gung-ho" exhibits on military technology and airpower. But unless the American Legion, with 3.1 million members, and possibly other veterans organizations became offended, the museum exhibit on the A-bomb could seem, in early 1990s planning, reasonably safe.

Thus, in prospect, for curators, for the museum, and for the Smithsonian Institution itself, the risks, when judged from 1992 or early 1993, should have seemed small. The educational and intellectual benefits should have seemed substantial. And the problems of putting together an intellectually respectable exhibit should have seemed interesting, not daunting. Living the history forward in planning the exhibit, as the curators and others did in 1992 and 1993, they had no reason to be greatly wary. They could not foresee that they were embarking upon a painful adventure, one that would provoke massive hostility and lead to the press and others disregarding much of the accumulated historical scholarship on the A-bomb decision and pillorying the museum for presenting the "wrong" history.

Because 1995 would be a commemorative year, as the fiftieth anniversary of V-E Day and V-J Day, and thus "the last hurrah" for many World War II vets, 1995 might be a particulary uneasy occasion to discuss A-bomb issues. Only in retrospect, *but* not in prospect, would this problem of commemoration loom large as a painful difficulty. In prospect, it could have added to the sense of opportunity.

CONCEIVING OF THE EXHIBIT: EDUCATING THE PUBLIC

Deciding in the early 1990s to feature a large exhibit on the *Enola Gay* and the use of the atomic bomb for 1995, the fiftieth-anniversary of the bombing of Hiroshima and Nagasaki, the director and curators at the National Air and Space Museum (NASM), a part of the Smithsonian Institution, began to think about how to construct such a display. In line with newer conceptions of museum practice that had evolved in the past two decades, they concluded that simply presenting the *Enola Gay*, perhaps with a brief placard, would be inadequate. Artifacts, whether technological or otherwise, do not simply tell their own "story." Their significance, as with the B-29 that dropped the bomb on Hiroshima, required a substantial prose exposition (a script), possibly accompanied by various pictures and related objects. To provide less information, in the judgment of the NASM director, Dr. Martin Harwit, an astrophysicist, and the curators, would have been a failure to meet the institution's fundamental obligation: to educate the public.

Thus, the decision was made, in effect, not to emulate what the Air Force Museum at Wright-Patterson Air Force Base was doing in exhibiting *Bockscar*, the B-29 that dropped the "second" bomb, the plutonium weapon, on Nagasaki. In that exhibit, the text ran about 170 words, in three brief paragraphs, culminating with a single sentence about this particular plane's place in history: "It dropped the second atomic bomb on Nagasaki on August 9, 1945, thereby bringing World War II to a conclusion."[162] Those twenty words, in the guise of a simple description of fact, actually contained a hotly disputed contention: that the Nagasaki bombing had been necessary, that it had significantly helped end the war, that the emperor would not have otherwise intervened, and that the Japanese government would not have sought a conditional peace without the bombing. Obviously, that text also omitted the whole context of World War II and the decision to use the bomb on Japan. And it also avoided any implication that the use of the bomb, even the first one, had ever been a subject of historical or ethical controversy. Nor did that single sentence, or the rest of the text, ever mention that the bomb had killed at least 35,000 and possibly 60,000 Japanese along with some Koreans, that the bomb had missed its target by about $1^{1}/_{2}$ miles, that it had exploded over a Christian area of the city, and that it had also killed more than a dozen Dutch POWs. Viewers of the exhibit would also have not known from the brief text that Kokura had been the original target city, that it had been clouded over on that fateful day and thus made the ordered visual drop of the bomb impossible, and therefore that *Bockscar* had moved on to the secondary-target city, Nagasaki.

From the beginning, Dr. Harwit and his NASM curators intended to distill the available scholarship into an exhibit, featuring the *Enola Gay*, to explain, among other matters, the decision to use the bomb, the context of A-bomb use in World War II, and the impact of the bombing for postwar history. In this conception, the exhibit would describe, and explain, that World War II in the Pacific, beginning for the United States with Pearl Harbor, seemed to be "A Fight to the Finish." That meant discussing Japan's atrocities and aggression, its use of kamikaze attacks, and America's fire-bombing of Japanese cities. A segment of the script, on "Delivering the Bomb," would discuss the development of the B-29 itself, the activities of Colonel Paul Tibbets and his 509th Composite Group, which had been created to deliver the A-bombs, and the dropping of two bombs. In rich detail, with numerous photos and related artifacts, a segment, tentatively entitled "Hiroshima, 8:15 A.M., August 6, 1945 / Nagasaki, 11:02 A.M., August 9, 1945," aimed to convey "the personal tragedy" of the death, destruction, and entire exhibit.[163]

One part of the intended exhibit was to look at the last days of the war—the roles of the A-bombs (and the Soviet declaration of war) in producing Japan's surrender. That meant discussing the emperor's intervention, and also America's ambiguous response to Japan's conditional-surrender offer. In the prospectus for this part, the curators wrote:[164]

> This section of the exhibit is important because it provides visitors with information about the controversial question as to whether atomic bombs were needed to shock the Japanese government into ending the war and whether the human suffering they produced was outweighed by the lives saved by an early surrender. These are, of course, difficult moral and political questions and the Smithsonian Institution can take no position in that regard. All the exhibit can do is to provide visitors with the information needed to think more deeply about these questions.

In sketching the "Conclusion: The Legacy of Hiroshima and Nagasaki," what was to be the last part of the exhibit and of the text, the prospectus suggested loosely connecting the atomic bombings to the nature of the Cold War, providing a video to give a range of perspectives on the atomic bombing by possibly the 509th vets or Paul Fussell, briefly noting the great buildup in postwar nuclear arsenals and the issues of proliferation, and thus suggesting the "potentially dangerous future for all civilization." It was kind of a catch-all conclusion, one described in little more than a page and, unlike much of the rest of the planned exhibit, seemingly lacking sharp focus.[165]

The prospectus speedily provoked angry criticism from some veterans, leading Dr. Robert McCormick Adams, the head of the Smithsonian, to review the planning documents in summer 1993 and to urge serious changes. Though trying to minimize his own objections, he stressed that the exhibit should not focus on the atomic bombing but, rather, "should be an exhibit commemorating the end of World War II, taking appropriate note of the atom bomb's central role in one theater [of the war], and seeing that decision-point as a decisive determinant of [future] decades of strategic and political thinking ..." Thus, he wanted the title revised, from "The Crossroads: The End of World War II, the Atomic Bomb, and the Onset of the Cold War," to, basically, "The End of World War II and the Atomic Bomb." He admitted that he did not really care about the title "Crossroads," but he seemed to think that his proposed title, perhaps by eliminating the reference to the Cold War, would protect the Smithsonian from assaults. Strangely, despite his fears of focusing on the atomic bombings, he retained the reference to the bomb in the title. Perhaps he did not want to appear to be emasculating the original purpose and focus, and possibly he was somewhat ambivalent. In addition to some surgery on the title, he also proposed eliminating the introductory section to the exhibit. Adams explained, "we can reply to critics concerned about the atomic bomb as the subject of an exhibit from any direction that this is essentially an exhibit commemorating the end of World War II and naturally also examining its sequala."[166]

The planning documents had also spoken of the exhibit as a commemoration, but certainly not as a celebration. In their plans, NASM would seize upon the fiftieth anniversary to explore, and to allow visitors to consider, "a thoughtful and balanced re-examination" of many key events and themes related to the "decision" to use the A-bomb. Adams also spoke of "commemorating," but he may have had a different conception of tone and purpose. He certainly had a quite different conception of the focus—mostly on the war, possibly in Europe and Asia, and far less on the bomb.

He worried, he stated, that sections of the planning document "treat fully and sympathetically the horrors of the bombing—the fire-bombing as well as the atom bomb—but do not present in adequate depth what were perceived as the horrors experienced during all of the land invasions culminating with Okinawa." He wanted a shift in emphasis. He left unclear whether that meant less on the horror of the bombings, or more on the many American dead and wounded at Iwo Jima and Okinawa, among other invasions, or whether Adams really wanted less on the one subject and more on the other.[167]

This concern could, and sometimes did, prove to be fundamental—not simply to the curator's later "script" (the text of description and explanation) but also to the pictures and related artifacts. Making clear the horrors of the invasions, especially for American troops, could help explain why Truman and his associates easily used the atomic bomb on Japan. Yet, emphasizing the horrors of invasions, especially if the script and pictures downplayed the horrors of the bombings, could shift the emotional balance of the presentation. To potential viewers, to other independent assessors, and to eager critics, this matter of "balance"—and what constituted balance—could speak to issues of explaining the bomb's use, characterizing its meanings to Japanese in 1945, and also implicitly justify or implicitly criticize the bomb's use on Japanese non-combatants.

At the risk of undue didacticism, the issue of "balance" warrants considerable attention as readers in 1995 and afterward think about what treatment in pictures, and also in words, would constitute balance. Should the pictures of A-bomb dead and injured equal the number of those of American soldiers killed and wounded? Or in an exhibit on the bomb, and not primarily on the war, should the focus on the bomb lead to many more pictures of those injured or killed by the bomb? Or should those killed and injured by the A-bomb receive "equal" treatment with those killed in the fire-bombings, and should each of these sets of pictures and artifacts be equal in number to those of American soldiers who were injured and wounded? And then, perhaps, should there also be an equal number of pictures of the various Asians killed and tortured by Japanese troops? Obviously, a call for "balance," given such varied treatments, even if all were based on good intentions, does not necessarily resolve the problems of visual representations.

In addressing Secretary Adams's concerns, one of the two major exhibit-curators chose, perhaps wisely, not to focus on this issue of "balanced" pictures and representation. He instead stressed that Adams's critique, when stripped of some evasive words, was really quite blunt: Don't focus on the A-bomb, but put it into an exhibit emphasizing the ending of both the European and Pacific wars. Having made that point, the curator, Dr. Tom Crouch, went on to state in his letter to Harwit:[168]

> I think that what really worries the Secretary is the fact that any morally responsible exhibition on the atomic bombing of Japan has to include a treatment of the experience of the victims. He knows we cannot escape that ... Some of our visitors, perhaps a very high percentage of them, are going to be upset by the powerful images, objects, stories and voices in the Hiroshima-Nagasaki unit [of the large exhibit].
>
> Do you want to do an exhibition intended to make veterans feel good, or do you want an exhibition that will lead our visitors to think about the consequences of the atomic

bombing of Japan? Frankly, I don't think we can do both.

In that response, Crouch undoubtedly did not think he was speaking about all veterans, but he probably did mean to refer to many World War II veterans and others, and possibly also to many of their organizations. He did apparently believe that any exhibit that stressed the suffering and death at Hiroshima and Nagasaki would risk offending the sensibilities, and political beliefs, of an appreciable number of veterans. Such an exhibit, he implied, could at least lead to the questioning of whether the atomic bombings had been necessary, wise, and just. In his view, apparently, it was the raising—even without the answering—of these questions that was anathema to some substantial number of veterans.[169]

Apparently, NASM's prospectus for its exhibit underwent more revision during the summer of 1993. The new plan, entitled "The End of World War II, the Atomic Bomb, and the Onset of the Cold War," emphasized six themes for the exhibit: "Japan's aggression in East Asia and subsequent attack on Pearl Harbor; issue of allied casualties as war progressed: rationale for decision to drop atomic bomb; missions against Hiroshima and Nagasaki; role of atomic bomb in ending the war; the enormous technological impact of nuclear age." This conception meant beginning virtually with the historical context, which the curators described as, "First of all Japanese aggression and atrocities prior to American entry into the Pacific War." The curators had in mind, as they explained, "the Japanese invasion of China and her manifest aggression while attempting to grab a 'Greater Prosperity Sphere.'" That also included "the herding of thousands of Koreans and other people into prostitution for the use of Japanese soldiers."[170]

Probably relying partly upon air-force historian Herman Wolk's 1975 essay, the curators planned to discuss in some depth that the air force's mass bombing of Japan was intended to do "whatever was necessary to defeat Japan as quickly as possible with the least loss of American lives." Like Wolk, the curators asserted that "General Arnold at Potsdam in July 1945 stated ...that it was not necessary to drop the atomic bomb." In what was to be the exhibit's final major section, they planned to include "footage of the [A-bomb] missions, interviews with survivors, and the crew members." They also expected to include Arnold's judgment that the atomic bombings had provided Hirohito with "a way out [of the war.]"[171]

If the likely objections to the exhibit involved its written interpretations, this brief planning document, if implemented, should have seemed adequate to deal with most reasonable concerns about providing a historical context for the A-bomb decision. But the leadership of the Air Force Association, a pro-service group composed of air force veterans and allied with the aerospace industry, had grave objections to the entire exhibit. Meeting in November 1993 with NASM's Harwit and his two exhibit curators (Crouch and Dr. Michael Neufeld), *Air Force Magazine* editor John Correll complained about the balance, interpretation, and use of artifacts. In that November session, he charged, according to his later report, that the script's words about Japan's terrible wartime behavior did not outweigh "an emotion-grabbing artifact like a little girl's lunch box," which was left after the atomic bombing. He feared, in short, that this lunchbox might emotionally dominate the substantial part of the *Enola Gay* in the exhibit. He worried that the lunch box might triumph.[172]

To create "balance," Correll wanted pictures of dead GI's and of the victims of various Japanese atrocities. To Correll, the inclusion of pictures of suffering GIs, injured in battle, was insufficient. But apparently, Harwit feared that stressing Japanese atrocities and emphasizing dead GIs in pictures would make the use of the bomb, incorrectly, in his judgment, seem an American act of revenge. That, he felt, was unfair to Americans.[173] As a former serviceman involved in postwar nuclear testing and as a Czech emigré, Harwit may have been especially sensitive on this subject.

In Correll's argument, his own emphasis on pictures of

Japanese atrocities and dead GIs was important to provide the historical context for the A-bomb "decision," and to indicate that this context also justified the decision. Without a number of pictures of dead GIs and Japanese atrocities, he feared, artifacts like the lunch box would shape the interpretation for viewers. He seemed to fear that the exhibit would evoke sympathy for the dead and injured of Hiroshima and Nagasaki.[174]

Correll's November contentions, as well as arguments by later critics of the exhibit, often focused on the need to stress Japanese atrocities. Part of that argument, reflecting Fussell's 1981 essay, was that Japan's atrocities justified America's use of virtually any weapon, even against Japanese non-combatants. There was, in that argument, an apparent belief in the collective responsibility of peoples: Whatever the Japanese government or its army did, meant that Japan's non-combatants could, and should, be massively killed, In 1993, Correll, like most Americans in 1945, rejected the earlier ethical standard of the immunity of non-combatants.

At this November 1993 meeting, Correll also complained about the pre-Hiroshima casualty estimates for the American invasion(s) of Japan. He wanted high numbers; apparently the script-writers presented him with much lower numbers, and he seemed aggrieved that Truman's postwar claim of a "half-million" saved American lives would not be included. On the basis of this discussion, Correll concluded that the script would not provide any specific pre-Hiroshima casualty estimates. In his judgment, that was unacceptable and reflected the script-writer's bias. He believed that high numbers were a "key point in the decision to drop the bomb." Correll concluded that the museum's reluctance to provide pictures of Japanese atrocities and of dead GIs, and to give high casualty figures, was all part of the plan "to tilt the balance toward the point we believe they are really trying to make, and to which we object."[175]

It is not precisely clear what Correll thought NASM's "point" was. Apparently, at minimum, raising questions about the use of the A-bomb was, in his judgment, irresponsible, ahistorical, prejudiced, anti-military, anti-nuclear, anti-air force, and close to being unpatriotic. Whether he actually distinguished between raising questions, which the curators sought to do, and giving answers, which they claimed they did not want to do, remains unclear. He obviously felt strongly that the exhibit, though featuring the *Enola Gay* (only part of it fuselage could fit), was giving or suggesting only one line of answers.

He may sincerely have not fully realized that many patriotic Americans, including Arnold, Eisenhower, MacArthur, Leahy, King, and LeMay, among others, had raised questions about Hiroshima. In his own magazine, in 1975, official air force historian Herman Wolk had even contended that some of these men had thought before Hiroshima that the invasion was unnecessary, that Arnold had opposed the use of the A-bomb, and that a few others had implied that it would be unnecessary.[176]

The problem seemed to be that Correll, unlike Stimson, who had viewed the atomic bombing as the "least abhorrent choice," did not want any implication that those injured or killed by the bomb merited any sympathy. He seemed to feel that no Japanese in World War II, even non-combatants, could be "innocent victims." For Correll, the moral, political, and historical issues were clear: The use of the bomb had been necessary, wise, and just. He emphatically affirmed the Hiroshima narrative in its most enthusiastic form. He seemed unconcerned, and perhaps largely uninformed, that the scholarship of the past thirty years, including McGeorge Bundy's own work, had challenged important parts of that orthodox history.

What Harwit and the script-writers did not anticipate in late 1993 was that Correll's version of the A-bomb history would triumph, that the museum would be pilloried for its planned exhibit, that some sentences would be skillfully taken out of context to pummel the museum and the exhibit, and that many critics, including respected journalists, would reveal how little they knew about the development of the scholarship on the A-bomb "decision" in the years since the early 1960s. What would frequently triumph, in the virtual "war" over the exhibit, would be the view that there was only one history of the atomic bombing, that Truman and Correll had it right, and that anything else was foolish at best, and possibly anti-American in purpose.

THE DRAFT-SCRIPT: MOSTLY MINOR CRITICISMS AND ACCOLADES

Despite Smithsonian secretary Adams's criticisms in summer 1993 and Correll's complaints, the exhibit's script, in its first version, a January 1994 draft, adhered rather closely to NASM's earlier conceptions. Entitled "The Crossroads: The End of World War II, the Atomic Bomb and the Origins of the Cold War," the script was divided into five units, as the 1993 prospectus had indicated, and it sought to distill the current scholarship into a narrative, with some causal analysis, to explain the use of the bomb, to discuss the actual delivery, to focus also on the human tragedy of the bombings, and to treat briefly the legacy. Compressed into about 50,000 words of text, not counting pictures and the usually short captions, the draft-script was, basically, an informed, respectable effort.

The aim of the curators had not been to do original scholarship, but, rather, to do what a good textbook does: Build upon the established scholarship, often rely heavily upon narrative and evocation, indicate and briefly discuss the major interpretative issues, inform the reader (in this case also the exhibit viewer) how most historians have treated these questions, sometimes hedge when the questions are not resolved and when there are complicated disputes over documents, and place the issues in an informative context. Such work, as with a good college textbook in history, cannot (and should not) be judged by historians of the A-bomb, or by others, on whether the text provides a clear, persistent, precise argument, but, rather, on whether it seeks roughly to follow the loose scholarly consensus, despite continuing vigorous disputes among scholars on many of the main A-bomb issues.

More than some important books and articles on the A-bomb decision, the draft-script presented the general context of World

War II in the Pacific: Japan's 1930s aggression, its atrocities, its attack on Pearl Harbor, the bloody land battles, the costly U.S. invasions of Iwo Jima and Okinawa, among others, and the fire-bombing of Japan's cities. The general aim, despite some possibly desultory segments on the American home front, was to enable readers to understand some of the salient features of the Pacific war. All this was done in about 54 pages (including pictures and captions), with the text probably totaling about 7,000 words.

Two sentences, totaling under 40 words, from this section were later to attract great attention: "For most Americans, this [Pacific] war was fundamentally different than the one waged against Germany and Italy—it was a war of vengeance. For most Japanese, it was a war to defend their unique culture against Western imperialism." These two sentences, when quoted by unfriendly critics, were often portrayed as anti-American and pro-Japanese, as naive and uninformed.

Though they were probably not the best-cast sentences to get at some important themes—of stronger American anti-Japan feelings and bitter charges because of Japan's "stab in the back" (Pearl Harbor), and of the rank-and-file Japanese understanding of the war—these two sentences were introducing, perhaps too briefly, important issues about the war. The sentences were not outlandish, or unpatriotic, or pro-Japanese. They were also embedded in a larger relevant context, one that unfriendly critics usually ignored when complaining that the draft-script did not treat Japanese atrocities, the "rape of Nanking," and other similar matters.

Here is the entire page (also on page 3 in this volume) from the original text in which those two fateful sentences appear:

In 1931 the Japanese army occupied Manchuria; six years later it invaded the rest of China. From 1937 to 1945, the Japanese Empire would be constantly at war.

Japanese expansionism was marked by naked aggression and extreme brutality. The slaughter of tens of thousands of Chinese in Nanking in 1937 shocked the world. Atrocities by Japanese troops included brutal mistreatment of civilians, forced laborers and prisoners of war, and biological experiments on human victims.

In December 1941, Japan attacked U.S. bases at Pearl Harbor, Hawaii, and launched other surprise assaults against Allied territories in the Pacific. Thus began a wider conflict marked by extreme bitterness. For most Americans, this war was fundamentally different than the one waged against Germany and Italy—it was a war of vengeance. For most Japanese, it was a war to defend their unique culture against Western imperialism. As the war approached its end in 1945, it appeared to both sides that it was a fight to the finish.

Perhaps if this segment of the script, rather than other pages, had also mentioned the racism on both sides in the Pacific war, the argument about the U.S.-Japan war being different from the U.S.-Germany and U.S.-Italy war would have been more clear. And maybe a few more words in one key sentence to make strikingly clear that the phrase about "Western imperialism" was a statement about Japanese perceptions, and not the curator's own judgment, would also have helped clarify matters. Yet, in the context of other pages, the curator's meanings were not really ambiguous. Careful critics, examining this full page of script text, could simply have asked for some polishing, what two then-sympathetic air force historians called "tweaking," in order to make minor but very useful improvements.[177]

The U.S.-Japan war, as historian John Dower had earlier argued, was a "war without mercy," and thus rather unlike the European war. In many places in the script, especially in the treatment of the bloody land battles, these themes received emphasis. In handling one very troubling matter, the response by each side to soldiers' efforts to surrender in the Pacific war, the script tried deftly to avoid giving offense to Americans when it stated: "Americans were reluctant to take prisoners and

Japanese officers and NCOs often shot those attempting to give up." Actually, an American Joint Chiefs document from mid-1944 had been less oblique on crucial aspects: "Evidence of the refusal of our [American] troops to accept their [Japanese] surrender has reached the Japanese who believe that offers to surrender will not be accepted."[178] The implication in that JCS document was that American troops not infrequently killed Japanese soldiers when they tried to surrender.

Much of what the curators called "unit 1" in their script, the lengthy first segment, was devoted to the costly casualties suffered by American ground forces in island invasions, and the air force's shift, beginning with the March 1945 fire-bombing of Tokyo, to area attacks (saturation bombing) on Japan's cities. Here, the script writers were leaning heavily upon the work of Sherry and Schaffer, and possibly on Wolk's essay, too, along with parts of the multivolume official air force history. The scholarship was sound, and the only reasonable criticism, raised by two air force historians, was that the script should make clear that these attacks on enemy non-combatants were not, simply, an autonomously conceived air force policy.

The two official air force historians—Richard Hallion, the chief historian, and Wolk told the curators, "President Franklin D. Roosevelt was the leading American official advocating the bombing of Japanese cities 'heavily and relentlessly.' Outraged by Japanese brutality in China, Roosevelt indicated even prior to December 7, 1941 [Pearl Harbor], that he wanted to see Japanese cities bombed. Arnold and [General Lauris] Norstad (and then LeMay in the Pacific) were under enormous pressure from Roosevelt and Marshall. Somewhere in the script there should be a sentence or two pointing this out."[179]

In rephrasing, the script could have taken Hallion's and Wolk's interpretation, softened it somewhat to acknowledge more ambiguities in the evidence than they admitted, and indicated the desires of Marshall (who was quoted in the script) and of Roosevelt. The large troubling interpretive question—of direct orders versus a general context of expectations—could have been skillfully hedged.

Probably these two air force historians were also correct, when focusing on the pictures in "unit 1," that there could be "more images [of] the Japanese brutality to subject peoples, 1931–1945."[180] The text itself was clear on this matter, but some additional pictures might have made more dramatic to viewers the fact of Japan's wartime atrocities against other Asian peoples. And that suggested that the single page on the 1931–41 background (quoted earlier in this essay and also appearing on page 3 of this book) might have been extended. Perhaps another few hundred words in the text would have further clarified, and could have developed, the otherwise very quick tour of the history of 1931–41. Of course, that could have required the curators to get into a difficult set of subjects—Japan's conception of its Co-Prosperity sphere, its contentions that it was displacing European colonialism in Asia and "liberating" Asian peoples by bringing them into Japan's Empire, and the economic (and sometimes political) presence of the United States in Asia.

The intellectual core of the draft-script was "unit 2," entitled "The Decision to Drop the Bomb." Conceptually, it was obviously the most difficult, because, despite a loose consensus by historians on some matters, interpretive disputes vigorously continued. This section treated the issues fairly, focused on a number of controversies involving the bomb's use and possible missed opportunities for otherwise ending the war, and often intentionally hedged, with the curators not coming to explicit conclusions.

Was the use of the bomb a decision, in the robust sense, as some analysts have suggested, or the implementation of an assumption, as others have contended. The draft-script intentionally, and shrewdly, never sharply confronted this question. Instead, the script provided evidence, usually cast in a narrative, that leaned toward the "assumption" framework. The script did quote General Leslie Groves's judgment, as well as Stimson's statement, both of which suggested the "assumption" framework. But neither statement was tied tightly to such a framework, tho the script did note that most analysts were close to the "assumption" position.

Along the way, the script-writers skillfully focused on a number of controversies. On the first, whether the bomb would have been used on Germany, they correctly stated that most historians agree that it would have been. The script did briefly note (without providing a citation) Groves's and others' thinking, as early as May 1943, about probably targeting Japan, partly because the Japanese were less likely to learn anything significant from the bomb if it failed to explode. The uncited source, the minutes of the May 5, 1943 Military Policy Committee, involving Conant and Vannevar Bush, the head of the Office of Scientific Research and Development, along with an admiral and two generals (Groves was one), stated:[181]

The point of use of the first bomb was discussed and the general view appeared to be that the best point of use would be on a Japanese fleet concentration in the Harbor of Truk. General Styer suggested Tokio but it was pointed out that the bomb should be used where, if it failed to go off, it would land in water of sufficient depth to prevent easy salvage. The Japanese were selected as they would not be so apt to secure knowledge from it as would the Germans.

Whether or not racial attitudes, as the script suggested, played some role in proposing that the target be Japan remains a matter of some controversy. The script shrewdly hedged by casting this in the subjunctive ("may have").

Many analysts of the A-bomb issues had focused, at least briefly, on the subject of Japan's pre-Hiroshima peace feelers. Alperovitz and some others had concluded that there was clear evidence that Japan had been very near surrender, but other historians including Bundy and Bernstein have challenged such contentions. Necessarily, in one of the script's sections labeled "Historical Controversies," it dealt with the question of whether the United States had ignored Japan's "peace initiative." Perhaps the question could have been phrased as one about "peace feelers" and not an "initiative," though no member of the advisory board apparently was troubled by this slight shift in phrasing. The script briefly summarized the fact that historians disagreed on the subject, and noted that some historians "have argued that the Japanese initiative was far from clear in its intentions." The script, while acknowledging that this issue of a missed opportunity was speculative and could not be decisively resolved, stated, "It is nonetheless possible to assert, at least in hindsight, that the United States should have paid closer attention to these signals from Japan." One advisory board member proposed softening this statement by inserting "wish" in place of "assert."

Had the script had space, and it probably did not, a fuller discussion of these peace signals, and of the deep split in the Japanese leadership, would have been desirable. Perhaps a July or August 1945 cable, from Japan's Ambassador Sato in Moscow to the Foreign Minister (Togo) in Tokyo, could have made clear that Japan's government had never really formulated any reasonable possible terms before Hiroshima for peace. One example would have been Ambassador Sato's August 3rd message to Togo: "So long as we propose sending a Special Envoy [nothing is likely to happen]." The day before, Togo had admitted that his divided government could not agree on peace terms.[182]

It would be decidedly unfair to blame the Japanese leadership for the use of the A-bomb, but the script might have tried to make explicit what was implicit at many junctures in "unit 2" and elsewhere: Japan's leadership, by continuing the war, unknowingly created a situation in which the bomb could be—and was—used. Such an explicit analysis, perhaps building on some of the emerging scholarship on the emperor's role, might have suggested that he was more influential before Hiroshima in the Japanese government than many earlier scholars had assumed. It might have been interesting, though admittedly very speculative, for the curators, relying upon the emerging scholarship, to have tried to cast a few paragraphs on this general theme of the emperor's activities and what he might have done.[183]

In all fairness to the curators, nobody on the advisory board including Akira Iriye, who is an expert in both modern Japanese and modern United States history, or Bernstein, who had begun to wonder about these matters, made such suggestions to the curators. That is largely because the framing of the A-bomb issues mostly in terms of America's use of the bomb necessarily focuses attention on American decisions, assumptions, behavior, and missed opportunities. Perhaps had army historian Edward Drea or John Dower been on the board, and because they were informed about the emerging scholarship on the emperor, either might have suggested this approach. It would only have involved a few hundred words at most and it would have had the advantage of broadening the script somewhat and making it more truly international in focus. Thus, there was a small missed opportunity for an additional enriching approach.

In the post-Hiroshima years, former Under Secretary of State Grew, Stimson in his 1948 memoir, Butow, and many others had raised a somewhat different issue: Could the war have been ended earlier and without the A-bomb if the United States had guaranteed the emperor's position? Most of the major studies, between 1965 and 1990, had dealt, at least briefly, with this troubling issue. There was no scholarly agreement, and the script made clear some of the complexity, the nature of the dispute among scholars, and the possibility that there had been a lost opportunity. It was a fair, necessarily brief treatment of one of the major "controversies," and that is precisely how the script labeled it.

In view of the great controversy over the role of anti-Soviet motives in American policymakers use of the bomb on Japan, any intellectually responsible script had to deal with this issue. The curator's draft-text emphasized that most scholars had rejected the anti-Soviet-motives-as-crucial argument and had generally concluded, in the words of the script, that President "Truman and his advisers saw the bomb first and foremost as a way to shorten the war." That statement reflected the judgments of Wolk, Bundy, Bernstein, Feis, and the earlier Sherwin (his

1975 book), and intentionally placed Alperovitz and Messer on the margin. Intelligently, the script did go on to acknowledge that most of the recent A-bomb scholarship had seen anti-Soviet motives as, at least, a confirming reason, among others, for Truman not seeking "to halt the dropping of the bomb."

For many laypeople, and some historians, the issue of a possible pre-Hiroshima warning or demonstration of the bomb has also raised questions. The script briefly explained many of the reasons why each possibility was not pursued, acknowledged that there had been some fears of endangering American servicemen or producing a dud, and avoided coming to any conclusion on the merits of these proposals.

Deeply rooted in the historical literature on the A-bomb is the question, as phrased by the draft-script in one of its "Historical Controversies," "Was an Invasion Inevitable if the Atomic Bomb Had Not Been Used?" Quite properly, despite problems with the Strategic Bombing Survey report, the script quoted its conclusions that "in all probability" the November invasion would not have occurred, and "certainly" the war would have ended before January 1946. The script also acknowledged that others had serious doubts about the Survey's contention. Building on the loose consensus among A-bomb scholars, the script concluded, "Some combination of blockade, firebombing, an Emperor guarantee, and a Soviet declaration of war would probably have forced a Japanese surrender." That hedge of "probably" was essential and reasonable. The script went on to conclude, contrary to Alperovitz, that this had not been clear to Truman.

Strangely, the script's treatment of pre-Hiroshima casualty estimates for the United States somewhat confused matters by omitting a crucial qualifying phrase and by also omitting some other information. The draft stated that spring 1945 military staff studies had placed likely American casualties in the Kyushu operation at 30,000–50,000 (which was correct for the range for Marshall, MacArthur, and Admiral Chester Nimitz)—but failed to include the words, *in the first 30 days*. Probably someone had simply left out that phrase in typing, and at least three members of the advisory board did catch this error. What the draft also failed to explain is that the JWPC had forecast (in a "guess" estimate) about 132,500 American casualties in the entire Kyushu campaign. For the script-writers, that omission undoubtedly seemed unimportant, because they were including a much higher number, 268,000 casualties, by Admiral Leahy, drawn from their interpretation of his summarized words at the June 18, 1945 White House meeting on the Kyushu invasion. Only later, when Leahy's diary entry for that date was focused upon, would various interpreters conclude that he, like Marshall, probably meant under 70,000 American casualties. The script very reasonably challenged the postwar contention (without citing Truman's memoirs as a key source for the claim) of over a half-million American dead. That half-million or even a higher number, the script stressed, would have been about twice the total number of American lives lost (292,000) in all theaters in almost four years of war.

In the last page and a half of "unit 2," the curators raised the question that analysts cannot avoid, "Was the Decision to Drop the Bomb Justified?" They carefully avoided answering the question, but instead summarized parts of the controversy, stressed that alternatives "are clearer in hindsight," noted that "many analysts" thought that the bombs had "ended the war quickly and saved lives," and also stated that other analysts "have argued that the atomic bombings were unnecessary," that a number of alternatives were available, and that Truman used the bomb "anyway because he wished to intimidate the Soviets."

Not to have mentioned the Alperovitz interpretation, especially since it had been joined by Messer and Sherwin, as well as some others, would have been intellectually unacceptable. It was part of the scholarly dialogue, accepted by some, rejected probably by many more, and thoughtfully critiqued by a few. But precisely because it was part of the serious intellectual dialogue— even though Bundy was withering in his brief assault on it— required that a responsible project include it. A project's task was to reflect, in part, the nature of scholarly thinking—and not to impose the curator's own historical judgment in such cases.

The script made clear that Alperovitz's interpretation was far from the consensus, and that the rough consensus was that Truman had primarily used the A-bomb to save American lives and shorten the war. In their rather deft phrasing, the curators did not make clear whether anti-Soviet motives were secondary and essential to the decision, or simply confirming and thus a "bonus." They seemed to imply the "bonus" interpretation, but it was difficult to be certain.

At least three members of the advisory board—the two air force historians and Bernstein—suggested reworking or deleting the few statements, scattered through the script, suggesting the centrality of anti-Soviet motives in shaping American decision making on the bomb. In their judgment, though perhaps the two air force historians and Bernstein would have disagreed on the rephrasing, all three men believed that these scattered sentences made too much of anti-Soviet purposes.

In the script's concluding segment of "unit 2," curators made clear that "most historians ...agree that there was scarcely any 'decision to drop the bomb.'" Truman merely approved the preparations already underway; the Manhattan Project had a great deal of momentum and the strategic bombing of German and Japanese cities made atomic bombing easier to accept."

That was a statement quite similar to Bundy's analysis, and to Bernstein's also. It was at odds with Alperovitz and Messer, and possibly the later Sherwin, but rather close to the views of Wolk and the earlier Sherwin, among others. In general, in this "unit's" analysis of the A-bomb decision and on the matter of missed opportunities, the script had usually ably reflected, or distilled, much of the major scholarship. It was a very creditable effort as a first draft.

In length, the core of the script was the unit (3) on "Delivering the Bomb." It was often full of the necessary "gee whiz" aspects that museums focusing on technology feel obligated to present. For many viewers, however, with a deep interest in the details of technology, the information on the development of the B-29 and on the problems in flights could be richly illuminating. The establishment, organization, and problems of the 509th Composite Group, created under Tibbets to drop the bomb, received substantial attention, replete with some "human-interest" anecdotes. More unsettling, undoubtedly, were the references to Japanese executions of captured American airmen, and the statistical information on the number of B-29s downed and the number of men lost as a result. It was a "unit" that would make viewers painfully aware of the perils, of the efforts, and of the heroism of air force members in the Pacific war.

Despite the difficulties in the "second" A-bomb mission, culminating in the attack on Nagasaki, "unit 3," and especially its latter sections, is designed as a narrative of triumph and heroism. The curators provided earlier, in this "unit," the evidence of the doubts, annoyance, and envy of others on Tinian who wondered why the 509th during the months before August 6, 1945, received special privileges when the group did not seem to be contributing to the ending of the war. As the script makes dramatically clear, attitudes at Tinian changed abruptly on August 6th, with the bombing of Hiroshima. Capturing the enthusiasm, the script has a segment entitled "A Hero's Return," briefly describing the award received by Tibbets on his return from that successful bombing mission: "To Tibbets' surprise [General Carl] Spaatz greeted him, shook his hand, and then pinned a Distinguished Service Cross to his rumpled overalls."

Perhaps in intentional dramatic contrast, "unit 4," originally described as the emotional center of the exhibit, focused on "Ground Zero": Hiroshima and Nagasaki. The actual text was about the same length as that of the intellectual core, "unit 2" on the decision to use the bomb. But unlike that "unit," "Ground Zero" was not at all explicitly analytical. Rather, it was richly descriptive and painfully evocative, capturing much of the horror and the human tragedy of what the A-bombs meant when they detonated over Hiroshima and Nagasaki, with deadly blast, heat, and radiation. In the exhibit were: the schoolboy's jacket, left by the youngster, Tetsuo Kitabayashi, killed in Hiroshima;

brief mention of the worshippers in Nagasaki who died at their prayers in the Catholic cathedral and elsewhere; the water bottle that belonged to a young Hiroshima schoolgirl, Yoshiko Kitamura, whose body was never found; and the scarred lunch box of another Hiroshima student, Reiko Watanabe, whose body was also never found. (It was her lunch box that Correll in late 1993 had complained about, when focusing upon the artifacts and images in the exhibit.) Among the other artifacts were the half-destroyed Buddha from Hiroshima and a remaining head of an angel from Nagasaki's Catholic cathedral, suggesting the bomb's indifference to religious differences and to beliefs, also.

The fifth "unit" in the draft-script discussed, sometimes in desultory ways, "The Legacy of Hiroshima and Nagasaki." The text stated that the atomic bombings had "played a crucial role in ending the Pacific war quickly," mentioned that there was still dispute about whether the bomb had been necessary, and noted briefly that some analysts thought that the first bomb was necessary but not the second one. The "unit" briefly discussed the difficulties of achieving a surrender because of the continuing Japanese and American differences over the guarantee of the emperor, mentioned that a third A-bomb could soon have been available at Tinian, and stressed that Truman said that he did not want to use another atomic weapon and kill "all those kids." In a loose fashion, the draft-script connected the atomic bombings to the early Cold War, and did correctly emphasize that the bombing of Hiroshima had spurred Stalin to accelerate and greatly expand what had previously been a small Soviet A-bomb project. In the last pages, this "unit" briefly discussed among other subjects the failed Baruch plan for international control, the growth of nuclear arsenals, the dangers of proliferation, the problems of nuclear waste, and the hopes and fears that the bomb had nurtured. Taking no stand on whether the bomb had produced the so-called "long peace," the absence of a shooting war for roughly 45 years between the two superpowers, the script noted that deterrence "seemed" to make a crucial difference but that the deterrence system, if it failed, could also produce the destruction of human civilization. Undoubtedly seeking to avoid a controversial stand on a hotly contested set of issues, the script did not directly suggest that the Cuban missile crisis, which was briefly mentioned, might have been partly created by the deterrence system itself.[184]

At the winter 1994 meeting of the advisory board for the *Enola Gay* exhibit, the only strong dissent came from Sherwin, a former naval officer and one of the recognized major historians of the A-bomb. He complained that the anti-Soviet theme for use of the bomb was muted in the script. More importantly, he feared that the script and the related small artifacts were virtually irrelevant, because the plan to display much of the *Enola Gay* meant that the plane, both physically and emotionally, would dominate the exhibit. In his judgment, that constituted a celebration of the bombing and the plane. It was obscene and unwarranted, he contended. The *Enola Gay* was a plane that had brought massive death, and unnecessarily,[185] he said.

Apparently the other board members preferred to spend their time discussing, and seeking to improve, the script and the exhibit. They did not challenge the basic plans, but operated within the framework of those plans, which they generally endorsed. Unlike Sherwin, they rejected or minimized anti-Soviet themes and generally welcomed the effort to display the *Enola Gay* in an exhibit about the atomic bomb.[186]

The two air force historians—Hallion who was technically a member of the board, and Wolk who had come along to the session and thus was an informal member—provided substantial praise. Don't worry, they told Michael Neufeld, the curator who had done much of the writing. He was dismayed by Martin Sherwin's criticism. "Chin up," Hallion scrawled in a penned note at the session. "You've got a great script, and nobody—except Marty—is out to emasculate it."[187]

They also presented the NASM curators with three pages of comments, much of which focused on details involving the air force in World War II. They did properly worry about some scattered sentences on anti-Soviet motives and the bomb decision, and about the script's casualty numbers, as well as the need to make more clear that Truman had been deeply concerned about American casualties in an invasion and therefore had hoped that the use of the bomb would end the war before November and the Kyushu operation. They also suggested more discussion of Japanese aggression in the 1930s and early '40s, more images (pictures and artifacts) focusing on Japan's "brutality to subject peoples," and some added clarification of what was to prove, in the hands of later unfriendly critics, one of the script's two fateful sentences: "For most Japanese, it was a war to defend their unique culture against Western imperialism."[188]

These gentle criticisms, which were quite helpful, were designed, as Hallion and Wolk said, "to give the script a better contextual balance." Significantly, they had begun their comments with this statement, "Overall, this is a most impressive piece of work, comprehensive and dramatic, obviously based upon a great deal of sound research, primary and secondary." At the end of the three typed pages, Hallion had penned, "Again—an impressive job. A bit of 'tweaking' along the lines here, should do the trick…" Those words probably summarized the judgments, despite minor criticisms, by most advisory board members.[189]

THE TRIUMPH OF THE HIROSHIMA NARRATIVE:
A DEFEAT FOR HISTORY?

During the winter of 1993–94, *Air Force Magazine* editor John Correll, along with some other Air Force Association members and war veterans, launched a campaign against the script and the entire exhibit, charging that the project was politically biased, pro-Japanese, and anti-American. Correll contended that the museum had gotten the A-bomb history wrong, did not appreciate the air force, and had to be corrected. His assault upon their exhibit was, significantly, the continuation of the Association's criticism of a NASM exhibition of World War I airpower. In the judgment of Correll, that World War I program had been designed "to debunk and discredit airpower."[190] Because NASM had, until Harwit's appointment, been virtually an adjunct to the aerospace industry and the Association, along with the air force, Correll and others seemed angry that "their" institution had slipped out of their control. They strongly desired to recapture it.[191]

Whereas the Association's complaints about the World War I exhibit had attracted little interest among veterans or the media, the *Enola Gay* display was different. The issues were closer to the present, and passions were likely to be stronger. Thus, there was attention, and interest, when the Association, often using distortions, condemned the A-bomb exhibit. The Air Force Association claimed that it only wanted the "truth" in the exhibit, and that the "truth" about the use of the bomb and the conduct of World War II was simple and that it was, in fact, the Association's version.

Shrewdly, the Association, in its publicity, never admitted that A-bomb history had been a hotly contested terrain for years, that its own magazine had published an article indicating high-level, pre-Hiroshima, military objections to the use of the A-bomb, and that a number of military leaders, including Arnold and LeMay, had questioned the use of the bomb after Hiroshima.[192] Instead, the Association basically revived much of the 1945–60 version of the Hiroshima narrative, added a few dashes of newer information, and contended that there was no justifiable controversy about why the bomb had been used or whether it should have been used.

Strangely, Harwit of the Air and Space Museum did not fight back. By nature, he was inclined to compromise, not fight, and such tactics had made him a successful and respected administrator. Probably, also, he did not appreciate the potential power of the Association: It could organize other veteran's groups, gain great sympathy in the media, and reach to Congress itself. Choosing not to conduct a counter-campaign, the Museum did not issue explanatory press releases, or op-ed articles (with a few belated exceptions), or seek to enlist the advisory board for the exhibition in a counter-campaign. That nine- or ten-member board was a reasonably prestigious and diverse group, which also included at least a few veterans, and it might have been helpful in asserting that the original script was, basically, a good job, as the two air force historians had stated in writing.

But those two historians, and especially Hallion, soon defected from their February 1994 support for the script, which in their judgment had required only "tweaking." Whether they yielded to Association pressures, as some suspected, or whether they simply reappraised their earlier opinion for autonomous reasons, they basically reversed their earlier positions. In a July 1994 statement, the Office of Air Force History, where Hallion was the chief historian and Wolk a longtime staff member, announced the following judgments: NASM's planned exhibit "is not the kind...that the air force would have done for the *Enola Gay*. The air force would have chosen a context emphasizing B-29 organization, development, production, training, command, and the evolution of bombing policy and strategy."[193] Small parts of that conception, and especially the discussion of the shift in bombing policy, had been in the original NASM exhibit. But it, unlike this air force conception, had centrally focused on the use of the A-bomb, largely because it was the A-bomb that made that particular B-29 famous. The *Enola Gay* was, thus, not a typical bomber, but in an important way an unusual bomber.

Never acknowledging Hallion and Wolk's February 1994 judgment, the Air Force History pronouncement continued: "The...Museum's approach raises substantive issues of context and balance that cannot, in our view, be resolved by revisions." The statement went on to assert, unfairly, that the curators [and hence the script] have a point of view, namely, that the bomb should not have been dropped, and that it was dropped primarily to impress the Soviet Union."[194] The draft-script had actually seemed agnostic on the issue of whether the bomb was necessary; it generally emphasized that Truman's primary purpose was to save American lives and end the war quickly, and, despite some misconceived scattered sentences, had clearly stated that Alperovitz's view was rejected by most historians.

The air force historians in June 1994, like Correll in 1993 and 1994, were also worried by another matter. The script had indeed focused on the air force's shift to bombing cities, with many deaths of non-combatants. The air force historians feared, as did Correll and some others, that such bombing (really saturation bombing) might well be found immoral in 1995. In their judgment, the depiction in the "Ground Zero" display of the remains of the dead and injured could add to the likelihood that the World War II bombing of Japan's cities, as for the *Christian Century* and Catholic critics in 1945, might even be classified as "atrocities."[195] Such conclusions were anathema to Correll and the air force historians, who wanted to emphasize, further, that Japan had started the war, that it had committed many atrocities, and thus, by implication, that enemy non-combatants could not be "victims." There were only "legitimate" targets.

The script had deftly stayed away from making such judgments, or even intentionally implying any such conclusions. Probably most members of the advisory board regarded the World War II bombing as necessary and ethical. A few undoubtedly believed otherwise. But the script never indicated a position on this matter.

During the late spring or early summer, the American Legion, whom Harwit invited to participate as part of his effort to pick up allies and isolate the Air Force Association, actively joined the assault upon the script. Far more powerful than the Association, and with many more members, and with Legion posts in many towns, the Legion was a far more formidable foe for Harwit and NASM than the Association.[196]

In dealing initially with the Legion, Harwit sought to mollify the organization's leaders and rank-and-file members. By his direction, his curators were compelled in the summer and autumn of 1994 to allow the Legion to do considerable editing of the script. The result, to the distress of the working curators, was a destruction of the solid historical scholarship and a reconfiguration of visual parts of the exhibit.

The Legion managed to purge the script of many statements

about the long-run historical controversy over the bomb's use. Under Legion "guidance," the approach in the script came closer to Truman's longtime postwar assertions and to Stimson's 1947 article: The bomb had been necessary, there were no alternatives, it was used after careful consideration, and it ended the war speedily and saved many American lives.

In the process of yielding to the Legion, the script-writers were compelled to remove, among other key statements, the postwar doubts uttered by both General Eisenhower and Admiral Leahy about the use of the bomb. To the Legion, apparently, such judgments by WWII military leaders could not be part of the exhibit. Obviously, Ike's and Leahy's comments, even though they had clearly been treated in the script as post-Hiroshima judgments, were likely to open challenging questions about the morality and necessity of the 1945 A-bombing of Japanese cities. The Legion's aim, like the Air Force Association's, was to define such questions as virtually unpatriotic and certainly as reflecting a poor understanding of history. Anything that clashed with the original Hiroshima narrative was, basically, unacceptable.

The Legion's efforts, like the earlier Air Force Association's demands, received considerable support from a trusting American press. Significantly, virtually none of the news correspondents and columnists, as well as editorial writers and newscasters, had read the original script in 1994. Instead, they generally believed what the Association and the Legion said about the script. In the aftermath of Vietnam and Watergate, and before the Republican triumph in the November 1994 elections, the national press had often been critical of authority. But on this subject, involving the A-bomb script, they simply did not do their basic homework—reading the script itself.[197]

Perhaps as troubling, they generally did not know that there had been a long controversy about why the bomb had been used, whether it was necessary, why alternatives had not been pursued instead, whether those alternatives would have been successful, and whether the use of the bomb was just. In 1994, most

American journalists, and perhaps as large a percentage of congressional members, would probably have been shocked to learn that John Foster Dulles, Thomas Finletter, Eisenhower, Leahy, Douglas MacArthur, Ernest King, Henry Arnold, John J. McCloy, Herbert Hoover, and other notables had raised such issues soon after Hiroshima. Presumably, most journalists and politicians also did not know that *U.S. News*, the *Chicago Tribune*, *Christian Century*, executives of the Federal Council of Churches, and others had raised similar questions in the aftermath of the atomic bombings.

In some measure, the veteran's groups also benefited from the belief, promoted by them and uncritically accepted by many journalists, that only the vets could know the "true" history of the bomb. By that conception, reaching well beyond Paul Fussell's earlier claims, experience in the war enabled the vets to define historical knowledge. Latter-day historians, especially if they seemed to violate the Hiroshima narrative, were rather easily dismissed. After all, they had not fought in World War II. How could they claim to know the history of the bomb's use?

Few journalists or politicians seemed to recognize that they were accepting a very peculiar conception of how historical knowledge is constructed. After all, just how could a GI's experience in the Pacific in World War II, even if he fought in bloody battles, help him, years later, to know why key decision makers in Washington in 1945 had chosen to drop A-bombs on Japanese cities? Understanding the context of that period was certainly essential. But it was not adequate. The road to substantial historical understanding of past, high-level political decisions, made in Washington, is by studying the archives, often using memoirs, and relying also on any wartime or postwar interviews. It is not a perfect process, and honest analysts can, and do, disagree in interpreting and assessing evidence. But the process does rely upon warranted evidence. However painful the experience of GIs in the Pacific, or elsewhere, their experience did not provide them—unless they acted as historians and also studied sources—with the requisite information to "explain" the crucial issues involving the use of the atomic bomb.

Empowered by the belief that the Legion could, and would, define the "true" history, its representatives also assailed the casualty estimates in the script. The original draft, as at least three advisory-board members had pointed out, had confused matters. But the Legion wanted, basically, to impose on the script Stimson's 1947 claim of a million American casualties. Under duress, the script-writers yielded, while undoubtedly knowing that the weight of historical evidence undermined such astronomical claims. The curators knew that a million American battle casualties in the last stages of war against Japan would have approximately equaled the total number of battle casualties (including 292,000 dead and 672,000 wounded) suffered by the United States in the entire war, in all theaters, over nearly four years.[198]

To the Legion, the Association, and many vets, the American casualty estimates were crucial. High numbers could justify the use of the bomb, and block both doubts and challenges. Low numbers, in turn, might open questions, provoking dialogue and doubt. In short, a million was useful, if not essential, in defining the "true" A-bomb history.

Despite NASM's many concessions on the script during the summer and autumn, the Legion was still unhappy. Their officials wanted more "cleansing" and a more "politically correct" text: the elimination of any suggestion that the atomic bombing of Japan was controversial, that any notables had ever questioned it, or that it might have been unnecessary. And the curators and Harwit, despite efforts at compromise, were unwilling to disregard all the historical evidence and provide exactly what the Legion in effect was decreeing: Stimson's 1947 history, minus the anguish, as the Smithsonian's text in 1995.

In November 1994, a group of A-bomb scholars, decrying what they called the evisceration of the script, met with Harwit to protest, to ask for justifications, to challenge his claims of evidence, and to plead for a restoration of many of the purged themes and statements. In that mid-November discussion, the subject of the casualty estimates was one of about a dozen issues. In challenging the "one million" figure, and demanding to see Harwit's documents supporting that number (the curators apparently had none), one historian pointed out that the mid-June 18, 1945, White House meeting's estimate for the Kyushu operation had only been about 63,000 American casualties. For evidence, he cited Leahy's diary entry of June 18th that Marshall had said that the operation would "not cost in casualties more than 63,000 of the 190,000 combatant troops..."[199]

At this November meeting, Harwit seemed unwilling to budge on the one million estimate. But apparently he later studied Leahy's diary entry, acknowledged that Marshall's June 18th advice to the President was important, and concluded that Leahy had probably reached about the same number as Marshall. As a result, in early January 1995, Harwit informed the Legion that he was going to integrate this new information, from Admiral Leahy's June 18th diary, into the script's text on pre-Hiroshima casualty estimates.[200]

Perhaps predictably, that angered the Legion.[201] High numbers were important to them. They charged Harwit with violating an agreement by revising the script, and they were angry that an advisory board member, whom they believed Harwit had chosen to consult, was the source for these new numbers. Strangely, the Legion was unwilling to ackowledge that the advisory board member had, basically, informed Harwit of a crucial historical source: Admiral Leahy's report on General Marshall's advice to President Truman.

The Legion, picking up substantial congressional support, called for a cancellation of the script, probably desired the firing of Harwit, and wanted an investigation of the National Air and Space Museum, its script-writing curators, and the entire *Enola Gay* project.[202] What the Legion wanted, basically, was just the display of the Hiroshima bomber as part of a celebration. Probably the dispute over the revision in casualty numbers had been the pretext that the Legion had been seeking in order to achieve total victory. Until then, it had only received substantial but never total concessions from Harwit and NASM.

Under assault from the Legion, the Air Force Association, Congress, vets, and the press, the Smithsonian Institution caved in. Recognizing that Congress provided over 70 percent of the Smithsonian's total funding, and facing assaults from powerful groups, while lacking countervailing support, Smithsonian secretary I. Michael Heyman in late January 1995 announced the basic cancellation of the script and the creation of a display that would feature the *Enola Gay*. It was exactly what Tibbets had requested: Just put the Hiroshima bomber in the museum.

Denying that the Smithsonian had surrendered, Heyman explained that the original conception of the exhibit had been fundamentally flawed. It was impossible to have both an analysis and a commemoration, he said. In 1995, the fiftieth anniversary of the end of World War II and the atomic bombings, he decreed that NASM should commemorate, not analyze, the decisions and events.[203]

Undoubtedly, Heyman, as a shrewd bureaucrat, understood that the dispute was not simply about the atomic bomb. Rather, the dispute was sometimes a symbolic issue in a "culture war," in which many Americans lumped together the seeming decline of American power, the difficulties of the domestic economy, the threats in world trade and especially Japan's successes, the loss of domestic jobs, and even changes in American gender roles, and shifts in the American family. To a number of Americans, the very people responsible for the script were the people who were changing America.[204] The bomb, representing the end of World War II and suggesting the height of American power, was to be celebrated. It was, in this judgment, a crucial symbol of America's "good war," one fought justly for noble purposes at a time when America was united. Those who in any way questioned the bomb's use were, in this emotional framework, the enemies of America. The Air Force Association, the Legion, many individual vets, segments of Congress, and parts of the media accepted, and promoted, that interpretation.

Illustrative of these themes, one advisory board member, who was publicly identified with the lowered casualty estimates, received a number of angry letters. In those letters, people spoke of the need to kill the "little yellow bastards," asked whether the board member had fought in the war, decried the "power" of Hillary Clinton, worried about the loss of American values, deplored the domestic economy's problems, worried about the decline of the American family, and castigated an alleged intellectual elite for not understanding an "obvious" truth: The bomb had been necessary.[205]

In March 1995, testifying before a congressional subcommittee, Heyman explained what he had in mind, besides displaying the long-planned section on the *Enola Gay*, for the redesigned exhibit: "I am just going to report the facts. Something along the lines of, "This clearly led to the conclusion of the war immediately and resulted in saving untold numbers of lives by avoiding the necessity of invasion."[206]

But of course, as many college-level history students could have explained, these were not "facts," but *interpretations*.[207] Presumably, Heyman, a former law school professor, understood what he was doing. His interpretation, presented as obvious "fact," was very close to Truman's postwar assertions and to Stimson's 1947 article. But even Stimson, in 1948, had partly backed away from that Hiroshima narrative. It was that very 1947 version that Bundy, once Stimson's "scribe," had challenged forcefully in 1988.

How surprised many of the script's foes might have been to discover that McGeorge Bundy, a World War II officer in the Pacific and later an architect of America's Vietnam policy, had chosen to reinterpret, and to question, the A-bomb decision. His own role in the Hiroshima narrative—first as a ghostwriter and then as a partial critic—suggests the confusing complexity of America's efforts to come to terms with its Hiroshima past. That effort has, indeed, been embedded in larger culture wars. But it would also be unfair, and too simple, to reduce the dispute over the A-bomb to a battle in the culture war. It is both more, and less, than that.

WHOSE HISTORY WILL TRIUMPH?

The dispute is over the effort, fifty years after Hiroshima, to come to terms with America's early nuclear past. With deep divisions within America over whether or not the bombing was necessary, moral, and wise, a well-publicized planned exhibit, in the Smithsonian, was barred from distilling the existing scholarship on the A-bomb for popular consumption. It was a struggle over history in multiple ways, with heated passions, with feverish polemics, with Congressional hearings, and with deep concern about how to represent a contested part of America's past. To all, history clearly mattered. The question was, who would shape it?

In the short run, in the Smithsonian and in the media, the American Legion, the Air Force Association, and their allies triumphed. But elsewhere in some parts of America, that victory is viewed with suspicion and distaste. The very clash over the cancelled NASM exhibit may, ironically, spark a heightened interest in the issues of A-bomb history. Perhaps more Americans will become curious about the A-bomb events, how historians have treated them, why a near-consensus emerged by the early 1990s, why it is being challenged in the mid-1990s, and how the A-bomb decision should be understood. That may lead more Americans to wonder, and to question, whether the 1945 use of the A-bomb was necessary and just, and why the United States dropped atomic bombs on Japanese cities.

In seeking to raise those issues, to provide the distilled scholarship to viewers, the museum's director, Martin Harwit, and its curators may ultimately be successful. Not only will the "purged"[208] script receive attention, but large questions have been emphasized in the struggle over A-bomb history. It is unfortunate that Harwit paid the price of being forced to resign, that the curators have been unjustly pummeled, and that some analysts of the A-bomb decision, who questioned it, have been savaged too.

* The author is grateful for the assistance—for either counsel or for sources, or both—of Gar Alperovitz, Kai Bird, Herbert Bix, Larry Bland, Charles Brower IV, McGeorge Bundy, Robert Butow, Alvin Coox, Conrad Crane, John Dower, Edward Drea, Robert Ferrell, Peter Galison, Marc Gallicchio, Gian Gentile, Allison Gilmore, Chuck Hansen, Gregg Herken, James Hershberg, Richard Hewlett, David Holloway, Linda G. Holmes, Edward Linenthal, Rufus Miles, Richard Minear, Robert Newman, Martin Sherwin, Stewart Udall, J. Samuel Walker, Michael Wallace, and Herman Wolk, among others. The ideas developed in this essay have emerged from research and writing partly funded by many institutes and foundations including the Ford Foundation, NSF, the Truman Library Institute, the MacArthur Foundation, Stanford's Center for International Security and Arms Control (CISAC), and the National Endowment for the Humanities, among others. Many of these ideas were presented in seminars and lectures in the U.S. and abroad, and the author is especially grateful to Stanford colleagues and students, as well as visiting Coe fellows and Lilly fellows, for providing useful responses. Librarians and archivists in the U.S. and abroad, with numerous collections containing materials on the A-bomb's history, on the conduct of World War II, and on wartime and postwar science and foreign policy, have greatly assisted the author.

Footnotes

1. "Possible Statement By The President," February 13, 1945, with H.H. Bundy to the Secretary, March 3, 1945, Harrison-Bundy (H–B) Files 74, Manhattan Engineer District Records (MED Records), Record Group 77, National Archives, Washington, D.C.

2. Truman, public statement of August 6, 1945, in *Public Papers of the President: Harry S. Truman,* 1945 (Washington, D.C., 1961), pp. 197, 199.

3. For different estimates on Hiroshima in 1945, see Committee for the Compilation of Materials on Damage Caused by the Atomic Bombs on Hiroshima and Nagasaki, *Hiroshima and Nagasaki* (New York, 1981), translated by Eisei Ishikawa and David Swain, p. 353; and untitled data sheet (1945), Bonner Fellers Papers, Hoover Institution Archives, Stanford, California.

4. Richard Hewlett and Francis Duncan, *Atomic Shield, 1947/1952* (University Park, Pa., 1969), p. 672.

5. General Thomas Handy to General Carl Spaatz, July 25, 1945, in Harry S. Truman, *Memoirs,* I, *Year of Decisions* (Garden City, N.Y., 1955), pp. 420–21.

6. Truman, radio address, August 9, 1945, in *Public Papers: Truman,* 1945, p. 212.

7. Sen. Richard Russell to Truman. August 7 1945, Official File (OF) 197 misc., Truman Papers, Truman Library, Independence, Missouri.

8. Truman to Russell, August 9, 1945, OF 197 misc., Truman Papers.

9. Barton J. Bernstein, "The Perils and Politics of Surrender: Ending the War with Japan And Avoiding the Third Atomic Bomb," *Pacific Historical Review,* 46 (Feb., 1977), pp. 3–17.

10. Henry Wallace Diary, August 10, 1945, Wallace Papers, University of Iowa, Iowa City, Iowa.

11. Samuel McCrea Cavert to Truman, August 9, 1945, OF 692A, Truman Papers.

12. Truman to Cavert, August 11, 1945, OF 692A, Truman Papers.

13. Bernstein "Perils and Politics of Surrender," pp. 17–25.

14. George Gallup, ed. *The Gallup Poll* (New York, 1972), I, pp. 531–32. Ten percent disapproved, and five percent had no opinion. There was virtually no difference by gender, age, or education.

15. Poll data in Thomas Graham, *American Public Opinion on NATO, Extended Deterrence, and use of Nuclear Weapons,* CSIA Occasional Paper No. 4 (Kennedy School of Government, Harvard University, Cambridge, Mass.), pp. 82–83.

16. McGill, Morrison, and Guest, all quoted in Michael J. Yavenditti, "American Reactions to the Use of Atomic Bombs on Japan, 1945–1947"(Univ. of California, Berkeley Ph.D. thesis, 1970), pp. 250–256.

17. Yavenditti, "American Reactions to Use of Atomic Bombs," pp. 186–192.

18. G. Bromley Oxnam and John Foster Dulles to Truman, August 22, 1945. OF 692A, Truman Papers.

19. Report of the Commission on the Relation of the Church to War in the Light of the Christian Faith, "Atomic Warfare and the Christian Faith" (Federal Council of the Churches of Christ, March 1946), in Arthur H. Compton Papers, Washington University, St. Louis, Missouri.

20. Yavenditti, "American Reactions to Use of Atomic Bombs," p. 199.

21. Press release, September 12, 1945, Fellers Papers, box 3, Hoover Institution. Also see D. Clayton James, *Years of MacArthur* (Boston, 1975), II, p.775.

22. U.S. Strategic Bombing Survey, *Japan's Struggle to End the War* (Washington, D.C., 1946), p. 13.

23. See, for example, interrogation with Prince Konoye, November 9, 1945, Records of the U.S. Strategic Bombing Survey, RG 243, National Archives; and Barton J. Bernstein, "Compelling Japanese Surrender Without the A-Bomb, Soviet entry, or Invasion: Reconsidering the U.S. Bombing Survey's Early Surrender Conclusions" *Journal of Strategic Studies* (forthcoming). Also see Robert Newman's forthcoming essay on the Survey in the *Pacific Historical Review* (1995).

24. Norman Cousins and Thomas K.Finletter, "A Plea for Sanity," *Saturday Review of Literature* (June 15, 1946), p.72.

25. John Hersey, "Hiroshima," *New Yorker* (August 31, 1946).

26. Hersey, *Hiroshima* (New York, 1946), pp. 68 and 60.

27. For other views, see Michael's J. Yavenditti, "John Hersey and the American Conscience: The Reception of 'Hiroshima,'" *Pacific Historical Review,* 42 (February 1974), pp. 24–49.

28. Cousins, "the Literacy of Survival," *Saturday Review of Literature* 29 (September 14, 1946), p. 14.

29. James B. Conant to Harvey Bundy, September 23, 1946, September 23, 1946, Conant (Harvard) Presidential Files, Pusey Library, Harvard University. This section of the present essay on Stimson's 1947 article draws heavily , and sometimes uses phrasings, from Barton J. Bernstein, "Seizing the Contested Terrain of Early Nuclear History: Stimson, Conant, and Their Allies Explain the Decision to Use the Atomic Bomb," *Diplomatic History,* 17 (Winter 1993), pp. 35–72. Because that essay provides full documentation on sources, this afterword purposely is not generally duplicating that substantial documentation, and readers who want full documentation can rely upon that 1993 essay. James Hershberg, *James B. Conant* (New York, 1993), appearing about a year after that early 1993 essay, also provides a similar interpretation.

30. Conant to Harvey Bundy, September 23, 1946; and Conant to McGeorge Bundy, November 30, 1946, Henry L. Stimson Papers, Yale University, New Haven, Connecticut.

31. Henry L. Stimson, "The Decision to Use the Atomic Bomb," *Harper's Magazine,* 194 (February 1947), pp. 97–107.

32. "Notes of the Use by the United States of the Atomic Bomb," September 25, 1946, marked as draft 3, with the initials of HHB (presumably Harvey Bundy) in the upper right, and located in Top Secret Documents of Interest to General Groves #20, MED Records.

33. Stimson to Felix Frankfurter, December 12, 1946, Stimson Papers.

34. Frankfurter to Stimson, December 16, 1946, Felix Frankfurter Papers, Library of Congress, Washington, D.C.

35. Stimson, "The Decision to Use the Atomic Bomb," p. 102, and also see p. 106.

36. William Leahy Diary, June 18, 1945, Leahy Papers, Library of Congress, with a copy also in Leahy Papers, Wisconsin Historical Society, Madison, Wisconsin.

37. Minutes of June 18, 1945 meeting in U.S. Department of State, *Foreign Reactions of the United States: Conference of Berlin (Potsdam)* (Washington, D.C., 1960), I, pp. 907–908.

38. Marshall to MacArthur, August 7, 1945, Douglas MacArthur Papers, MacArthur Library, Norfolk, Virginia, and also in Marshall Papers, Marshall Library, Lexington, Virginia.

39. Stimson, "The Decision to Use the Atomic Bomb," p. 107.

40. Stimson, "The Decision to Use the Atomic Bomb," p. 105. A forthright state-

ment would have made clear that he was disagreeing with the Survey's conclusions, and would not have implied agreement.

41. Grew to Stimson, February 12, 1947, Grew Papers, Houghton Library, Harvard University.

42. Stimson and Bundy, *On Active Service* (Boston, 1948), p. 629. In his book, Stimson also made clear that he had been ethically uneasy in 1945 about the area bombing of Japanese cities. Ibid.., pp. 622–623.

43. General Bonner Fellers to Herbert Hoover, March 10, 1947, Post-Presidential Papers, Herbert Hoover Presidential Library, West Branch, Iowa.

44. Richard Norton Smith, *An Uncommon Man: The Triumph of Herbert Hoover* (New York, 1984), pp. 349–350.

45. Hoover to Fellers, March 12, 1947, Post-Presidential Papers.

46. Hoover, "Views on Nations Policies as to the Atomic Bomb for North American Newspaper Alliance," September 27, 1945, Hoover Papers, Hoover Presidential Library.

47. See Barton J. Bernstein, "Introduction," Szilard, *The Voice of the Dolphins and Other Stories* (Stanford, Calif., 1992), pp. 3–23.

48. Bernstein, "Introduction," Szilard, *Voice of the Dolphins,* pp. 17–21, and Szilard, "My Trial," reprinted in *Voice of the Dolphins,* pp. 103–14.

49. Szilard, "A Personal History of the Atomic Bomb," University of Chicago *Roundtable* 601 (September 25, 1949) pp. 14–15.

50. Walter Millis, ed., *The Forrestal Diaries* (New York, 1951), p. 78.

51. Millis, ed., *Forrestal Diaries,* p. 74.

52. Millis, ed., *Forrestal Diaries,* p.76.

53. See, for example, Barton J. Bernstein, "Understanding the Atomic Bomb and the Japanese Surrender: Missed Opportunities, Little-Known Near Disasters, and Modern Memory," *Diplomatic History* (Spring 1995), pp. 263–266. (All page citations to this article are from galley pages, and thus page numbers may slightly shift.)

54. Eisenhower, *Crusade in Europe* (New York, 1948), p. 443.

55. Quoted in "Ike on Ike," *Newsweek* (November 11, 1963), p. 108. For severe doubts about the accuracy of Eisenhowers's postwar recollections about his 1945 conversation, see Barton J. Bernstein, "Ike and Hiroshima: Did He Oppose It?" *Journal of Strategic Studies* 10 (September 1987), pp. 377–89. But clearly Eisenhower chose to raise doubts *after* Hiroshima.

56. Leahy, *I Was There* (New York, 1950), p. 441. Many analysts have projected backward, and thus questionably, Leahy's postwar attitudes, but his wartime diary provides no support for such a judgment.

57. Arnold, *Global Mission* (New York, 1949), pp. 596–98.

58. Arnold, *Global Mission,* p. 598.

59. Ernest J. King and Walter M. Whitehill, *Fleet Admiral King* (New York, 1952), p. 621.

60. Bernstein, "Understanding the Atomic Bomb and the Japanese Surrender," *Diplomatic History,* pp. 252–55.

61. P.M.S. Blackett, *Fear, War, and the Bomb* (New York, 1949): and Baldwin, *Great Mistakes of the War* (New York, 1949), esp. pp. 88–113. These two works receive more substantial discussion in Barton J. Bernstein, "The Atomic Bomb and American Foreign Policy 1941–1945: An Historiographical Controversy," *Peace and Change* 2 (Spring 1974), pp. 1–5: and Baldwin's is also treated in Barton J. Bernstein, ed., *The Atomic Bomb* (Boston, 1976), pp. 33–34.

62. McCloy, *The Challenge to American Foreign Policy* (Cambridge, Mass., 1953), pp. 41–43. He was describing himself, when discussing the one individual, and he had also told Forrestal a similar version in 1947. See Millis, ed., *Forrestal Diaries,* pp. 70–71. But the absence of confirming evidence in various diaries for June 18, 1945, including those of McCloy (Amherst College Library), Leahy, Stimson (Yale University), and also Forrestal (Princeton University), as well as in the official minutes, raises some doubts about McCloy's claim, which seemed to grow with clarity over time. Kai Bird, *The Chairman* (New York, 1992) puts great faith in McCloy's recollections of this meeting.

63. Butow, *Japan's Decision to Surrender* (Stanford, Calif., 1954), p.132.

64. Butow, *Japan's Decision,* pp. 132–35.

65. Butow, *Japan's Decision,* p. 158.

66. Butow, *Japan's Decision,* p. 180.

67. Butow, *Japan's Decision,* p. 231.

68. Herbert Feis, *The Atomic Bomb and the End of World War II* (Princeton, 1966), pp. 36, 41, 44, 47–49, 59, 89, 100, 103, 108, among others.

69. Feis, *The Atomic Bomb,* p. 194.

70. Feis, *The Atomic Bomb,* p. 191.

71. Feis, *The Atomic Bomb,* p. 191–193.

72. Feis, *The Atomic Bomb,* pp. 199–200.

73. Feis, *The Atomic Bomb,* pp. 186–95.

74. Gar Alperovitz, "the Trump Card," *New York Review of Books* (June 15, 1967), and reprinted in Alperovitz, *Cold War Essays* (New York, 1970), with a Feis-Alperovitz exchange of letters (pp. 133–136).

75. Byrnes in "Was A-Bomb A Mistake?" *U.S. News and World Report* (August 15, 1960), pp. 65–66.

76. Joseph Grew, *Turbulent Era* (Boston, 1952), II, pp. 1446–1473.

77. Lewis L. Strauss, *Men and Decisions* (Garden City, 1962), pp. 163–200; and Edward Teller, with Allen Brown, *The Legacy of Hiroshima* (New York, 1961). For Teller's pre-Hiroshima position, which differs substantially from his post-Hiroshima claims, see Teller to Leo Szilard, July 2, 1945, J. Robert Oppenheimer Papers, Library of Congress.

78. Stimson Diary, May 15, 1945, Yale University Library, New Haven, Connecticut.

79. Stimson Diary, May 31, 1945,

80. Stimson Diary, June 6, 1945.

81. Stimson Diary, July 21 and 22, 1945.

82. Stimson Diary, July 24, 1945.

83. Poll data in Graham, *American Public Opinion,* p. 67.

84. Alperovitz, *Atomic Diplomacy* (New York, 1965), p. 14 (on assumption) and pp. 241-42 (on the hedges and conclusion).

85. See Bernstein, "The Atomic Bomb and American Foreign Policy," pp. 9–15.

86. This controversy, in updated form, can be surveyed in Gar Alperovitz and Robert Messer, "Marshall, Truman, and the Decision to Drop the Bomb," *International Security* 16 (Winter 1991/92), pp. 204–14, and Bernstein, pp. 214–221.

87. See, for example, Barton J. Bernstein, "Hiroshima and the End of World War II...,"(paper at Society for Historians of American Foreign Relations, 1992).

88. Martin J. Sherwin, *A World Destroyed* (New York, 1975); and Bernstein, "Roosevelt, Truman, and the Atomic Bomb: A Reinterpretation," *Political Science Quarterly* 90 (Spring 1975), pp. 23–62; Bernstein, "The Atomic Bomb and American Foreign Policy"; and Bernstein, ed., *The Atomic Bomb.* I refer to myself in the text in the third person, as Bernstein, rather than using pronouns (I, me, my) not in attempted coyness nor strained modesty, but because the personal pronouns are often likely to distract readers and focus undue attention upon the author, rather than on the discussion of A-bomb issues.

89. Bernstein, "Doomsday II," *New York Times Magazine* (July 27, 1975); and Sherwin, *World Destroyed,* pp. 233–36. For a possible dissent, see Butow, *Japan's Decision,* pp. 163–64. For a challenge, see Robert Newman's forthcoming book, ch. v.

90. Wolk, "The B-29, the A-bomb, and the Japanese Surrender," *Air Force Magazine* 58 (February 1975), pp. 55–61.

91. Wolk, "The B-29, the A-bomb," p.58. Readers should consider whether this statement,

if it had been present in the Air and Space Museum's *Enola Gay* script, would have been pummeled as unpatriotic, insensitive, and pro-Japanese. Obviously, in 1975, in this magazine, Wolk's words were not misunderstood, though his phrasing was careless.

92. Wolk, "The B-29, the A-Bomb," p. 59.

93. Wolk, "The B-29, the A-Bomb," p. 60–61.

94. Wolk, "The B-29, the A-Bomb," p.61.

95. January 1971 poll data in Thomas Graham, *American Public Opinion on NATO,* p. 60.

96. Alsop, in "Was the Hiroshima Bomb Necessary? an Exchange," *New York Review of Books* (October 23, 1980), pp. 37-40.

97. Joravsky, in "Was the Hiroshima Bomb Necessary?" pp. 40–41.

98. Alsop, in "Was the Hiroshima Bomb Necessary?" p. 37.

99. Paul Fussell, "'Thank God for the Atom Bomb'—Hiroshima: A Soldier's View," *New Republic* (August 22 & 29, 1981), pp. 26–30. See William Manchester, *American Caesar: Douglas MacArthur* (New York, 1978, paperback), p. 513. His source note cites two sources, but each is irrelevant to the quotation and statement about a million U.S. casualties.

100. Fussell's essay is reprinted in expanded form in Fussell, *Thank God for the Atom Bomb and other Essays* (New York, 1988), pp. 1–27, and see p. 17.

101. Michael Walzer, "An Exchange on Hiroshima." *New Republic* (September 23, 1981), pp. 13–14, and reprinted in Fussell, *Thank God,* pp. 23-28 with Fussell's *New Republic* rebuttal and with his postscript (pp. 29–35).

102. Walzer, "An Exchange," p. 14.

103. Martin J. Sherwin, "Hiroshima and Modern Memory," *Nation* (October 10, 1981), pp. 329, 349–53.

104. Bernstein, "Understanding the Atomic Bomb and the Japanese Surrender," pp. 263–266.

105. Historian Larry Yates, working for Truman biographer Robert Donovan, was probably the first independent scholar to find this diary, probably in 1978. For citations to the three publications, by Edward Mark, Robert Ferrell, and Bernstein, see J. Samuel Walker, "The Decision to Use the Bomb: A Historiographical Update," *Diplomatic History* 14 (Winter 1990), p. 103, note 10.

106. Truman, "Potsdam diary," July 17,18, 25, 1945, Truman Papers.

107. Bernstein, "Truman at Potsdam: His Secret Diary," *Foreign Service Journal,* (July/Aug. 1990), pp. 30–32. These issues of interpretation are developed further in Bernstein, "Marshall, Truman, and the Decision to Drop the Bomb," pp. 218–19, and in similar ways in Bernstein, "Understanding the Atomic Bomb and the Japanese Surrender," pp. 266–69.

108. Robert Messer, "New Evidence on Truman's Decision," *Bulletin of the Atomic Scientists* 41 (August 1985), pp. 50–56. Walker, "The Decision to Use the Bomb," is more inclined to view Messer's essay as truly agnostic about Alperovitz's position (p. 104).

109. Alperovitz, *Atomic Diplomacy* (New York, 1985), pp. 24–25, 32–33, 35–47.

110. Alperovitz and Messer, "Marshall, Truman, and the Decision to Drop the Atomic Bomb."

111. Barton J. Bernstein, "The Myth of Lives Saved by A-Bombs," *Los Angeles Times*, July 28, 1985, sec. 4, pp. 1, 2; Rufus Miles, "The Strange Myth of Half a Million Lives Saved," *International Security* 10 (Fall 1985), pp. 121–140; and Bernstein, "A Postwar Myth: 500,000 U.S. Lives Saved," *Bulletin of the Atomic Scientists* 42 (June/July 1986),pp. 38–40.

112. Truman, *Memoirs*, I, p.417.

113. Memoir draft 1, p. 249, draft 2, p. 683; draft 3, p. 804, Post-Presidential Memoirs, Truman Papers. There is also another draft 1, which on p. 1291k(a) has the higher numbers found in later drafts and in the published memoir.

114. Fussell, *Thank God*, p. 5. Fussell claims that there were 7,000 allied casualties per week in July 1945, but he has been unable to provide any substantiating sources for this claim. Fussell to Richare Minear, October 28, 1993; and Bernstein to Fussell, November 28, 1994. U.S. casualties in July probably averaged under 1,600 per week, and possibly under 1,400.

115. Joint War Plans Committee (JWPC) "Details of the Campaign Against Japan," JWPC 369/1. June 15, 1945, file 384 Japan (5-3-44), Records of the Army Staff, RG 319, National Archives.

116. Minutes of June 18, 1945 meeting in *Foreign Relations: Potsdam*, I, p. 907; Joint Staff Planners, 697/2, July 9, 1945, Records of the Joint Chiefs of Staff, RG 218, National Archives.

117. Leahy Diary, June 18, 1945. Leahy, *I Was There*, p. 384 printed the same sentence.

118. Edward Drea, *MacArthur's Ultra* (Lawrence, Kan., 1992), pp. 214-25.

119. Drea to Bernstein, March 15, 1995; David Westheimer, *Lighter Than a Feather* (Boston, 1971), pp. 125, 249

120. This document is excerpted in ch. xv of the unpublished "Medical Service in the Asiatic and Pacific Theaters" (Center for Military History) and was provided by the Center, with the generous and skillful guidance of Drea. Apparently, this unpublished chapter did not come to his attention until after his book had been issued. My efforts to trace the chapter back to the full document, in the National Archives holdings, failed in 1994. Perhaps some scholar will be successful. The total casualties in the unpublished chapter, to be precise, were 394,859, and battle casualties were stated as 124,935. My efforts to find other medical-planning documents for other Pacific campaigns also failed, but perhaps others will compare pre-battle estimates with actual battle results in late 1944 and 1945.

121. Hull to Eaker, September 13, 1945; Eaker to Hull, September 14, 1945; and Arnold to FEAF [Far Eastern Air Force], September 14, 1945, all in OPD 704 PTO, Records of War Department General Staff, RG 165, National Archives. In spring 1995, *Military History Quarterly* published two articles—one by Edward Drea and one by Peter Maslowski—coming to sharply different conclusions about casualties in the Kyushu invasion. Robert Newman, "What New Consensus?" *Washington Post*, November 30, 1994, has also suggested high numbers. He has generously shared with me a July 21, 1945 memo of high numbers by a nonmilitary adviser, W.B. Shockley to Edward Bowles, "Proposals for Increasing the Scope of Casualty Estimates, July 21, 1945. Bowles Papers, box 34, Library of Congress.

122. Col. R.F. Ennis to Chief Strategic Policy Section, S & P Group, OPD, "Use of Atomic Bomb on Japan," April 30, 1946, file ABC 471.6 Atomic (17 August 1945), box 570; and Col. C.H. Bonesteel to General Weckerling, January 29, 1946, box 566, both in Records of the War Department and Special Staff.

123. Bernstein, "A Postwar Myth," p. 40. In 1990, Samuel Halpern, claimed that the June 1945 refutation by U.S. military officials of "500,000 dead" proved that this number was "bruited about" in official Washington at high levels. That is tantamount to asserting that a physicist's letter rejecting an autodidact's design for a frictionless machine indicated that the design was "bruited about" among physicists. Such a claim conflates "bruited about" with an idea being taken seriously, and is therefor deceptive. Halpern also claimed, strangely, that Truman, whose World War I experience Halpern overlooked, did not know the difference beween the meaning of "casualty" and "fatality." Such a contention allowed Halpern to argue that Truman may have meant 500,000 *casualties*, not 500,000 *dead*. Halpern's contention may have been clever but it is unconvincing. If taken seriously, however, this 500,000 casualty figue would translate into "only" about 125,000 dead, which is far from Truman's many statements during his presidency. Halpern to Bernstein, August 27, 1990, and Bernstein to Halpern, October 1, 1990. Apparently Halpern has chosen to circulate his August letter but to disregard, or claim never to have received, the October 1990 rebuttal. Admittedly, Halpern's letter did not request a reply, nor did Bernstein's. Also see Bernstein to Halpern, May 14, 1995, written after Orange County (California) vets offered to share their copies of Halpern's 1990 letter with UC (Irvine) scholars.

124. Truman to James Cate, December 12, 1952 (handwritten letter); David Lloyd to President, January 6, 1953, both in PSF (President's Secretary's File) 112, Truman Papers; and see Barton J. Bernstein, "Writing, Righting, or Wronging the Historical Record," *Diplomatic History* 16 (Winter 1992), pp. 163–72. In December 1994, a copy of this article was sent to commander William Detweiler of the American Legion, but he still cited the "doctored" letter as an authoritative source, and thus simply seemed to dismiss the article and the archival sources on which it was based.

125. Efforts to gain a focused response on this matter have failed: Manchester has either disregarded letters or sent copies of letters that are not on the subject of source notes for the casualty numbers. Bernstein to Manchester, February 15, 1994, January 29, 1995, February 21, 1995, March 7, 1995, Bernstein note on apparent Manchester form letter, March 23, 1995, and Manchester to Bernstein, April 1, 1995 (which disregarded the question), and Bernstein to Manchester, April 19, 1995, and May 19, 1995. For additional doubts about Manchester's

scholarship, James Zobel, MacArthur Library, to Bernstein, March 28, 1995.

126. David McCullough, *Truman* (New York, 1992), pp. 400–01. Despite the prizes for the book, most historians who work on the Truman presidency regard this volume as naively adulatory, poorly researched, and indifferent to the scholarly literature. This assessment seems to range across the spectrum, regardless of whether the historians seem pro- or anti-Truman.

127. General Thomas Handy to General Hull, June 1, 1945, with Marshall's memo of agreement (Marshall to Stimson, June 7, 1945), all in regard to Herbert Hoover's memo, forwarded down the line from Truman. See file OPD 336 TS, Records of War Department General Staff, and Bernstein, "Postwar Myth," p. 30 and also note 7. Also see Marshall to Stimson, June 15, 1945, with G.A.L. (General George A. Lincoln), "Memorandum of Comments on 'Ending the Japanese War,'" June 14, 1945, which dismissed Herbert Hoover's "estimate of 500,000 to 1,000,000 American lives [to be saved]" as deserving "little consideration." Lincoln did not know that Hoover was the author of this memo, which Lincoln easily rejected.

128. Tony Capaccio, "'Truman' Author Errs on Japan Invasion Casualty Memo," *Defense Week* (October 11, 1994), pp. 1, 8–9

129. This statement intentionally minimizes the significance of Shockley to Bowles, "Proposals for Increasing ...Estimate," July 21, 1945, which was an analysis at a much lower level and not by a military expert.

130. Robert Ferrell, *Harry S. Truman* (Columbia, Mo., 1994), p. 213 does contend that a million U. S. casualties was possible. His book was not available when the *Enola Gay* script was initially being put together; Robert Newman, whose work was not then available, may be moving toward support for this number in his forthcoming (post-spring) 1995 book.

131. John Dower, *War Without Mercy* (New York, 1986), esp. p. 205

132. Dower's analysis, in his book, deepened and provided rich sources to substantiate the general proposition, normally taught well before Dower's book, of this basic distinction in popular American attitudes toward America's German and Japanese enemies.

133. Michael Sherry, *The Rise of American Air Power* (New Haven, Conn., 1987); Ronald Schaffer, *Wings of Judgment* (New York, 1985)

134. Schaffer, *Wings of Judgment*, p. 135.

135. Robert P. Patterson to George Harrison, August 2, 1945, H-B #8.

136. Harrison to Patterson, August 8, 1945, H-B #8.

137. Forrestal to Truman, August 8, 1945, Forrestal Diary; copies at Princeton University Library and Naval Archives, Washington D.C. For a similar point, see Truman to John Snyder, August 8, 1945, Records of the Office of War Mobilization and Reconversion RG 240, National Archives.

138. Stimson Diary, August 9, 1945.

139. See Stimson Diary, August 10, 1945; Forrestal Diary, August 10, 1945; and Leahy Diary, August 10, 1945; and Bernstein, "Perils and Politics," pp. 2–18.

140. Barton J. Bernstein, "Eclipsed by Hiroshima and Nagasaki: Early Thinking About Tactical Nuclear Weapons," *International Security* 15 (Spring 1991), pp. 160–171 Some similar points were later made in Marc Gallicchio, "After Nagasaki: General Marshall's Plan for Tactical Nuclear Weapons in Japan," *Prologue* 23 (Winter 1991), pp. 396–404.

141. John McCloy, memorandum of meeting, May 29, 1945, Records of the Secretary of War, May 29, 1945, RG 107, National Archives.

142. Bernstein, "Eclipsed by Hiroshima," pp. 160–62

143. Major General Clayton Bissell to Chief of Staff (Marshall), "Estimate of Japanese Situation for Next 30 Days," August 12, 1945, OPD Exec Files, box 12, RG 165, courtesy of Colonel Charles Brower IV.

144. McGeorge Bundy, *Danger and Survival* (New York, 1988) p. 64.

145. Bundy, *Danger and Survival*, p. 67; and see Stimson Diary, June 1 and 6, 1945.

146. Bundy, *Danger and Survival*, p. 87; and *Foreign Relations: Potsdam*, I, p. 883.

147. Bundy, *Danger and Survival*, p. 92.

148. Bundy, *Danger and Survival*, p. 88.

149. Bundy, *Danger and Survival*, pp. 77–79; and Stimson Diary, July 24, 1945.

150. Bundy, *Danger and Survival*, p. 93.

151. Bundy, *Danger and Survival*, p. 96.

152. Bundy, *Danger and Survival*, p. 96.

153. Bundy, *Danger and Survival*, p. 97.

154. Walker, "Decision to Use the Bomb," p. 110 has phrased the near-consensus differently and thus his meaning, despite his earlier discussion in that essay on p. 108, has sometimes been misunderstood, when he stated that scholars agreed "that the bomb was not needed to avoid an invasion of Japan and to end the war *within a relatively short time*" (emphasis added). He was not saying that scholars agreed that, without the bomb, the war would *definitely* have ended before November 1, 1945, the date for the invasion. Unlike Walker's 1990 historiographical essay, the present essay (the afterword to this volume) reaches into 1995, but the treatment of literature on the use of the A-bomb ends generally with publications from the mid-1992 period, when the curators began doing their early research on the subject. Thus, in addition to not discussing Leon Sigal's *Fighting to a Finish* (Ithaca, 1988), a study in organizational behavior that has had little influence on A-bomb discussions, and Richard Rhodes' *The Making of the Atomic Bomb* (New York,

1987), which provides little interpretation amid its narrative, the present essay does not discuss the 1992 book by Kai Bird on McCloy, with its generally Alperovitz-like argument; William Lanoutte's biography of Szilard, which often comes close to Alperovitz; Stanley Goldberg's various essays on Groves and the Manhattan Project, which seem close to the "definite" camp; John Ray Skates's *The Invasion of Japan* (Columbia, S.C., 1994), which has little to say about the A-bomb decision; Ferrell's *Truman*, which is decidedly anti-Alperovitz; Hershberg's *Conant*, which is close to Sherwin's work; or Robert Pape, "Why Japan Surrendered?" *International Security* 18 (Fall 1993), pp. 154–191, which is poorly informed, seems not to know much of the salient literature, and was criticized by Bernstein in a 1995 CISAC-Stanford seminar. Apparently Bruce Lee, "Why Truman Bombed Hiroshima," *Wall Street Journal*, May 5, 1995, is seeking to challenge much of the revisionist work in his forthcoming book; but his *Journal* article makes dubious claims about having "uncovered" new sources, thereby implying that others had not previously used them. Most, if not all, of his *Journal* article's cited sources have been used by others, and the document that was featured had been published at least 7 years earlier by another writer, Bernstein to *Wall Street Journal*, May 15, 1995; and Sherwin, *World Destroyed* (1987 edition), pp. 335–36.

155. Committee for the Compilation, *Hiroshima and Nagasaki* p. 369 places the death totals at 340,000 by 1950, but provides lower numbers on pp. 113–16. For lower numbers, see U.S. Strategic Bombing Survey, *The Effects of Atomic Bombs on Health and Medical Services* (Washington, D.C., 1947), pp. 55-56. On A - bomb and conventional bombing fatalities, see also Sherry, *American Air Power,* pp. 413–14, notes 43 and 44. The issue of American (and Allied) lives allegedly saved by the A-bomb is more complicated also because many former Japanese-held POWs believed that the A-bomb saved their lives, and that they would have been slain, on earlier orders from high Japanese officials, if the November invasion had occurred. The chief documentary support for this contention is an August 1, 1944 source (from the "Journal of the Taiwan POW Camp H.Q. in Taihoku, entry 1 August 1944"), part of the British Division's International Prosecution Section, generously provided by Linda G. Holmes. The problem with this 1944 source, among other matters, is that it is from 1944, and it is not clear that the 1944 policy endured into 1945 and would have been implemented, if it did endure, amid the invasion of 1945. The absence of 1945 confirming documents, as POWs and Holmes point out, may be explained by the specific 1945 orders, from high Japanese levels, that POW camps should destroy all incriminating evidence of poor treatment or plans to eliminate POWs. See Chief, POW Camps Tokyo, 30 August 1945, certified as Exhibit 2687, also courtesy of Linda Holmes. The sources on this issue—of likely Japanese behavior in the invasion toward POWs—seem less than firm but obviously lean in the direction of ex-POWs' contentions.

156. Poll data for October 1986 in Graham, *American Public Opinion,* p. 45.

157. December 1994 poll data from Roper Center, University of Connecticut (Storrs), courtesy of Stanford University Library and Richard Fitchen.

158. November 1994 poll data from Roper Center, courtesy of Stanford Library and Fitchen.

159. December 1994 poll data from Roper Center, courtesy of Stanford Library and Fitchen.

160. On the question of a racial theme for using the bomb, 3 percent agreed strongly

and 5 percent somewhat that such a motive operated, but 19 percent disagreed somewhat and 60 percent strongly disagreed. For white/black breakdowns, the results were 3 percent (white) and 5 percent (black) agreed strongly and 4 percent (white) and 9 percent (black) agreed somewhat, while 17 percent (white) and 31 percent (black) disagreed somewhat and 70 percent (white) and 45 percent (black) disagreed strongly. Despite differences, what is striking is the overall rejection of the contention, and the additional fact that whites were far more likely than blacks, and in large numbers, to reject the contention strongly. December 1994 poll data from Roper Center, courtesy of Stanford Library and Fitchen.

161. Ideally, for this analysis of what constituted reasonable expectations in 1992 and into at least mid-1993, there should be poll data from that period, not from late 1994. Quite probably, however, the numbers were about the same and possibly even more anti-bomb in the 1992 to mid-1993 period, especially because that was a period before many media, spurred by the *Enola Gay* exhibit, published articles, editorials, and columns which generally assumed that there were no justifiable questions about the 1945 use of the A-bombs and that their use on Japanese cities had been necessary, just, and wise, and probably had contributed to the so-called "long-peace" also. The data from November 1991 are very similar to the anti- and pro-bomb data for late 1994 in cases where similar (or the same) questions were asked.

162. Statement ("Boeing B-29 'Superfortress'"), provided by the Air Force Museum.

163. National Air Space Museum (NASM), planning document. "The Crossroads: The End of World War II, the Atomic Bomb, and the Onset of the Cold War," July 1993, in *Documents in the Enola Gay Controversy* (henceforth *Documents*), an unpaginated collection provided by *Air Force Magazine* and the Air Force Association.

164. "The Crossroads," July 1993, in *Documents*.

165. "The Crossroads," July 1993, in *Documents*.

166. Bob Adams to Martin Harwit, July 17, 1993, in *Documents*.

167. Adams to Harwit, July 17, 1993.

168. Tom Crouch to Martin Harwit, "A Response to the Secretary," July 21, 1993, *in Documents*.

169. Crouch to Harwit, "A Response ..." July 21, 1993.

170. NASM, "A Proposal—The End of World War II, the Atomic Bomb, and the Onset of the Cold War," no date but between July–September 1993, *in Documents*.

171. NASM, "A Proposal—The End of World War II, The Atomic Bomb, ..."

172. John T. Correll, "Memo for the Record [on] Subject: Meeting at Air & Space Museum ," November 23, 1993, *Documents*.

173. Correll, "Memo for the Record...," November 23, 1993.

174. Correll, "Memo for the Record ...," November 23, 1993.

175. Correll, "Memo for the Record ...," November 23, 1993.

176. In an April 1994 article, "The Decision That Launched the Enola Gay," *Air Force Magazine,* and in the footnoted version in *Documents,* Correll briefly noted Arnold's pre-Hiroshima judgment that, in Correll's words, "the bomb was not a military necessity." Typically, Correll did not link that "evidence" to any larger interpretation about why the bomb was used or whether it was, indeed, necessary. Correspondence with Correll made clear that he did not know much about the archival sources or the historical literature on the A-bomb issues. Bernstein to Correll, May 5, 1994; Correll to Bernstein, May 12, 1994; and Bernstein to Correll, May 23, 1994.

177. Dick Hallion and Herman Wolk, "Comments on the Script, 'Crossroads: The End of World War II, the Atomic Bomb and the Origins of the Cold War,'" probably February 7, 1994, courtesy of Edward Linenthal.

178. Combined Chiefs of Staff, "Anglo-American Outline Plan for Psychological Warfare Against Japan," CCS 539/4, May 21, 1944, file PD 385 Japan (12-7-43), Records of Headquarters U.S. Air Force, RG 341, National Archives. The JCS were members of the CCS. Allison Gilmore, "We Have Been Reborn," *Pacific Historical Review* (forthcoming) places Japanese surrendering soldiers at over 19,000 in the Southwest Pacific alone.

179. Hallion and Wolk, "Comments on the Script," probably February 7, 1994.

180. Hallion and Wolk, "Comments on the Script," probably February 7, 1994.

181. Groves, "Military Policy Committee Minutes," May 5, 1943, folder 23A, MED Records.

182. Sato to Togo, August , August 3, 1945, in No. 1228, Magic - Diplomatic Summary: and Togo to Sato, August 2, 1945, in No. 1225, Magic - Diplomatic Summary, Records of the National Security Agency, RG 457, National Archives.

183. In the United States, historian Herbert Bix, in his earlier work, had somewhat indicated that he was moving in this interpretive direction. His essay in the Spring 1995 *Diplomatic History* further develops this line of analysis.

184. For example, Barton J. Bernstein, "Reconsidering the Missile Crisis: Dealing with the Problems of American Jupiters in Turkey," in James Nathan, ed., *The Cuban Missile Crisis Revisited* (New York, 1992), pp. 55–130.

185. Discussions with Edward Linenthal and Sherwin.

186. Discussions with Edward Linenthal and Sherwin.

187. Hallion handwritten note on Hallion and Wolk, "Comments on the Script, 'Crossroads...,'" probably February 7, 1994.

188. Ibid.

189. Ibid.

190. John Correll, "War Stories at Air and Space," April 1994, in *Documents.*

191. Stanley Goldberg, "Smithsonian Suffers Legionnaires Disease," *Bulletin of the Atomic Scientists* 51 (May/June 1995), pp. 30–31

192. See "The Decision that Launched the Enola Gay," p. 27, in *Documents* for a minor exception.

193. Office of Air Force History Position, "Comments on "The Last Act: The Atomic Bomb and the End of World War II," July 12, 1994, in *Documents*.

194. Office of Air Force History Position, July 12, 1994.

195. *Christian Century* (August 29, 1945), p. 975 ("America's Atomic Atrocity"), cited in Yavenditti, "American Reactions to Use of Atomic Bombs," p. 237. For high-level U.S. military fears about "atrocity" charges, see Murray Green, card-note on August 24, 1945 Guam meeting (from Carl Spaatz Papers, Library of Congress), in Green/Arnold Papers, U.S. Air Force Academy, Colorado Springs, Colorado. For Japanese efforts to promote such charges, see "Magic" No. 1255, September 1, 1945, and Foreign Minister Mamoru Shigemitsu in "Magic" No. 1269, September 15, 1945, Records of the National Security Agency, National Archives. The fact that Japanese officials promoted "atrocity" charges should not lead to the conclusion that American critics and others were "pawns" of this Japanese effort. Critical readers should recognize that most U.S. contentions that the use of the A-bomb was an "atrocity" were rooted in deeply held values at the time, and therefore cannot be explained as the result of Japanese manipulation. For a different view, see Bruce Lee, "Why Truman Bombed Hiroshima," who also claimed that these "Magic" documents, declassified in 1978, had *recently* (presumably in 1993-95) been declassified and "uncovered" by Lee. His claim is false, and suggests remarkable sloppiness, at best.

196. For a different interpretation of the Legion's role, see testimony by Herman Harrington, May 11, 1995, before the U.S. Senate Committee on Rules and Administration.

197. While the coverage in the *New York Times* was usually an exception to these generalizations, the treatment in the *Washington Post* seemed unusually unfair, not just ill-informed. See also Kai Bird and Martin Sherwin to Don Graham et al., April 28, 1995. For a lame but spirited defense, see Meg Greenfield, editorial page editor of the *Washington Post*, who claims that the editorial board read "those bulky drafts of the final versions of the [exhibit] script." If she meant even three drafts, that could have taken two days, and thus seems unconvincing. (Greenfield to Bird and Sherwin, May 10, 1995, courtesy of Bird.) For a critique of poor coverage on PBS, see Bernstein to MacNeil/Lehrer Newshour, February 27, 1995, and reply, Tom Bearden, March 16, 1995, who claims that the NASM script was not available and therefore that he could not read it. In fact the script was available—but not easily so. Usually, reporters had to go to NASM to read it, and that was obviously inconvenient, which may have helped deter some reporters. In a case where MacNeil/Lehrer seemed to misreport matters in a news program, and was therefore asked for a video out-take or at least the voice-track of the original interview, MacNeil/Lehrer has provided nothing after over 13 weeks.

198. Data in U.S. 50th Anniversary of World War II Commemoration Committee (Pentagon), *World War II Information Fact Sheets* (probably 1995), unpaged, but see first page.

199. Barton Bernstein, Kai Bird, Carole Gallagher et al., to Harwit, "Recommendations

regarding 'The Last Act: The Atomic Bomb and the End of World War II,'" November 17, 1994, in *Documents*. At this meeting, I spoke initially for the group, and I introduced the issue of Leahy's diary, with Marshall's estimate of 63,000 U.S. casualties.

200. Harwit to Hubert Dagley, American Legion, January 9, 1995, in Documents.

201. On earlier Legion hostility and proposals for cancellation of the exhibit, see William Detweiler to National Commander's Advisory Committee, January 4, 1995, in *Documents,* which *preceded* by five days Harwit's letter about revising casualty numbers.

202. Detweiler to Department Commanders and Adjutants, January 18, 1995, with press release statement, in *Documents*. Firing Harwit is possibly implied, not stated, in these sources.

203. *New York Times,* January 31, 1995.

204. These themes were especially strong in letters (over 50) that I received in 1994-95 from various critics of the script.

205. These themes are also in letters of protest received.

206. *Washington Times,* March 11, 1995, quoted in Kai Bird, "Hiroshima in Modern Memory," (unpub. March 1995 paper), p. 5. See also *Washington Post*, May 19, 1995, p. D-6 for a "mea culpa" by Heyman and an NASM curator.

207. The analysis presented in this entire afterword essay on the struggle over history assumes, epistemologically, that there is a reality, that meaningful statements can be made about it, that rules of evidence can be roughly agreed upon, and that history is about a "reality," and not just an arbitrary construction in which each person, using different rules and procedures, writes and interprets both "facts" and causal connections, as well as complex descriptions. Thus, this essay intentionally rejects some radical forms of "social constructionism," but it does acknowledge the roles of epistemic communities in formulating knowledge and that they are not independent of larger social concerns. For a useful discussion of some of these issues, see Peter Norvick, *That Noble Dream* (New York, 1988), though he too easily dismisses the epistemological issues in his treatment of the question of what "objective" history means. At the risk of indulging in what some may term jargon, this afterword essay might be classified as "neo-positivist." In many ways, this afterword seems close to the epistemological assumptions, later explicated by Thomas Kuhn in his *The Essential Tension*, after the dispute over the meanings and implications of his *The Structure of Scientific Revolutions*.

208. Veteran's organizations, unwilling to acknowledge their role in what their critics call "censorship," seek to avoid such charges. See, for example, the May 11, 1995 testimony by Harrington if the Legion and R.E. Smith of the Air Force Association, U.S. Senate Committee on Rules and Administration. For Japan's much greater inability to come to terms with its World War II past, especially its aggression and atrocities, see, for example, *New York Times*, May 22, 1995, p. 4; and the useful work by historian Saburo Ienaga, *The Pacific War* (New York, 1978); as well as *New York Times*, October 8, 1989, p. 10.

Index to *The Crossroads: The End of World War II, The Atomic Bomb and the Origins of the Cold War*

Philip Nobile, born in Cambridge, Massachusetts, is the author of *Intellectual Skywriting: Literary Politics and the New York Review of Books* and *United States of America vs. Sex: How the Meese Commission Lied About Pornography* (with Eric Nadler). A former syndicated columnist and staff writer at *Esquire* and *New York*, Nobile has published in *The New York Times*, *The Washington Post*, *The New York Review of Books*, *The Village Voice*, *Commonweal*, *The National Catholic Reporter*, *Playboy*, and *The Scarsdale Inquirer*. He studied for the Catholic priesthood and holds graduate degrees in philosophy from Boston University and the Catholic University of Louvain in Belguim. He lives in New York City where he annually runs the marathon.

Dr. Barton J. Bernstein is professor of history at Stanford University and co-chair of the International Relations Program and the International Policy Studies Program. A leading revisionist scholar, Bernstein is the editor of *The Atomic Bomb: The Critical Issues* and several landmark monographs on the bomb. His article in the January/February 1995 *Foreign Affairs*, "The Atomic Bombings Reconsidered," set the intellectual ground for the 50th anniversary debate. Bernstein was also a pivotal figure in the controversy over the Smithsonian's *Enola Gay* script. He was a member of the exhibit's Advisory Board and led the battle against the "historical cleansing" of the museum's review of the destruction of Hiroshima and Nagasaki.